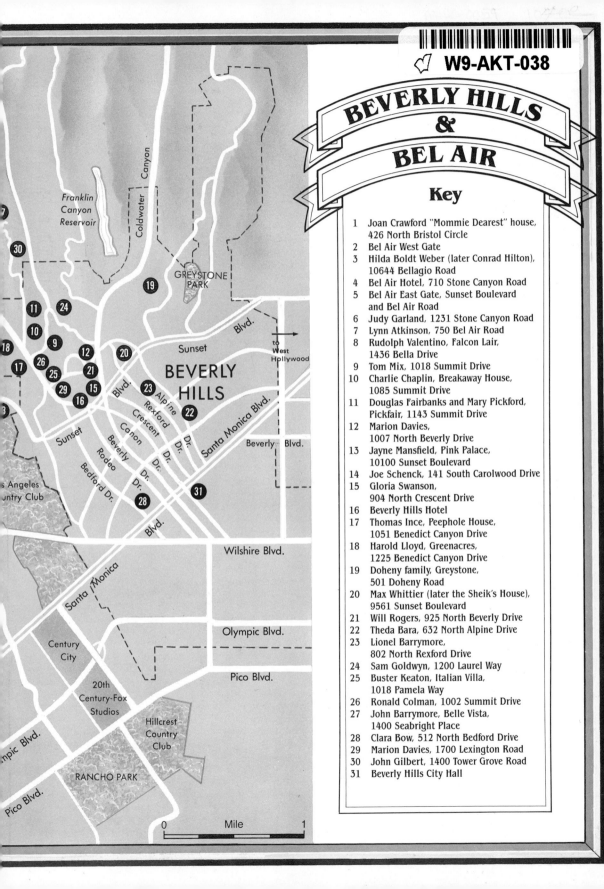

W9-AKT-038

BEVERLY HILLS & BEL AIR

Key

1 Joan Crawford "Mommie Dearest" house, 426 North Bristol Circle
2 Bel Air West Gate
3 Hilda Boldt Weber (later Conrad Hilton), 10644 Bellagio Road
4 Bel Air Hotel, 710 Stone Canyon Road
5 Bel Air East Gate, Sunset Boulevard and Bel Air Road
6 Judy Garland, 1231 Stone Canyon Road
7 Lynn Atkinson, 750 Bel Air Road
8 Rudolph Valentino, Falcon Lair, 1436 Bella Drive
9 Tom Mix, 1018 Summit Drive
10 Charlie Chaplin, Breakaway House, 1085 Summit Drive
11 Douglas Fairbanks and Mary Pickford, Pickfair, 1143 Summit Drive
12 Marion Davies, 1007 North Beverly Drive
13 Jayne Mansfield, Pink Palace, 10100 Sunset Boulevard
14 Joe Schenck, 141 South Carolwood Drive
15 Gloria Swanson, 904 North Crescent Drive
16 Beverly Hills Hotel
17 Thomas Ince, Peephole House, 1051 Benedict Canyon Drive
18 Harold Lloyd, Greenacres, 1225 Benedict Canyon Drive
19 Doheny family, Greystone, 501 Doheny Road
20 Max Whittier (later the Sheik's House), 9561 Sunset Boulevard
21 Will Rogers, 925 North Beverly Drive
22 Theda Bara, 632 North Alpine Drive
23 Lionel Barrymore, 802 North Rexford Drive
24 Sam Goldwyn, 1200 Laurel Way
25 Buster Keaton, Italian Villa, 1018 Pamela Way
26 Ronald Colman, 1002 Summit Drive
27 John Barrymore, Belle Vista, 1400 Seabright Place
28 Clara Bow, 512 North Bedford Drive
29 Marion Davies, 1700 Lexington Road
30 John Gilbert, 1400 Tower Grove Road
31 Beverly Hills City Hall

DREAM PALACES

ALSO BY CHARLES LOCKWOOD

BRICKS & BROWNSTONE

MANHATTAN MOVES UPTOWN

GREENWICH VILLAGE

SUDDENLY SAN FRANCISCO

DREAM PALACES

HOLLYWOOD AT HOME

CHARLES LOCKWOOD

THE VIKING PRESS · NEW YORK

First published in 1981 by The Viking Press
625 Madison Avenue, New York, N.Y. 10022
Published simultaneously in Canada by
Penguin Books Canada Limited

Portions of this work appeared originally in *Smithsonian* magazine
in slightly different form.

LIBRARY OF CONGRESS CATALOGING IN PUBLICATION DATA
Lockwood, Charles.
Dream palaces.
Bibliography: p.
Includes index.
1. Moving-picture actors and actresses—
Homes and haunts—California—Hollywood.
2. Hollywood (Calif.)—Dwellings.
I. Title.
PN1993.5.U65L57   791.43′028′0922   [B]   81-65260
ISBN 0-670-28461-0   AACR2

Designed by Beth Tondreau
Printed in the United States of America
Set in V.I.P. Bembo

TO
ISAAC MALITZ
AND
RANDOLPH HARRISON

ACKNOWLEDGMENTS

This book would not have been possible without the many people who shared their recollections of old Hollywood with me, showed me through their homes, or simply offered their goodwill and encouragement: Ellen Alperstein, Juan Alvarez, Val Arnold, Lawrence Barker, Doug Bartoli, Trudy Blankenberg, Lawrence Block, Brian Bounous, Sam Burchell, Emile Cuhel, Gordon Curtis, Marshall Davidson, Phyllis Diller, Barbara Dixon, Crosby and Linda Doe, Mike Donaldson, Tony and Elizabeth Duquette, Allan Dwan, Tony and Nitsa Elite, Alan Emery, Douglas Fairbanks, Jr., Joan Fontaine, James Fraser, John Free, Lillian Gish, Mike Griffin, Peter Grimes, Howard and Jean Harrison, Edith Head, Hugh Hefner, Frank Hewitt, Thomas Holtz, Liz Hough, Landon Y. Jones, Donald Lewis, Willard J. Lewis, George Livermore, Anita Loos, John Loring, Les and Janice Marshall, Robert and Kathy McBain, Charles McLaughlin, Hugo Mentz, Paul Merar, Lou Miano, Roger Mohovich, James Packer, Raymond Page, Jeff Park, Barbara Poe, Deborah Reimer, Buddy Rogers, Don Rogers, David Rowinski, Robert Register, David Santos, Don Schneider, Stephen Severson, Mike Silverman, Gloria Swanson, Thomas Howard Tarantino, Albert and Donna Thatcher, Ed White, Mark Williams, Jon Winder, Carter Wiseman, and Elaine Young. Also, my special thanks to James Harbison, Jr., and Thomas Stritter for their moral support and good counsel, to Alison Luchs for her advice and friendship, and to Carolyn Patterson for her suggestions and introductions during my first months in Los Angeles.

I did most of my research at the Academy of Motion Picture Arts and Sciences, the American Film Institute, the Beverly Hills Public Library, the Huntington Library, the Los Angeles Public Library, the New York Public Library, and the Santa Monica Public Library. Terry Roach and Robert

Cushman were particularly helpful during my research at the Academy of Motion Picture Arts and Sciences.

For providing the vintage photographs in this book, I must thank Michael Back, Robert Cushman, Tom Dardis, Oliver Dernberger, Bettye Ellison, Lillian Gish, Alan Jutzi, Richard Lamparksi, Bruce Brooks Pfeiffer, Frank Piontek, Virginia Reidy, Donald Schneider, Allan Smith, Bruce Torrence, Don and Alice Willfong, and especially Marc Wanamaker of the Bison Archives. His knowledge of the old Hollywood is just as remarkable as his picture collection. Randolph Harrison took the present-day photographs of the stars' homes.

I have enjoyed working with my literary agent, Maxine Groffsky, whose sense of what an agent should do goes above and beyond the call of duty. Thank you, Maxine.

And I have been incredibly fortunate that Amanda Vaill was *Dream Palaces'* editor at Viking Press. Over the past three years, Amanda and her assistant, Susan Leon, have offered me good advice and splendid editing. Their commitment and enthusiasm to this book have been unfailing—and vital to its completion. I cannot thank Amanda or Susan enough.

My greatest appreciation goes to two friends: Isaac Malitz, who first showed me Los Angeles and whose kindness has meant so much to me since I have lived here, and Randolph Harrison, whose encouragement and friendship have helped me through some of the more trying parts of this book. I dedicate *Dream Palaces* to them.

CONTENTS

INTRODUCTION

About ten years ago in New York City, I watched the classic 1950 film *Sunset Boulevard* for the first time on late-night television. Confined to a sixteen-inch screen and interrupted by commercials, the movie was interesting but not much more. In 1976 I saw *Sunset Boulevard* again, this time at a revival movie theater in San Francisco with an appreciative audience, and I was both enchanted and a little appalled.

In the film, a struggling young Hollywood screenwriter named Joe Gillis, played by William Holden, unexpectedly turns his car into the driveway of an overgrown estate on Sunset Boulevard, just west of Beverly Hills, and stumbles into the eerie fantasy world of Norma Desmond, a once renowned but now almost forgotten, half-mad silent-movie actress, played by Gloria Swanson. Living in the decaying Spanish-style palazzo that she built during her heyday in the 1920s, Norma Desmond still imagines herself a great star, and *Sunset Boulevard* proceeds from there.

Never having visited Los Angeles and not much of an old-movies buff, I felt as though I had glimpsed another world through *Sunset Boulevard*, namely Hollywood's golden era of the 1920s, with gods and goddesses for stars and at least one Isotta Fraschini in the garage of every star's Beverly Hills mansion. I saw *Sunset Boulevard* several more times, and I was hooked. I became fascinated by the Hollywood of the 1920s and 1930s—not so much by the films of that era or the motion picture industry, but by how the stars of that period lived, outside the studio walls and exaggerated press releases. Specifically, I wanted to look into their personalities, their homes, their social lives: to find out what it was really like to be a star at that time. Out of this fascination came *Dream Palaces*.

As an architectural writer, I was curious to explore the much-maligned Southern California landscape and visit some of the legendary move-star homes, such as Douglas Fairbanks and Mary Pickford's Pickfair or Rudolph Valentino's Falcon Lair. And as a social historian, I wanted to meet some of the old-time stars, producers, and directors before it was too late and I could only learn about this amazing Hollywood era from books and yellowing newspaper clippings.

One of my most pleasant meetings of this sort was with director George Cukor at his estate in the Hollywood Hills, just above that section of Sunset Boulevard known as the Sunset Strip. There were no bristling iron gates here, not even a glimpse of an impressive house sitting far back from the street on a broad expanse of perfectly cut, perfectly green lawn. Just a simple black door in a blank high masonry wall along the road. Taking the telephone receiver from a box next to the door, I announced myself to a secretary. A buzzer sounded, and I opened the door and entered another world magically hidden behind the wall. Splashing water and flowers—the scent of flowers—everywhere. A large inviting white neoclassical-style house. The contrast between the road and this scene on the other side of the wall was so startling that I felt like Dorothy in *The Wizard of Oz* when she awakens in the little Kansas house after the cyclone, opens the door, and steps into a bright and cheerful-looking Oz.

A few minutes later I was sitting with George Cukor inside the house, drinking coffee, talking about Hollywood and about the people he had known, the stars he had directed, from Ronald Colman and Greta Garbo to Katharine Hepburn and Spencer Tracy. I asked, "If you were in my shoes, Mr. Cukor, how would you approach this book?"

"With a sense of humor," he replied, without a moment's hesitation. "Don't go 'oohh! aahh! Hollywood!' and have a lot of preconceived notions. That's stupid. And it's been done before. Really get involved in your subject and always have a sense of humor."

That sounded like good advice, and that is what I have tried to do with this book.

DREAM PALACES

CHAPTER ONE

As the black chauffeur-driven Isotta Fraschini town car moved slowly through the streets of downtown Los Angeles on the evening of July 10, 1926, Rudolph Valentino and the exotic Polish-born actress Pola Negri sat in the limousine's passenger compartment on their way to the preview of his latest movie, *Son of the Sheik*. Valentino's studio, United Artists, had billed the evening at Grauman's Million Dollar Theater as a preview, not a full-fledged premiere, and so no searchlights scanned the sky over the Spanish-style theater and no long lines of Rolls-Royces and Pierce Arrows dropped off dozens of stars and studio executives beneath the marquee. But thousands of Valentino's fans had still gathered outside faithfully, to see their idol arrive and perhaps get close enough to catch his eye, even touch him.

When the Isotta Fraschini pulled up in front of the theater, the crowd erupted into cheers, and then nearly broke through the police lines when Valentino and Miss Negri stepped out of the car: Valentino graceful in full evening dress, searching the crowd with his sensual dark eyes, and Negri wearing a clinging silver sheath gown, a diamond tiara, and a pearl necklace for the occasion. Valentino waved to the ecstatic mob, took Miss Negri's hand, and hurried into the theater.

He was clearly worried; even the sight of several hundred adoring fans did not reassure him. *Son of the Sheik* had already been playing inside the theater for over an hour, and he was going to make an appearance in front of the audience when the film was over. Waiting in

Rudolph Valentino and Hungarian actress Vilma Banky in Son of the Sheik (1926), *his last film.*

Several hours before the July 10, 1926, preview of Son of the Sheik, *Valentino's fans had already started gathering outside the Million Dollar Theater in downtown Los Angeles to see their idol arrive that evening. Who would have dreamed that Valentino would be dead just six weeks later?*

the cavernous Baroque-style lobby, Valentino chatted absentmindedly with friends and wondered what the audience thought of the film, which was a farfetched combination of beautiful scenery, desperate bandits, dancing girls, and desert sandstorms.

Valentino had not wanted to make this movie, a sequel to his wildly popular *The Sheik*. But he needed money, lots of money, because he was broke and still recklessly spending himself into debt furnishing and remodeling his Falcon Lair estate. *The Sheik* had made nearly three million dollars a few years before, and if *Son of the Sheik* did that well, Valentino would earn a million of his own. Besides, his career needed another hit badly. His popularity had slipped in the past year, because recent films such as *Monsieur Beaucaire*, *Cobra*, and *The Eagle* had not equaled earlier triumphs.

He need not have worried as he stood in the lobby of the Million Dollar Theater. When *Son of the Sheik* was over, the sound of applause, even cheers, drifted into the lobby. The tension was broken, and Valentino smiled for the first time that evening. This was more than polite applause. He knew that the audience really liked what it had seen.

Uniformed ushers briskly opened the double doors into the theater auditorium, and Valentino strode down the aisle toward the stage. The applause and cheers grew louder, and he had to wait several minutes before he could thank everyone for coming. Then the audience started applauding again, and he walked out of the auditorium, smiling and waving to his friends along the way.

After the preview and the party, Valentino headed for home, this time alone, along Sunset Boulevard. The chauffeur sat in the open driver's seat, wearing the uniform Valentino had designed for him—it was taupe, that shade of tan so popular in the 1920s. Valentino sat in back, in the five-person passenger compartment upholstered in taupe-colored Italian broadcloth, accented by silver mountings and panels inlaid in two-toned walnut and silver. He could, if he wished, talk to the chauffeur through a speaking tube, but actually that was unnecessary. A panel of buttons in the enclosed passenger compartment lit up signs on the dashboard that read "turn right," "slow down," "speed up," and half a dozen other instructions—an elegant refinement in a car that, some said, was the most beautiful and expensive in Hollywood. Valentino had purchased the chassis and eight-cylinder, dual-carburetor engine from the Isotta Fraschini factory in Italy and then hired a custom coachworks to build the limousine body out of aluminum, not steel, so that the car would be faster and more maneuverable. The entire body—even the wood spokes in the wheels—was painted a high-luster black lacquer, except for the boxy hood and cowl, which were aluminum polished to a mirror finish.

Soon this splendid car left suburban Hollywood and entered Beverly Hills, where Sunset Boulevard turned into a broad, curving, smoothly paved street that separated the Beverly Hills "flats" from the more fashionable foothills of the Santa Monica Mountains. A twenty-five-foot-wide bridle path ran down the center of Sunset Boulevard, separating the opposite lanes of traffic, and on either side of the street, behind thick hedges or brick walls and formal-looking iron gates, stood the stucco Spanish-style or half-timbered Tudor mansions of millionaire businessmen and Hollywood greats, darkened and silent now in the dawn.

But Valentino's car also passed some reminders of Sunset Boulevard's recent past as an unpaved country road: the one-room school house at Alpine Drive, the empty lots in the flats that had been farmed only two or three years earlier, and the rugged land at the start of the foothills, where sportsmen still hunted rabbits and deer to the consternation of nearby residents.

Where North Crescent Drive crossed Sunset Boulevard, Valentino's car passed Gloria Swanson's twenty-two-room Spanish-style mansion, which was almost hidden among the palms and acacia of her three-acre estate, and then the genteel Mission-style Beverly Hills Hotel and its acres of fragrant gardens, also on the right. Then the limousine turned right and down-shifted for the ascent up Benedict Canyon Drive, which was lined by short, scrawny-looking date palms planted just a few years earlier.

Narrow, steep-sided, and still largely empty, Benedict Canyon was sacred ground for movie fans. On the right, comedian Buster Keaton was building a twenty-room Italian-style villa with lovely terraces, fountains, and sweeping staircases on a three-acre knoll overlooking the canyon. A few hundred yards beyond, the car passed Summit

ABOVE: *Valentino in* Son of
the Sheik.

RIGHT: *A hopeless clotheshorse, Valentino chose this casual country-
gentleman outfit from the 44 different
hats, 124 shirts, 37 vests, and 24 pairs
of riding boots in his closets at Falcon
Lair. And that was just the beginning
of his wardrobe.*

Drive, perhaps the most sought-after address in Beverly Hills, a narrow dirt road that wound up into the hills past Charlie Chaplin's Spanish-style mansion, cowboy star Tom Mix's flamboyantly decorated home, and Douglas Fairbanks and Mary Pickford's fabled Pickfair, the comfortable, vaguely Tudor home that was the White House of Hollywood.

Just before Angelo Drive, the late director Thomas Ince's Spanish-style mansion flashed by, reflected in its front-yard pond. Next on the left was the hill where comedian Harold Lloyd was building his several-million-dollar Greenacres estate, complete with its own 110-foot-tall waterfall, 800-foot-long canoe pond, and 9-hole golf course on the 22-acre grounds.

At what is now Cielo Drive, Valentino's car slowed down and turned left to drive into the barren hills above Benedict Canyon. The narrow dirt road clung to the steep hillside, and the Isotta Fraschini slowed to a crawl to make several treacherous hairpin turns before climbing one last hill and stopping in front of a nine-foot-tall stucco wall—painted taupe—and the gates at 1436 Bella Drive. The Gothic script letters on top of the right gatepost read "Falcon Lair." Here, on this promontory high above the twinkling lights of the city below, was Valentino's home, "an enchanted castle suspended high above the rest of the world"— or so said Pola Negri, who shared his public life at this time but not his private hours.

Even on this remote and strangely beautiful hilltop, Valentino's fans would not leave him alone, and he had built a wall around the house to gain some privacy. But the wall couldn't stop women who were desperate for a glimpse of their hero. Just one hour of love-making with Valentino would be enough to carry them through an entire lifetime, they told the private guards who caught them climbing over the wall or prowling through the house itself. To discourage such devotion, Valentino floodlit the house at night, and he loosed three Great Danes, two Italian mastiffs, and one Spanish greyhound in the courtyard and terrace.

The dogs started howling and sniffing excitedly at the inside of the gates when they heard their master's car on the road outside. A servant came out of the gatehouse, shooed away the dogs, and threw open the gates. The Isotta Fraschini pulled into the driveway, passed the small fountain on the left, and stopped in front of a Spanish-style main house with a red tile roof and taupe-colored stucco walls. A steel pennant with a stylized "V" in the center flew from the central tower.

The chauffeur hopped out of his seat, ran around the car, and opened the door of the passenger compartment. As the chauffeur stood at attention, Valentino stepped out of the car and walked through the front door of the house, which the butler was holding open. Then the chauffeur got back into the Isotta Fraschini, a little more slowly this time, and parked the limousine in the garage next to Valentino's 1925 French Avion Voisin four-passenger phaeton, with its taupe lacquer paint job, wire wheels, and red leather interior; his 1926 taupe Franklin coupe; and the black 1925 Chevrolet roadster he drove when traveling incognito. All these cars weren't the garage's only occupants. There was also a hundred-and-twenty-gallon gasoline tank, because going to a filling station was out of the question for a star like Valentino. The second floor of the garage housed the servants' quarters, which included a dining room, a kitchen, four bedrooms, and one bath.

Near the garage stood Falcon Lair's stables and twenty-dog kennels, with the same taupe stucco walls and red tile roof as the main house. An expert horseman, Valentino rode one of his four Arabians—Firefly, Yaqui, Ramadan, and Haround—through the empty hills near Falcon Lair every morning before going to the studio. His fans had heard about these early morning rides, and they started to annoy him as soon as he rode past the fence of his eight-acre estate. Valentino found a simple, though expensive, solution to this problem. He bought the empty six and eight-tenths acres adjacent to Falcon Lair so that he could ride the bridle path in solitude to the nearby estate of cowboy star Fred Thompson and screenwriter Frances Marion.

Valentino had bought Falcon Lair from a Beverly Hills realtor, George B. Read, for $175,000 in 1925, and he named the estate after the screenplay "The Hooded Falcon," which his second wife, Natacha Rambova, had written for him. Natacha had pestered him to buy an estate like this. She had complained bitterly that their eight-room home at 6776 Wedgewood Place in the Hollywood Hills just wouldn't do for a star of his magnitude. The house was too small, the neighborhood

Falcon Lair, on Bella Drive, in the hills above Beverly Hills' fashionable Benedict Canyon.

was going downhill, and the top movie people lived in Beverly Hills anyway. Natacha, however, never moved into Falcon Lair, because she left Valentino soon after he bought the property.

Valentino was reportedly heartbroken over the rift, but he didn't let his grief slow his plans to spend hundreds of thousands of dollars remodeling the estate to his liking. He completely redecorated the main house, erected the concrete wall, built the stables and kennels, and added the second-floor servants' quarters to the garage. In the two acres of level ground around the house, he planted more than fifty Italian cypress trees and laid out an Italian garden with several hundred rare European and Oriental shrubs.

Falcon Lair was Valentino's greatest extravagance: a star's showplace, a plaything, and the fulfillment of an escapist fantasy, all at once. Few movie stars had Valentino's highly developed sense of style, and even fewer dared to express themselves with such forthright individuality. From the outside, the main house looked like any other movie star's Spanish-style mansion in the 1920s, except for the taupe paint job and stirring views of Benedict Canyon. But few guests to Falcon Lair ever forgot what they saw once they stepped through the richly carved, solid-oak sixteenth-century Florentine front doors. Inside, the house looked like a set from one of Valentino's movies, only grander and more fantastic.

On one wall of the entrance hall hung a life-size portrait of a stern-faced Valentino, dressed in the full armor and costume of a Saracen warlord at the time of the Crusades, with a young woman seated on the ground, her legs crossed, looking up at him. The hall floor was travertine, and the walls were painted the ever-present taupe, as were the walls of every room in the house. Valentino had also carpeted the entire house—except for the entrance hall and dining room—in seamless taupe Axminster wool carpeting. The drapes in the living room, dining room, library, and Valentino's office were Genoese velvet, and the curtains in the three master bedrooms on the floor below were hand-loomed Italian linen net.

The living room, dining room, library, office, and two downstairs guest bedrooms were filled with expensive antiques Valentino had acquired during buying binges in New York and European auction houses—Turkish and Arabian furniture, carved Spanish screens, an eleven-thousand-dollar Italian player grand piano, several dozen fifteenth- and sixteenth-century Florentine chairs, a fifteenth-century French throne with a Gothic canopy, even a fifteenth-century French walnut chest that had been carved to look like the facade of a Gothic cathedral, down to the pointed arch windows and elaborate tracery.

Thousands of books, each one with a Rudolph Guglielmi Valentino bookplate, jammed the shelves in the library. Valentino had collected the works of standard nineteenth-century authors such as Victor Hugo, Charles Dickens, Goethe, Schiller, Alexandre Dumas, and even fifty-one volumes of the *Harvard Classics*. But Valentino's eclectic taste extended beyond these safe classics: Other titles included *A History of the Hat, Sport in Art in the Eighteenth Century, Spanish and Portuguese Gardens, Anatomy for Art Students, Russian Ballet in Western Europe, 1909–1920*, plus several hundred softcovers.

Valentino also collected armor and antique weapons. Several suits of medieval armor stood around the house, and he had hung a few favorites of his dozen guns and several dozen swords and daggers on the walls. The jumble of old furniture, books, and weapons made Falcon Lair look more like an expensive antique store or a slightly overdressed stage set than a comfortable house—as if the thirty-year-old Valentino was trying just a little too hard to act out his role as Hollywood star.

He certainly dressed the part. A hopeless clotheshorse, Valentino filled his dressing-room closets with 30 business suits, 10 complete dress suits, 4 riding outfits, 10 overcoats, 37 vests, 124 shirts, 7 dressing gowns, 60 pairs of gloves, 59 pairs of shoes, 28 pairs of assorted spats, and 110 silk handkerchiefs, each one monogrammed "RGV." He owned 44 hats, including one aviator helmet even though he didn't know how to fly an airplane. Valentino even kept elaborate costumes from *Blood and Sand* and *Monsieur Beaucaire* at home, because he liked to admire their fine materials and costly workmanship.

Valentino had bought dozens of gold and platinum cigarette boxes, cuff links and studs, wristwatches, card cases, scarf pins, match cases, and cigarette holders. His jewelry box held over thirty rings, including a 10-karat pigeon-blood ruby set in platinum, a 12-karat

Just twelve years before this photograph was taken, Rudolph Guglielmi Valentino was a penniless Italian immigrant in New York City, who claimed to be the son of impoverished nobility. Here he has become Valentino, the million-dollar-a-year Hollywood idol and the master of Falcon Lair, dressed to fit his carefully thought out and frightfully expensive at-home country-gentleman role.

Valentino and his taupe 1925 Avion Voisin four-passenger phaeton with its custom red leather interior and silver cobra radiator cap.

Valentino showing off one of his four Arabians at the Falcon Lair stables.

emerald in platinum, and a 40-carat sapphire in platinum—but his favorite piece of jewelry was the solid platinum slave bracelet that he wore around his wrist at all times.

Falcon Lair's antique-filled public rooms represented Valentino, the internationally revered Hollywood star. But in the bedroom the taste of Rudolph Guglielmi Valentino, the man and the private individual, expressed itself in the sleek avant-garde Moderne style. This was the most extreme room in the house, particularly because of its bewildering jumble of colors. The king-size bed had massive gold ball feet, and the headboard was lacquered dark blue. The sheets, pillowcases, and bedspread were crocus yellow—to set off Valentino's dozen pairs of yellow Japanese silk pajamas. On either side of the bed stood bright orange lacquered Moderne cabinets with the same gold ball feet. The two dressers were lacquered dark blue, and the overstuffed settee and upholstered armchair were covered in black satin.

The built-in perfume lamp on the orange lacquered round pedestal table at the foot of the bed filled the room with fragrance whenever the light was turned on, for the height of 1920s bedroom decadence. On the wall above the headboard of the bed hung a three-foot-square portrait of the Spanish dancer Señorita Gaditana, nude to the waist, reclining and facing the observer with her arms folded behind her head.

Valentino's fans expected him to live like royalty or, better yet, a deity, and he willingly obliged their expectations, because he loved all this luxury. Spending hundreds of thousands of dollars on Falcon Lair, however, did more than keep his fans happy and satisfy his ego. By unwittingly turning Falcon Lair into almost a parody of a silent-star's showplace, complete with stables, kennels, private guards, a wall, and a gate, Valentino had created a private compound where he could pursue his hobbies in peace and see his friends outside the public gaze.

Behind Falcon Lair's taupe walls, Valentino felt free to be himself, to wear dirty old clothes while he took car engines apart and put them together again. Other times, he'd quietly entertain a few friends, some of them movie stars like Charlie Chaplin, Marion Davies, or Lillian Gish, but mostly ordinary people he'd known since arriving in Hollywood as an unknown in 1917. Despite his effulgent wardrobe and platinum slave bracelet, Lillian Gish remembers Valentino as "simple, unpretentious, very much the Italian gentleman. His two great loves were horses and dancing. He had many talents; he designed riding clothes for Dorothy and me, and he was a good cook. Often on our return from an evening canter, he would go into our kitchen and cook spaghetti for us."

Falcon Lair was the tangible symbol of Valentino's international stardom and his amazing success in Hollywood. Just twelve years before he bought the estate, he had arrived in New York, in December 1913, an Italian immigrant in the steerage deck of an overcrowded steamer. In New York he claimed to be the son of impoverished Italian nobility, and he earned a living as a professional dancer in cabarets and nightclubs. After he came to Los Angeles in 1917, he earned a living, but just barely, working in the movies as an extra and doing occasional bit parts. Then the part of young Julio in *The Four Horsemen of the Apocalypse* catapulted him into stardom in 1921, and just five years later he was the master of Falcon Lair and the idol of millions.

CHAPTER TWO

For the several decades before it became one of America's biggest and fastest-growing cities in the 1920s, Los Angeles had been, briefly, a kind of earthly paradise. Surrounded by orange groves, barley fields, and the last of the Spanish and Mexican land-grant cattle ranches, Los Angeles was outgrowing its violent and vice-ridden small-town past by the 1880s; thereafter it began to gain some of the comforts, culture, and appearance of larger, more settled cities back east. But few other American cities enjoyed such a pleasant—and striking—location as Los Angeles. The climate was temperate all year long, and the local landscape included every conceivable terrain: grassy plains, hills, snow-capped mountains, ocean, even desert, all within a day's journey of the city.

The first settlers to put down roots in what would become Los Angeles found themselves on a flat plain that ended at the Pacific Ocean, where constant offshore breezes ensured a temperate and predictable climate. In summer, the temperature seldom climbed above 85 degrees Fahrenheit, and, after the hottest July and August days, it usually dropped into the 60s in the evening. In winter, the daytime temperature often reached the 60s or 70s and rarely fell below 40 degrees in the evening.

Los Angeles grew up along the Los Angeles River, which started in the mountains rising behind the San Fernando Valley and emptied into the Pacific Ocean near Long Beach. This was a river in name only. Los Angeles received an average of fifteen inches of precipitation a year, and almost all of this fell during the winter. For those few months, the rainfall and the melting snows in the mountains turned the Los Angeles River into a turbulent and muddy-colored stream, fed by numerous mountain creeks along its way to the ocean. During the rest of the year the only rainfall was an occasional nighttime sprinkling of heavy ocean fog, and the Los Angeles River turned into a dry gulch, the kind of California river that Mark Twain had fallen into and "come out all dusty."

With only one part-time local river and month after dry month of no rain, the coastal plain around Los Angeles originally was a virtual desert, covered with fields of bunch grass and occasional patches of chaparral. During the wet winter months these fields were green, but they quickly turned golden brown after the rains stopped in April.

Los Angeles' dry climate had its compensations: low humidity and day after day of sunlight, sometimes bright and glaring, other times softened by haze or ocean mist. Even during the rainy winter months there was plenty of sunshine, because precipitation actually fell only thirty-five to forty days a year. Nights of rain were often followed by sunny days, with the air cleansed to brilliant sharpness and the grass and chaparral green and glistening with moisture.

On these crystal-clear days, the Santa Monica Mountains loomed high above the coastal plain, looking rugged and barren except for patches of chaparral on the steep hillsides and clumps of small trees along an occasional stream in the canyons. These mountains, which began near downtown Los Angeles and stretched fifteen miles west to the Pacific Ocean, divided the coastal plain from the inland San Fernando Valley. Reaching 3059 feet at their highest elevation, the Santa Monica Mountains were the home of rabbits, coyotes, skunks, rodents, over two hundred species of birds, and more than a few rattlesnakes.

The view from these mountains was spectacular: to the south, the coastal plain bathed in sunlight, and to the southwest, the sparkling, limitless blue expanse of the Pacific Ocean, with Santa Catalina Island twenty-seven miles offshore, its mountain peaks rising over two thousand feet above the sea. Behind the Santa Monica Mountains lay the twenty-two-mile-long San Fernando Valley, and behind it the Santa Susana and San Gabriel mountains, the second mountain chain inland

Hollywood panorama, 1895, looking down on the Los Angeles coastal plain from Laurel Canyon in the Santa Monica Mountains, called the Hollywood Hills here. This pastoral scene did not last long. Shortly after the turn of the century, bungalow subdivisions began to replace these orange groves and barley fields, and in the teens moviemakers swarmed into Hollywood, turning the straitlaced middle-class suburban town into an international symbol of glamour and excitement—and scandal.

Ocean View tract in Monrovia, twenty miles northeast of Los Angeles, where—at the height of the late 1880s Southern California real-estate boom—land developers were luring buyers to their subdivisions with free picnics and circus acts, and even hanging oranges on ordinary trees to make the land look more fertile than it really was.

from the ocean. In the summer and fall months these mountains looked golden-brown in the hazy air, but they were snowcapped just a few weeks after the start of the winter rains.

Pacific Ocean breezes generally didn't get past the Santa Monica Mountains, and the San Fernando Valley was ten degrees hotter than the coastal plain and Los Angeles during the summer months—and about five to ten degrees cooler in winter. But the Santa Susana and San Gabriel mountains did protect the San Fernando Valley and Los Angeles from much of the desert heat and dust in the even hotter and drier Central Valley, the third inland plain from the ocean.

Nature had endowed Los Angeles with this remarkable combination of ocean breezes, almost constant sunlight, and easy temperatures. But it was man who turned Los Angeles into a garden spot. The missing ingredient had been water. But around 1870, Los Angelenos discovered artesian water beneath the dusty, grass-covered coastal plain—so much water that they didn't have to pump it out of the ground; it simply poured out of the artesian wells on its own.

With sufficient water year-round, almost anything thrived in Los Angeles, and it grew faster there than almost anywhere else in America. The palm, eucalyptus, acacia, pepper tree, and fragrant night-blooming jasmine, all of which have become an inextricable part of the Southern California landscape, were imported to Los Angeles at this time. Los Angeles' coastal plain and the inland San Fernando Valley emerged as one of the nation's richest farming areas. Thousands of poultry ranches, barley fields, vegetable farms, and orchards dotted the once arid fields of bunch grass and chaparral. Between March and early May, tens of thousands of orange, lemon, and grapefruit trees bloomed, and the air in Los Angeles was sweet. At night the mist from the ocean held this scent close to the ground, and the air turned into perfume.

A place like this couldn't remain a secret for long. During the 1870s and 1880s, books, magazines, and newspapers published glowing accounts of the Southern California landscape and climate.

In November 1885 the Santa Fe Railroad completed its Missouri Valley–Los Angeles line and began a rate war with its already established competitor, the Southern Pacific Railroad. From a previous high of $125, fares from St. Louis to the new Eden plummeted to $12, then to $8, $6, $4. On March 6, 1886, both railroads posted a $1 fare. The result was that thousands of Midwestern farmers and townspeople suddenly packed up their belongings and left for Southern California.

The first railroad immigrants to arrive in Los Angeles in 1886 found a backward, often violent trading and agricultural town of about fifteen thousand American and Mexican residents, where the streets were ankle-deep in dust or mud, depending on the season. Ornate two- and three-story Victorian-style downtown business buildings stood next to drab, weather-beaten adobes. Los Angeles had such a backward reputation that the Los Angeles *Times* once assured the rest of the country that the "people do not carry arms, Indians are a curiosity, [and] the gee string is not a common article of apparel here."

The flood of railroad immigrants quickly turned Los Angeles into a prosperous though often chaotic boomtown. The nation had never before witnessed an internal migration so large or so swift. In 1887, over a hundred and twenty thousand people arrived in Los Angeles on the Southern Pacific Railroad. Every day three or four Santa Fe trains pulled into town, jammed with hundreds more eager newcomers. The resulting real-estate explosion dwarfed earlier land booms in Chicago, Wichita, and Seattle. Real-estate "boomers" bought pieces of old Spanish and Mexican ranches, built a hotel, and opened some streets, and started the first few hundred feet of a railroad leading to downtown Los Angeles. Then they selected names for the towns—Morocco, Sunset, Ivanhoe—filed their subdivision maps at the county recorder's office, and presto! there were some new towns on the landscape.

Between January 1, 1887, and July 1, 1889, just thirty months, more than sixty new towns on 79,350 acres were mapped out in Los Angeles County. No location was too unlikely. If the boomers did not find a flat piece of ranchland at the right price, they planned their new community on a steep hillside and stressed its picturesque views. Desert towns were promoted as health resorts, and new communities on swampy land near the Pacific Ocean inevitably became "harbor cities."

The real-estate promoters did anything and everything to attract buyers. Many held "grand jubilee auctions," complete with brass bands, circus performers, and free lunches to lure crowds. Some developers even hung oranges on ordinary trees, to make the land look more fertile than it was.

Just about everybody got into the real-estate act. An Eastern visitor attended services at a Methodist church in downtown Los Angeles one Sunday. As the congregation filed out of the church, the minister shook his hand, asked if he were a recent arrival, then sold him a lot in a new subdivision!

One of these real-estate developers was Horace Henderson Wilcox, who arrived in Los Angeles from Topeka, Kansas, with his wife, Daeida, in 1883. Horace Wilcox's legs were crippled because of a childhood bout with typhoid fever, but this tragedy had not impeded him. He learned shoemaking as a child and used this skill to work his way through college; then, after receiving his degree, he became active in Ohio church and political affairs, eventually moving on to Kansas to make a fortune in real estate and help carry the state for Prohibition.

On his arrival in Los Angeles, Wilcox started subdividing property at the outskirts of the city, and he and his wife established themselves at the center of the city's religious, political, and charitable activities. It was about this time that *Mr.* Wilcox became known as *General* Wilcox, and shortly afterward that he bought a ranch about an hour's ride and eight miles northwest of town at the base of the Santa Monica Mountains.

But Horace Wilcox was too energetic a man to spend his life raising barley and tending the orange groves at his ranch. In 1887 he mapped the property into streets, blocks, and lots and built a gabled and turreted Queen Anne–style mansion on a dirt road that he named Wilcox Avenue. The town was named "Hollywood" by his wife, Daeida, who took the name from the country estate of one of their friends back in Ohio—or so the story goes.

Horace and Daeida Wilcox hoped that Hollywood would become more than just a real-estate venture. As devout Methodists and active Prohibitionists, they had an almost Utopian vision and wanted Hollywood to become a model of Christian virtue for the still violent, vice-ridden Los Angeles. The Wilcoxes barred saloons and liquor stores, and they offered a free lot to any church willing to build in Hollywood. Unfortunately only a handful of houses had been built in Hollywood when the Southern California land boom collapsed in 1889. Horace Wilcox died one year later. Daeida Wilcox married Philo Judson Beveridge in 1894, and she continued to donate free land to religious and community organizations, but Hollywood's growth had slowed to a standstill.

This lethargy was only slightly abated by the "Belgian hare craze," which gripped all Los Angeles around 1890. Under its spell, otherwise reasonable Angelenos decided that raising rabbits was a sure way to fortune: Rabbits, after all, ate a cheap diet of vegetables, but they provided plenty of meat for the family dinner table, and their fur was good for winter coats. Or so went the argument. Rabbit fanciers talked about the virtues of this or that pedigree, and prized "Belgian hares" sold for hundreds, even thousands, of dollars before the bunny boom ended just as abruptly as it had begun.

By then Los Angeles had another get-rich-quick scheme, and this one worked. On November 4, 1892, Edward Laurence Doheny, an unsuccessful thirty-six-year-old Wisconsin-born gold and silver prospector, and Charles A. Canfield, another miner and an old friend, struck oil near Colton Street and Glendale Boulevard in the middle of a residential neighborhood, about a mile northwest of downtown Los Angeles.

At first nobody—except the two grimy prospectors—got excited. Doheny and Canfield knew so little about oil exploration that they dug a five-by-seven-foot mining shaft with a pick and shovel to a depth of 155 feet before they switched to a sixty-foot-tall eucalyptus tree that they had hollowed out and sharpened into a makeshift drill. When they struck oil at 460 feet, the well delivered only seven barrels a day, which Doheny and Canfield bailed out with a bucket.

Los Angelenos already knew that modest amounts of oil lay beneath the city and surrounding coastal plain. At a few places like the La Brea Tar Pits, the oil bubbled to the surface and formed quagmires, which had trapped prehistoric animals thousands of years earlier. In many other spots, small amounts of oil seeped out of the ground and slowly thickened on contact with the air, the way pine sap turns into resin on a tree trunk. For centuries, local Indians had used the tarry brea to waterproof their woven baskets. More recently, Mexican and

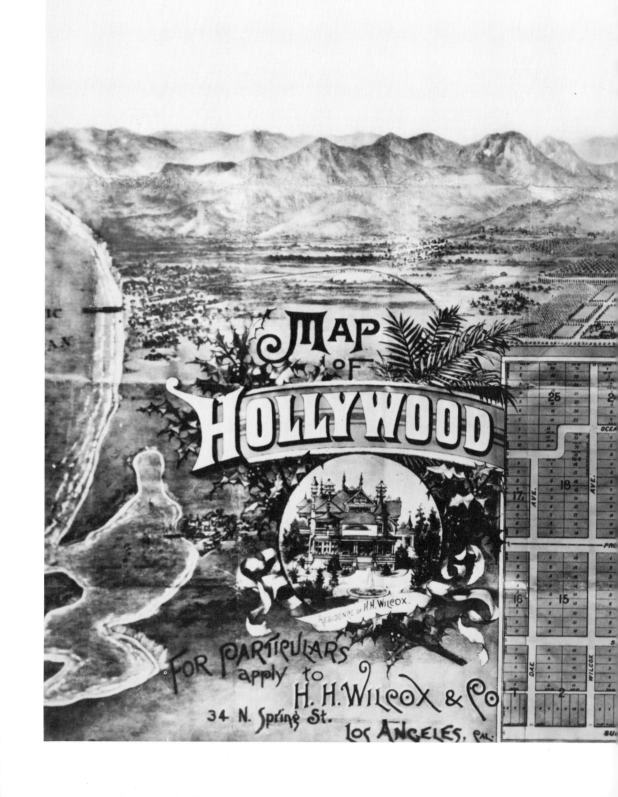

Horace and Daeida Wilcox, 1887. The Wilcoxes founded Hollywood in 1887, but they were more than get-rich-quick speculators. Devout Methodists and ardent Prohibitionists, the Wilcoxes hoped to make Hollywood a model of Christian virtue, and they barred saloons and liquor stores from the community, then offered a free lot to any church willing to build there.

The first map of Hollywood, 1887.

REFERENCES:
1 Hotel Hollywood.
2 Residence of H.H.Wilcox
3 Hollywood Depot.
4 Business Block of H.
5 Mt. Whittier.
6 Hotel Hollywood.
7 City Reservoir.
8 Soldiers Home.
9 Santa Monica.
10 Ballona Harbor.
11 Sunset Hotel.

American settlers collected it to caulk roofs and fence posts, to lubricate machinery, even to burn in the wood- and coal-starved Los Angeles basin. But no one took it seriously as fuel, since there didn't seem to be very much of it. When Doheny and Canfield's well started to produce forty-five barrels a day, however, people began to wonder if their homes or ranches were sitting over a fortune in black gold. And the Los Angeles oil boom was on.

Wildcatters swarmed into town, looking for land to lease and wells to drill. Homeowners trampled their gardens, ripped out palm trees, even moved or tore down their houses to make room for drilling rigs and oil derricks. Everybody worked quickly, lest a neighbor sink a well first and drain all the California crude from under nearby properties. One man installed a drilling rig in his backyard only to realize that he didn't have any place to dispose of the waste water and mud coming out of the ever-deepening shaft. Rather than lose precious time hauling the mud away, he simply dumped it into his basement.

Oil exploration spread beyond the original field, and by 1897, twenty-five hundred wells were pumping away in a half-mile-wide, several-mile-long area stretching south and west from Elysian Park to Vermont Avenue. Between 1897 and 1899, wildcatters brought in another five hundred wells in this new field, raising the total in Los Angeles to three thousand.

With almost no city regulations over the petroleum industry, Los Angeles became an oil speculators' paradise. Wildcatters drilled wherever they wanted—next to schools, churches, even fine homes. City streets were hopelessly torn up as teams of six or eight steel-shod mules pulled heavy drilling machinery and oil tanks. At times it seemed as if the petroleum companies wasted more oil than they pumped. Wagons filled with poorly sealed barrels of oil literally dripped their way from the wells to the refineries. So much oil drained into Echo Park Lake from nearby storage tanks that it caught fire and burned for three days in 1907. But nobody worried about wasting oil, because it was a glut on the market in turn-of-the-century Los Angeles, sometimes selling for as little as ten cents a barrel!

The oil boom was the first assault on the extraordinary quality of the Los Angeles environment. Entire streets and neighborhoods vanished under a forest of wooden derricks and a grimy film of oil. In some parts of town the smell of natural gas replaced the scent of orange blossoms, and the constant *ump-um ump-um* of oil pumps drowned out songbirds and made life miserable for families living nearby.

Even belated city ordinances at the turn of the century could not control the lust for black gold. Hundreds of property owners filed permits with the city to drill water wells. What could anyone do if they struck oil instead? Besides, the city was not enthusiastic about strict enforcement. As Mayor Meredith P. Snyder declared in 1897, "This is one of the leading industries in the city, and all legislation bearing on it should be liberal."

The oil boom was helping to turn Los Angeles into a twentieth-century city. Besides offering low-priced fuel for new local industries and providing thousands of jobs, the oil boom generated the capital to build homes and open streets, develop an ocean port twenty-five miles south of the city at San Pedro, and bring desperately needed water several hundred miles from the Owens River Valley for Los Angeles' productive farms and growing population. Every winter, tens of thousands of East Coast and Midwestern tourists poured into Los Angeles to escape the brutal weather back home. Many took jobs and never went home. Los Angeles' population jumped from 50,395 in 1890 to 102,479 in 1900 to 319,198 in 1910.

Hollywood, however, did not share in the new prosperity. It was too far from Los Angeles to become another suburb, it didn't have many oil wells, and it had become a slowly decaying backwater with a population of about six hundred permanent residents. Some of the Victorian houses built during the 1880s land boom were beginning to look run-down and a little old-fashioned.

Hardy Eastern and Midwestern tourists came to Hollywood to see the Cahuenga Water Gardens, where Edmund D. Sturtevant raised water lilies that were large enough for a child to stand on, or to visit Dr. C. J. Sketchley's Ostrich Farm in the foothills near present-day Griffith Park. But most of Hollywood remained barley fields, orange and lemon groves, and vegetable gardens, worth two hundred to four hundred dollars an acre, until a real-estate syndicate headed by General Moses Hazeltine Sherman, Eli P. Clark, and Harry Chandler bought

Los Angeles oil boom, Court Street, 1901. After Edward Laurence Doheny struck oil near downtown Los Angeles in 1902, homeowners trampled their gardens, even moved or tore down their homes to make room for drilling rigs and oil derricks. By the turn of the century, over three thousand wells were pumping away in Los Angeles.

BELOW: *Cahuenga Water Gardens, 1901, one of Hollywood's most famous attractions before the arrival of the movie studios in the teens.*

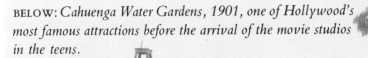

several citrus groves north of Hollywood Boulevard, between Cahuenga Pass and La Brea Avenue. This was a high-powered group: Sherman was a railroad and trolley millionaire; Clark was Sherman's brother-in-law and front man; and Chandler was the son-in-law of General Harrison Gray Otis, publisher of the Los Angeles *Times* (Chandler would later become publisher of the newspaper).

Hollywood real-estate men, however, wondered if Sherman, Clark, and Chandler hadn't made a dreadful mistake. The land they bought had been cheap, but the syndicate would never be able to make any money from subdividing the property into town lots, given the way Hollywood looked at the turn of the century. Potential lot buyers were attracted to successful real-estate subdivisions where they would have plenty of neighbors, local shopping, and the likelihood of rising property values.

So Sherman, Clark, and Chandler began to set the stage. Their grandly named Los Angeles–Pacific Railroad ran an electric trolley between Los Angeles and Hollywood every hour so that prospective lot purchasers didn't have to worry how they would get back and forth to work in town. The seven-mile trip took twenty-five minutes, and with a yearly commuter ticket, the one-way fare was seven cents.

In 1903, Sherman, Clark, and Chandler helped lead the campaign that made Hollywood an incorporated city. The same year George W. Hoover, one of their investors, built the Hollywood Hotel on unpaved Hollywood Boulevard, between Orchid and Highland avenues. An eclectic mix of Moorish and Spanish styles, the twenty-five-thousand-dollar frame hotel had thirty-three rooms, two baths, and a roof garden. More importantly, the Hollywood Hotel provided a physical focus for the community and offered visitors from Los Angeles a place to stay overnight.

Now Sherman, Clark, and Chandler were ready to put their first tract on the market. They posted SOLD signs on hundreds of unsold lots, and piled lumber and bricks on other vacant lots to give the impression that buyers were starting to build houses. And then, on May 3, 1903, they decorated their electric trolleys with flags and flowers for the run between Los Angeles and Hollywood; they hired a brass band to greet visitors; and late in the afternoon General M. H. Sherman spoke to the crowd that had gathered in front of the real-estate office. At the end of his speech, he pointed to the spurious SOLD signs nearby and the piles of building materials, broke into tears, and cried out, "Behold what God hath wrought!" This sales promotion was melo-dramatic and deceptive, but it worked. Modest frame bungalows and unpaved streets slowly replaced Hollywood's barley fields and orange groves—and Sherman, Clark, and Chandler made a tidy 60 percent profit on their investment.

Hollywood was changing from an isolated cluster of houses into a small town charmingly situated in the foothills of the Santa Monica Mountains, here known as the Hollywood Hills. In 1904, Sunset Bou-levard was completed from downtown Los Angeles to Laurel Canyon in Hollywood. A year later, Hollywood's first store, the Hollywood Cash Grocery, opened at the northeast corner of Cahuenga Avenue and Sunset Boulevard. The electric trolley between Los Angeles and Hol-lywood started running every fifteen minutes in 1905, and Hollywood got its first electricity, piped water, and telephone service that year.

Hollywood's population increased from 700 in 1903 to 4,000 in 1910. Horace Wilcox would have approved of these new people. They were, for the most part, sober, churchgoing middle-class families, and the town government did everything in its power to make Hollywood a safe and wholesome community for them. In its first year, the eight-member Board of Trustees outlawed the sale of liquor, except by pre-scription, closed billiard rooms and bowling alleys at eleven p.m. on weekdays and all day Sunday, and prohibited gambling and "disor-derly houses." Also banned were slaughterhouses, glue factories, gas-works, oil wells, and sanitariums. Another law forbade driving herds of more than two hundred horses, cattle, or mules, and herds of more than two thousand sheep, goats, or hogs through the streets. Finally, the Board of Trustees outlawed riding bicycles and tricycles on side-walks, even though there were only two short stretches of sidewalk in all of Hollywood at the time.

But there were signs that solid middle-class virtues were beginning to give way to the exotic and the fanciful: Arthur Letts, founder and owner of the Broadway Department Store in downtown Los Angeles, built a twenty-room house at 4931 Franklin Avenue in Hollywood, a few blocks west of Vermont Avenue. This house followed the half-timbered Elizabethan style, except for the large verandahs, which were a concession to the Southern California climate. Charles F. Harper, a hardware merchant, built a gabled and turreted mansion near Sunset Boulevard and Laurel Canyon, one of the two routes over the Santa Monica Mountains between Hollywood and the San Fernando Valley.

Paul De Longpre, an artist best known for his realistic flower paintings, bought four lots at Cahuenga Avenue and Hollywood Boulevard, not far from Cahuenga Pass, the other road over the Hollywood Hills, and planted them with flowers. The engineer and businessman Homer Laughlin, another gardening enthusiast, bought thirty-three acres in the foothills, just east of Vermont Avenue, but he was so obsessed with the idea of creating the perfect country estate that he would not build a house on the property until all the landscaping was planted *and* mature. From 1899, for the next twelve years, Laughlin's gardeners covered the gently rolling hills with more than fifty thousand trees, shrubs, and perennial flowers.

After going to all that trouble, Laughlin decided not to build a house on the property after all, and his son, Homer Jr., turned the thirty-three-acre estate into a stylish subdivision called Laughlin Park. Making every effort to maintain the site's natural beauty, Laughlin, Jr. laid out winding roads to preserve the contours of the hills and his father's careful years of gardening, and his architects had to approve plans for all new homes. All this work paid off. When Laughlin Park was opened to the public in October 1913, the Los Angeles *Times* proclaimed it "the last word in residential masterpieces."

Hollywood residents were delighted to read about this in the big-city newspaper. At last, important things were beginning to happen in their community, they reasoned: the annual Floral Parade in April, with its flower-covered carriages and automobiles proceeding down Hollywood Boulevard, its costumed men and women on horseback, and its Tilting Tournament, in which horsemen tried to spear white harness rings hanging from poles with their fourteen-foot lances; the opening of the twenty-four-room Lookout Mountain Inn at the top of Laurel Canyon, where Hollywood residents could eat chicken dinners in the dining room and admire the panoramic 270-degree view of the city below; the construction of the Hill Street Tunnel in 1909, which sharply reduced travel time on the trolley between Los Angeles and Hollywood; a presidential visit by William Howard Taft in 1910. Hollywood had arrived—and yet it was about to change so drastically, that the retired Midwestern farmers and Los Angeles businessmen would scarcely recognize their town in just a few years.

CHAPTER THREE

A few days before Christmas, 1913, Cecil B. De Mille, a struggling New York actor-turned-director, rented Jacob Stern's large faded yellow barn at the southeast corner of Selma Avenue and Vine Street in Hollywood. De Mille had just arrived in Los Angeles on December 20 with the cameraman Alfredo Gandolfi, the experienced director Oscar Apfel, the Broadway stage star Dustin Farnum, and Farnum's secretary, Fred Kley, and he was going to make a movie called *The Squaw Man* for the Jesse L. Lasky Feature Play Company.

This barn would be their studio. Actually, De Mille and his little production company didn't get to use the entire barn, because owner Jacob Stern still kept his horse and carriage in one corner. Actors changed their clothes in empty horse stalls, and De Mille had to put his feet in the wastepaper basket under his desk whenever Stern washed the carriage and flooded the barn floor. De Mille hired a young woman named Stella Stray to be his secretary, because she had her own typewriter. But De Mille wasn't perturbed by these makeshift conditions. He had high hopes for *The Squaw Man* and hung a large sign on the barn that read JESSE L. LASKY FEATURE PLAY COMPANY STUDIO.

Most Hollywood residents didn't care about De Mille's movie, and many didn't even know what was happening in the weather-beaten barn. When Jesse L. Lasky arrived in Hollywood from New York in January 1914, he stopped at the Hollywood Hotel, walked up to the desk clerk, proudly told the young man who he was, and asked for directions to his company's studio.

"Never heard of it," replied the desk clerk.

"Our director-general is Cecil B. De Mille," said a somewhat deflated Lasky.

"Never heard of him either," was the answer.

Lasky started to walk away, wondering what to do next, when the clerk called after him: "There's a bunch of people making pictures down on Vine Street. They might know where your company is. Go down the boulevard here to Vine and turn right. You can't miss the barn, on your left." Lasky heard the word "barn" and knew that he'd found his company.

The Squaw Man marked the start of a new era for Hollywood, for Los Angeles, and for the entire movie industry. Within a few years, a secluded and intensely respectable Los Angeles suburb had replaced New York as the capital of the motion picture industry, and the word "Hollywood" had become a symbol of glamour, excitement, and opportunity to millions of people across the nation and around the world.

Cecil B. De Mille was not the first filmmaker to work in Los Angeles. That distinction belongs to Francis Boggs, a director for Colonel William N. Selig, who shot several scenes of *The Count of Monte Cristo* near Laguna Beach late in 1908, because bad winter weather at the Selig Polyscope studios in Chicago had delayed completion of the film. After finishing the missing scenes, Boggs returned to Chicago. But the next winter he was back in Los Angeles and converted an empty Chinese laundry at Eighth and Olive streets into his production company's offices and dressing rooms; he also built a forty-foot-square stage on the vacant lot next door. Here Boggs filmed *The Heart of the Racetrack Tout*, the first movie made entirely in California.

Other East Coast and Midwestern directors followed Boggs' example. By the end of 1910, fifteen fledgling production companies were working in Hollywood, at least part of the year. And many more had come to Los Angeles because of the nearly year-round warm, sunny weather and the wide variety of scenery nearby. Southern California, moreover, was three thousand miles away from the New York headquarters of the Motion Picture Patents Trust, a monopoly that leading

Cecil B. De Mille, seated on the step of the truck, with the cast of The Squaw Man *(1914) near the faded yellow barn at Selma Avenue and Vine Street in Hollywood that served as the Jesse L. Lasky Feature Play Company's first studio. The* Squaw Man *was not the first film to be made in Hollywood, but it was one of the fledgling movie industry's first nationwide box-office successes and thereby accelerated the exodus of film companies from New York to Los Angeles.*

A scene from The Squaw Man *with the Hollywood Hills in the background.*

film and equipment manufacturers formed in 1909 to regulate the rapidly growing movie industry. Trust members agreed to sell film and equipment only to each other and to distribute their movies to exhibitors who promised to show only Trust-produced films.

But some independent producers still made movies with bootlegged film and equipment, and independent distributors handled these non-Trust films. The Trust filed lawsuits against the independents, and its strong-arm men harassed and even beat up producers, often when they were in the middle of making a picture. But the independents refused to be run out of business. They formed a protective association of their own and retaliated with lawsuits and violence. By 1913 the Trust's power was waning, but independents such as Cecil B. De Mille still felt safer working in Southern California than in New York.

Even though De Mille did not make the first movie in Hollywood, his Selma Avenue barn was soon pointed out as the place where Hollywood was born. When *The Squaw Man* was released in February 1914, it became one of the movie industry's first nationwide box-office successes. The film cost $15,000 to make, and it earned over $225,000. Within several years, the Jesse L. Lasky Feature Play Company Studio had taken over the two blocks around the De Mille barn, and the motion picture industry was quickly deserting New York for Hollywood.

But Hollywood's sober, God-fearing families didn't like the influx of movie people, and the factory-like studios were eyesores looming over the town's bungalows and citrus groves. Boardinghouse owners posted signs saying NO DOGS AND NO ACTORS, and local residents indignantly called the studios "gypsy camps." After all, the movie companies came from places like New York, and just that was enough to worry the retired Midwestern farmers who had moved out to Hollywood because Los Angeles was the wicked big city. Most actors and actresses, furthermore, had worked in vaudeville or on the Broadway stage before getting into the movies, and all "theater people" were morally suspect, at least according to prevailing middle-class mores at the turn of the century.

Old-fashioned bigotry was another reason for this antagonism. Hollywood residents generally were white Anglo-Saxon Protestants, whose families had been in this country for several generations. But

Mack Sennett's Keystone Kops, 1920. Early moviemakers used all of Los Angeles as one big movie set, to the annoyance of Los Angelenos who did not see any humor in chase scenes that snarled traffic and brought noisy film crews onto quiet suburban streets. Thousands of moviegoers, however, liked the bungalows, palm trees, and glorious scenery in the background of these films so much that they moved to Los Angeles.

most movie company leaders—men such as William Fox, Samuel Goldwyn, Jesse L. Lasky, Carl Laemmle, William Selig, and Adolph Zukor—were Jewish or foreign-born, and sometimes both. Most movie audiences around 1910, furthermore, were immigrant working families living in big cities, and their theaters were not much more than empty storefronts with a projector, several rows of folding chairs, and a sheet for a screen. In the first decade of the twentieth century, Hollywood didn't have any movie theaters, and the town fathers were determined to keep things this way. The ever-vigilant Board of Trustees banned all movie theaters in Hollywood in 1910.

The movie companies, of course, brought some of this trouble on themselves. Early production companies worked so quickly turning out ten-minute one-reelers and twenty-minute two-reelers that they didn't have time to build elaborate sets at the studio: It was quicker—and cheaper—to use all of Los Angeles as a big movie set. Many families' quiet Sunday outings were ruined when movie companies borrowed sprawling Griffith Park in the Hollywood Hills for country settings. Filming chase sequences invariably tied up traffic on busy downtown streets. Sometimes movie companies paid a family five dollars to film a scene at their front door, but more often a housewife heard strange noises and found an entire production company working on the front lawn.

The worst offenders were the film companies making Westerns. The movies may have been silent, but the noise of gunfire, cowboy whoops, and horses' thundering hooves during filming were not. Many cowboy extras were real-life cowboys, who didn't see any distinction between what they did for the camera and what they did after work. At the end of the day they raced their horses down quiet suburban streets, screaming and taking potshots at the carefully trimmed palm trees, while during the evening they got into furniture-breaking, window-smashing brawls in Los Angeles bars.

After 1910, however, the good people of Hollywood couldn't do much about the movie companies, because their town had become a part of Los Angeles that year. And Los Angeles was not going to restrict moviemaking seriously, because local business and civic leaders wanted to encourage any industry in the city, no matter what they personally may have thought of the production companies' conduct or the movie people's dubious morals, and no matter whether an organization named Conscientious Citizens collected over ten thousand signatures on a petition to run the movie companies out of town.

Still, the pillars of Hollywood orthodoxy were unhappy with the film people, and they were even more discomfited by the equally strange and even more exotic invaders who followed. In 1913, Adolphe and Eugene Bernheimer, two Oriental-art importers, completed a Japanese mountain palace at 1999 North Sycamore Street, on a seven-acre estate in the hills just west of Cahuenga Pass. Gifted with as much imagination as any movie director or set designer, the two brothers furnished the house with Japanese art and turned the grounds into terraced Japanese gardens, complete with a six-hundred-year-old pagoda.

Then, a few blocks away, Dr. Alfred Guido Randolph Schloesser built not one but two castles on a hillside east of Cahuenga Pass. A brilliant and wonderfully eccentric man, Schloesser had been a successful physician and surgeon in Chicago during the 1880s and 1890s, then went into mining and made his fortune. By the turn of the century, Schloesser was earning forty thousand dollars a month from his mining discoveries, and he liked to spend it. He visited Europe regularly, buying art for his growing collection as he went along. He went around the world once, crossed the equator several times, and traveled within seven hundred miles of the North Pole. A self-described "capitalist, art connoisseur, and music critic," Schloesser was also a would-be architect. When he first came to Hollywood in 1910, he built a castle called Glengary, which reputedly combined features from buildings at Oxford University, Glengary Castle in Scotland, and Nuremberg Castle in Germany, all in one gloriously eclectic hodgepodge. But Schloesser's real pride and joy at Glengary were the formal gardens, laid out by Mils Emitslof, who had been landscape architect to Queen Victoria and the Czar of Russia. He didn't, however, enjoy them for long: Only a year later he announced that Glengary, one of the largest houses in Hollywood, was too small, nothing more than "a satisfactory architectural experiment." Now Schloesser wanted to build the kind of castle he'd always dreamed about, and the only suitable location was a former lemon grove he had bought as a development project across the street from Glengary, and which his real-estate agents were marketing. Some families were already building bungalows on their newly purchased lots, but that didn't stop Schloesser. No other spot would do, and he started buying back the property, a lot at a time, sometimes spending three and four times what the families had paid only a few months earlier.

Schloesser's second home, Castle Sans Souci, completed in 1912 at the northwest corner of Franklin and Argyle avenues, looked every bit like a castle and then some: leaded glass windows, corner turrets, crenellated roof lines, even a several-story tower rising out of the middle. Schloesser's art collection, antiques, and books filled most of the rooms, which included a very un-castle-like Louis Quinze reception room. The main feature of Castle Sans Souci was a Gothic hall, fifty by twenty feet, with a twenty-five-foot-high beamed ceiling, stained glass windows depicting scenes of chivalry, suits of armor, and an organ loft. No one seemed to mind that beyond the stained-glass windows were Southern California lemon groves.

Hollywood residents may have smiled at Schloesser's eccentricities, but they were quite upset with Alfred Powell Warrington, a Norfolk, Virginia, attorney turned Los Angeles guru, who founded a Theosophical retreat named Kratona on a fifteen-acre site above Castle Sans Souci. Theosophy is a blend of Buddhism and Brahmanism; its followers believe that they establish direct mystical contact with divine principles through contemplation and revelation. Warrington had selected the Hollywood Hills for the Kratona colony because "a spiritual urge seems to be peculiar to all this section" and "the prevailing breezes from off the nearby Pacific gives physical tone to the surroundings." Besides, Warrington reported that the Hollywood Hills were "magnetically impregnated."

In the mid-teens, dozens of true believers flocked to Kratona, and Warrington quickly built a Moorish-Egyptian occult temple, a psychic lotus pond, a vegetarian cafeteria, several small tabernacles, a metaphysical library, and a Greek theater. At Kratona the faithful lived in apartment buildings with Islamic domes and horseshoe arches for doorways. By the late teens, Kratona was so popular that Warrington rented a hall on Hollywood Boulevard to teach courses in Esperanto, the Esoteric Interpretation of Music and Drama, and the human aura.

After Hollywood residents heard about psychic lotus ponds and the human aura, the motion picture industry began to look good by comparison. For one thing, the movies were outgrowing their crude beginnings in the mid-teens and starting to attract middle-class audiences, not just the urban poor. Feature-length films were replacing the one- and two-reelers, and *The Birth of a Nation*, which premiered in Los Angeles at Clune's Auditorium on February 8, 1915, was an unparalleled artistic triumph as well as a big moneymaker.

What's more, the movies *had* become big business in Hollywood and throughout Los Angeles. By 1915 the industry's annual payroll reached twenty million dollars, and many Los Angeles residents earned good money as extras, set carpenters, and wardrobe mistresses. The community of Hollywood was changing quickly as its population jumped from 4,000 in 1910 to 36,000 in 1920. Although thousands of residents were still hardworking, God-fearing Midwesterners, many more were liberal-minded young men and women attracted to Hollywood by the excitement, the jobs, and their dreams of stardom in the film industry.

Rather than regard movie actors and actresses with suspicion, most Los Angelenos began to idolize their favorites in the late teens—the slapstick comedian Roscoe "Fatty" Arbuckle, the mysterious "vamp" Theda Bara, the handsome heartthrob Francis X. Bushman, the comedian Charlie Chaplin, the athletic and wholesome Douglas Fairbanks, the delicately beautiful Lillian Gish, and "America's Sweetheart," Mary Pickford—plus dozens of now-forgotten names, such as Arthur Johnson, John Bunny, Florence Turner, and Jean, the first dog star.

At first, the movie companies did not exploit the public's thirst for celluloid heroes. Before 1910 most movie actors and actresses were little more than hired hands, who were paid five to ten dollars a day and did not receive any screen credit. Audiences, nevertheless, began to recognize some actors and actresses and gave the anonymous, larger-than-life faces names of their own. A childlike actress with golden curls

Castle Sans Souci, Hollywood, Cal.
Dr. Schloesser's Hollywood Residence.

OPPOSITE: *Castle Sans Souci, 1912. During the teens, the grandest homes in Hollywood belonged not to the newly arrived movie people but to rich eccentrics like Alfred Guido Randolph Schloesser, who built Glengary Castle in the Hollywood Hills in 1910, then erected the even larger Castle Sans Souci across the street two years later. And when virulent anti-German sentiment swept the United States during the First World War, Schloesser had a wonderful solution to his Germanic last name: He switched names with his house. Schloesser became Alfred Guido Randolph Castles and Castle Sans Souci became Schloesser Terrace.*

Cecil B. De Mille's thirty-dollar-a-month home in 1914 in Hollywood's Cahuenga Pass. The era of the extravagant dream palace and the "a star has to live like a star" ideal was still several years away.

named Gladys Smith was called "Little Mary" several years before she adopted the screen name Mary Pickford, and early cowboy star G. M. Anderson was nicknamed Bronco Billy. Fans named other actors and actresses for their studios—the Biograph Girl, the Vitagraph Girl, and the Imp Girl. Jean, the dog star, was the Vitagraph Dog.

Early producers had refused to divulge the names of their leading actors and actresses for fear that a well-known personality could demand a high salary. But Carl Laemmle, the nickelodeon-operator-turned-movie producer, was the first to realize that he could make even more money by promoting his top actors and actresses. In 1910 he hired Florence Lawrence, the Biograph Girl, away from Biograph Studios by raising her salary and promising her screen credits. Laemmle didn't mind paying Florence Lawrence more than other actresses, because he charged his distributors a higher rental for her films. And the distributors didn't balk, either, because Florence Lawrence's fans filled the theaters to see her movies.

Other producers also started to give their top players name billing, and soon, as movie companies competed for the valuable name talent, stars' salaries climbed to once unimaginable heights. By the mid-teens, known actors and actresses were demanding—and getting—$250 to $500 a week, and a few internationally famous stars were receiving $1,000 to $2,000 a week.

In the teens, most moviegoers didn't know much more about the stars than what they saw on the screen. Studio public-relations departments, gossip columnists, and movie magazines were just getting started and didn't tell fans much about their favorite stars' private lives. So most moviegoers naively assumed that the stars were the same people offscreen as they portrayed in films. If an actress played glamorous roles, she obviously lived that way at home. Or so many fans thought.

But that just wasn't true. In the teens, most movie stars lived quite simply in Los Angeles. They took hotel rooms or rented modest apartments and drove their own cars back and forth to the studio every day, if they owned an automobile. When Lillian Gish came to Los Angeles in 1914 to play Northern girl Elsie Stoneman in D. W. Griffith's *The Birth of a Nation*, she rented a five-room apartment with her mother and sister Dorothy on Hope Street, downtown. "We lived there, because it was cheap," she recalls, "and I could ride the streetcar back and forth to the studio."

Lillian Gish liked living in Los Angeles, because "the weather and the land were just like heaven." But many other movie people did not share her enthusiasm. "It's a shame to take this country away from the rattlesnakes," D. W. Griffith once declared. Anita Loos, who started writing movie scenarios for Griffith in 1912 as a teenager, thought Hollywood was not much better than a "dilapidated suburb."

Most movie people were older than the Gish sisters, and they were used to living in cities like New York and Chicago. After a long day's work at the studio, they wanted to go someplace for fun or just a good meal, and Hollywood didn't offer much. Bars were outlawed, and the town's two restaurants closed at nine o'clock. The only alternative was driving to downtown Los Angeles, and even there, restaurants, bars, theaters, and nightclubs did not measure up to New York standards.

The big weekly social event in Hollywood was the Thursday-night dance at the Hollywood Hotel, which Charlie Chaplin once described as a "fifth-rate rambling barn-like establishment" that "had bounded into prominence like a bewildered country maiden bequeathed a fortune." These Thursday-night dances were staid affairs, because Miss Mira Hershey, the elderly owner, had a finely developed sense of morality. She hired "a string quartet of lady musicians who could be counted on for refined selections," recalled Anita Loos in *A Girl Like I*. "No Charlestons, no Bunny Hops, sometimes a restrained Fox Trot, but more often waltz numbers. While poor Miss Hershey watched from the sidelines, jittering with affront, those movie actors purposefully made a sport of being caught in 'lewd' dancing and getting ordered off the floor."

Miss Hershey did not confine her watchful, though nearsighted, eye to the dance floor. She began to patrol the dining room when she learned that some guests were ordering more food off the menu than they were permitted under the American plan. Woe betide the guest caught with a second entree or an extra serving of peas. Before the glutton knew what was happening, Miss Hershey would swoop down on the table and snatch away the offending plate, fussing and muttering to herself all the while. Many diners, however, were too drunk to care,

Adolphe and Eugene Bernheimer's Japanese palace in the Hollywood Hills, just east of Cahuenga Pass, 1918.

BELOW: *Japanese gardens at the Bernheimer estate.*

because they had smuggled wine and liquor into the dining room against Miss Hershey's strictest orders.

Roscoe "Fatty" Arbuckle gave Miss Hershey the most trouble in the dining room. The 266-pound comedian liked to drink, and obviously ate more than his share. Worst of all, he played with his food. While sitting at the table, he'd carefully fold his linen napkin into a long, narrow strip and put a pat of butter in the middle. Then he'd snap the ends of the napkin apart and send the butter up to the ceiling, where it stuck until the heat caused it to fall down or drip on other guests below. The dining room ceiling was a mass of greasy spots, which made Miss Hershey understandably furious.

Miss Hershey even tried to control her guests' bedroom behavior. Before giving a room to young couples, she often asked them to produce a marriage license. Even a then unknown Rudolph Valentino and his first wife, Jean Acker, were not above suspicion. When Miss Hershey learned that some actors visited their lady friends by climbing through the ground-floor windows, she planted large cacti under each sill and regularly checked to see that an overly eager gentleman caller had not dug one up.

Despite Miss Hershey's strictness, by the mid-teens, the Hollywood Hotel had grown to one hundred rooms and sixty-six baths; it was a popular place with movie people because of its convenience to many studios. But most movie people found boardinghouse rooms or rented apartments if they planned to stay in Los Angeles for any length of time. Many lived in downtown Los Angeles, because its restaurants, bars, shops, and theaters reminded them a little of New York. Other movie people lived in Hollywood, because they liked its countrified atmosphere and wanted to be close to the studios. When Douglas Fairbanks arrived in Los Angeles in 1915, he rented a two-story house on North Highland Avenue. In the late teens, Gloria Swanson and her then-husband, Wallace Beery, lived in a bungalow village not far away, and their next-door neighbors were Raoul Walsh, an actor who became a director, and his wife, Miriam Cooper, who worked for D. W. Griffith and played Southern belle Margaret Cameron in *The Birth of a Nation*.

When Cecil B. De Mille started filming *The Squaw Man* at the end of 1913, he stayed at the Hollywood Hotel and then rented a small house at 6136 Lexington Avenue in Hollywood, a month later. "Though Mrs. De Mille and Cecilia [his daughter] were still in New York, I did not live alone," De Mille wrote in his *Autobiography*. "My companion was young, faithful, graceful . . . quite tame. She was a gray prairie wolf. I bought her for a scene in *The Squaw Man*." De Mille took the wolf to the studio on a leash for her scenes. At night, back on Lexington Avenue, he turned her loose in the living room. "While I read and as often as not fell asleep in my easy chair, the wolf would pace the four sides of the room, silently, intently, hour after hour through the night."

When his wife, Constance, and daughter, Cecilia, arrived in Hollywood early in 1914, the family rented a thirty-dollar-a-month cottage in Cahuenga Pass. Constance De Mille insisted that he get rid of the wolf, but De Mille quickly got another animal, this time a horse. The Hollywood Freeway now slices through Cahuenga Pass, but this was open countryside in 1914, and Cahuenga Boulevard was a bumpy dirt road, unsuited for automobiles. "Every morning Mrs. De Mille packed my lunch which I carried slung over my shoulder in a leather pouch, as I rode to work. Every evening the same leather pouch carried home the precious extra negative [of the day's shooting] to be stored in our attic."

The De Milles loved their modest home, but Cahuenga Pass was an inconvenient, if pretty, place to live for a rapidly rising director. De Mille was turning out almost one film every month, among them the highly regarded *The Call of the North; The Virginian,* which starred Dustin Farnum and Winifred Kingston; *Rose of the Rancho*; *What's His Name*, in which his daughter, Cecilia, played a little girl; *The Warrens of Virginia;* and *The Girl of the Golden West*. In 1915 the De Milles rented a large house on Hollywood Boulevard, better suited to their more elevated status. De Mille's partner, Jesse Lasky, and his wife, Bessie, took over the Cahuenga Pass cottage and promptly fell under its spell. Several decades later, Jesse Lasky wrote in his autobiography, "Although we had some luxurious houses later, Bess doesn't speak of any

Dorothy and Lillian Gish.

of them with the nostalgia she reserves for that first home of our own after five years of marriage."

Movie stars and studio executives could have lived much better than they did in the mid-teens. When Charlie Chaplin rented a several-dollars-a-week room at the Los Angeles Athletic Club, he was already a rich man and an internationally beloved comedian. Few actors had risen faster or farther than Chaplin, who had signed his first contract with an "X." In 1912 he was a little-known member of an English music hall act touring America, and his salary was fifty dollars a week. A year later, Mack Sennett signed Chaplin for Keystone Studios at a hundred and fifty dollars a week, but when Chaplin's contract expired after a year, Sennett discovered that he couldn't afford the star that he had helped create. In January 1915, Charlie signed with Essanay at $1,250 a week. A year later, he joined Mutual at $10,000 a week, plus a one-time bonus of $150,000. That wasn't the end of his amazing upward spiral. In 1917, Charlie agreed to make eight one- or two-reelers for First National in the next eighteen months for one million dollars. He was twenty-seven years old.

But Charlie Chaplin wasn't the highest-paid star in Hollywood in 1917. Mary Pickford also received a million dollars, the same amount as he, but for only twelve months of work. The movie studios paid these astronomical salaries as long as a star's presence virtually guaranteed a film's success at the box office.

Stars like Pickford and Chaplin lived modestly in the mid-teens, because the motion picture industry was still a novelty, and the stars didn't know how long the movies' popularity—or their huge salaries—would last. For all anyone knew then, movies might be a passing fad. In 1913, Cecil B. De Mille offered Dustin Farnum some stock in the Jesse L. Lasky Feature Play Company as payment for his lead role in *The Squaw Man*. Farnum refused the offer. All he wanted was cash and a train ticket back to New York. The stock was worth millions only a few years later. Even D. W. Griffith was uncertain of the future. He once confided to director Rex Ingram, "We are building on sand, Rex, just building on sand."

Besides, silent stars in the mid-teens didn't have the time to run large homes or use the expensive automobiles, yachts, and clothes that were to become *de rigueur* in the 1920s. "You must remember that film-making, in the teens, was a full-time job," declared Lillian Gish recently. "You worked twelve hours a day, seven days a week. Year in and year out. I did that for nine years. I didn't have the vitality to work and to lead a busy social life, and I don't know of anyone who did.

"Mother, God bless her, would have dinner ready for Dorothy and me when we got home from the studio after dark, and she didn't make us go through what we'd been doing all day. She'd put us to bed right away. We'd be so tired, and we always got up before dawn, at four or five in the morning. Then we'd be at the studio, ready to work when the sun was high enough in the sky. We didn't use artificial light in those days in California, just sunlight."

But the days when stars rented modest apartments and took the trolley to the studio were disappearing by the late teens. The movies were more successful than ever and had become America's leading mass entertainment, as well as an important influence on the country's values and dreams. Movie people soon began to settle down and spend a little of their money. The era of the dream palace was just around the corner.

CHAPTER FOUR

Once again, Cecil B. De Mille led the way—the first of the movie people to live in the grand style that befitted his position and income. In those days of low income taxes, he was saving two-thirds of his thousand-dollar-a-week salary and earning many thousands more every year from a profit-sharing plan with the studio; he had become one of Hollywood's leading directors. His first spectacle, *Carmen* (1915), starring opera singer Geraldine Farrar and box-office favorite Wallace Reid, was a popular and critical success; Charlie Chaplin even made a parody of the film the following year. During the First World War, De Mille put aside his plans for other showy productions and made several patriotic films, but once the war ended, he shrewdly sensed that Americans wanted to forget about suffering and sacrifice, and he started making sophisticated modern comedies that showed beautiful people wearing fashionable clothes, living and partying in expensively furnished homes. Drinking and adultery were very much in evidence (although true love and legal marriage always won by the end of the film): "See your favorite stars committing your favorite sins" was one of De Mille's favorite advertising slogans.

De Mille put Hollywood's first luxurious bathtub scene into his movie *Male and Female* (1919) and subsequently showed so many beautiful women taking milk baths that he became known as "the plumber's best friend." One plumbing-supply house even named one of its most expensive bathtubs "early De Mille."

Cecil B. De Mille, first member of the movie colony to live grandly, sits in front of his fifteen-room mansion in Hollywood's Laughlin Park neighborhood.

BELOW: *De Mille living room.*

Mary Pickford, age 30, plays a poor, rag-clad girl who marries a rich, handsome young man in Tess of the Storm Country (1922).

Mary Pickford and her mother, Charlotte, who negotiated her contracts with the studios, picked up her checks, even invested her fabulous earnings. And after Mary separated from her first husband, Owen Moore, in the mid-teens, Charlotte Pickford moved in with her devoted daughter.

Mary Pickford—without makeup or her famous golden curls—and her mother, Charlotte, outside their large but hardly palatial bungalow at 1403 Western Avenue in Hollywood, 1917 or 1918.

But the De Milles would have none of this extravagance in their own home, when in 1916 they paid $27,893, due over ten years, for businessman C. F. Perry's two-year-old Spanish-style estate in Hollywood's Laughlin Park subdivision. Their taste was quite conventional, even a little dowdy for the 1920s. They furnished their Laughlin Park mansion in an eclectic mix of Chippendale and Victorian furniture, some antiques, some reproductions. Constance De Mille bought fine Oriental carpets for the living room and paneled dining room, hung heavy printed linen curtains at the windows, and installed portieres in the doorways of the downstairs rooms.

The public, however, expected that the man whose street had been renamed after him (the house stood at 2000 De Mille Drive) and whose name was synonymous with movie spectacles and lavish bathtub scenes would live more grandly than this. One day Constance De Mille gave a tea party at their home "for the ladies of a certain very worthy religious organization. Two of the ladies," C.B. wrote in his *Autobiography,* "confessed to our maid their cherished secret yearning: *could* they have a glimpse of Mr. De Mille's bathroom? They were terribly disappointed. It was just a plain, comfortable, standard American bathroom, without a square inch of onyx or ermine, without even a tap over the tub for rose water or milk."

De Mille's Laughlin Park mansion may not have been architecturally flamboyant, but the director knew how to enjoy his money in other ways. He bought a gray Locomobile with a red leather interior, which he drove back and forth to the studio, usually well over the legal speed limit. Wife Constance, however, always used the family's chauffeur-driven limousine. De Mille bought a six-hundred-acre ranch, named Paradise, in the Sierra Madre mountains near Little Tujunga Canyon, where he raised alfalfa, grew fruit trees, and carried on affairs with young actresses on weekends. He spent over $250,000 for landscaping at Paradise and the Laughlin Park mansion.

In 1917 De Mille bought a 57-foot cruiser, the *Sea Bee,* to sail to Catalina or along the west coast of Mexico. Four years later he acquired a 106-foot yacht, the *Seaward,* which had a crew of seven and accommodations for eight guests. De Mille's other love was flying. In 1918

Mildred Harris (the first Mrs. Charlie Chaplin), Mary Pickford, Lillian Gish, Mrs. Gish, and Dorothy Gish.

he learned how to fly, bought an airplane, and took friends joyriding over Los Angeles and the Pacific Ocean.

Other studio executives and movie stars quickly followed De Mille's example and moved into large, comfortable homes in the late teens. The movie colony was settling down. Jesse Lasky lived in a Spanish-style mansion at 7209 Hillside Avenue, where La Brea Avenue dead-ends into the Hollywood Hills. The Lasky house boasted a film screening room—one of the first in a private house—a tennis court, a swimming pool, terraced gardens, plus more than a dozen servants.

In 1917, Mary Pickford rented a comfortable but hardly luxurious bungalow at 1403 Western Avenue, near Sunset Boulevard. By then Mary was separated from her first husband, Owen Moore, and shared the house with her mother, Charlotte. Two years later, Mary and her mother traded up: They moved into an eight-hundred-dollar-a-month mansion at 56 Fremont Place, a gated and guarded street of sixty houses off Wilshire Boulevard, about a mile west of Western Avenue.

When Charlie Chaplin married his first wife, Mildred Harris, on November 10, 1918, he bought a large though architecturally undistinguished stucco mansion at 2010 De Mille Drive, next to Cecil B. De Mille. This was quite a step up from a room at the Los Angeles Athletic Club, but it was still no dream palace. None of the movie people's homes in the late teens were. Most stars and studio executives rented or bought large homes that had been built for rich Los Angeles businessmen. Except for their generous size and good addresses, these houses were nothing extraordinary, and they did not yet aspire to the unabashed extravagance and abandonment to personal whims that characterized the great movie stars' mansions of the 1920s, such as Falcon Lair. But these houses were well suited for most stars' relatively simple and unexaggerated life-styles at the time. ✗

Of course, there were exceptions, notably the mysterious man-eating "vamp" Theda Bara, the product of one of Hollywood's first high-pressure public-relations campaigns. According to Fox Studio, Theda was the illegitimate daughter of a French artist and an Arabian princess, born in the shadow of a pyramid in Egypt, and her name was an anagram for "Arab Death."

All this was wonderful nonsense. Actually, Theda was Theodosia

Goodman, the daughter of a Cincinnati tailor, who had come to Hollywood and worked as an extra before she was "discovered" in 1914. But Theda's many fans would never have guessed the truth. With the help of her studio, she created the vamp, then maintained that image on the screen, in public, and even in private.

It was quite a potent image—perhaps best exemplified by her role in *A Fool There Was,* the six-reel 1915 film that made her a star. Based on Rudyard Kipling's poem about the man "who made his moan" to "a rag, a bone, and a hank of hair," *A Fool There Was* tells how John Schuyler, a rich, influential, overweight, middle-aged family man, traveling alone on a diplomatic mission of the utmost importance, is corrupted by the vampire, a wicked woman who snares honorable men with her primitive, almost magical sexuality, and then destroys the hapless creatures as they grovel at her feet with passion. With her pale white skin and deeply set dark eyes, Theda Bara looks every bit the vampire—especially when, as she heads for Schuyler's ship, a ragged, unshaven derelict stops her near the dock. This pitiful-looking creature is one of her former lovers, and he was a handsome young man just a year ago. But the vampire ensnared him, used him, and tossed him aside. "See what you have made of me," he groans, "and still you prosper, you hellcat!"

Schuyler is no match for her: "Kiss me, my fool!" she commands—and he does. At that moment, Schuyler's fate is sealed. He forgets about the President's mission and dawdles for two months on the Italian Riviera with the vampire, becoming puffier and shakier with every scene. Finally, dismissed by his government and estranged from his family, disgraced, drooling, and bleary-eyed, Schuyler is reduced to dragging himself across the thick carpeting of the Fifth Avenue mansion he has rented for the vampire, as his mind's eye recalls the scenes of his earlier sins in quick succession. He is put out of his misery when he crawls through an open stair railing and falls onto the floor of the vestibule below. The last title card reads: "So some of him lived, but the soul of him died." In the final scene, Theda Bara stands triumphant in the vestibule, wearing a black velvet gown and a string of pearls, smiling wickedly as she idly tosses rose petals on Schuyler's broken body.

Theda Bara, wearing this diaphanous white gown, looks ladylike, almost virginal, outside her 649 West Adams Boulevard home. But onscreen, Theda played an insatiable man-eating vamp, who was the illegitimate daughter of a French artist and an Arabian princess, born in the shadow of a pyramid in Egypt. Even her name was an anagram for Arab Death—or so the studio publicity agents told the public.

Theda Bara in her home, which she furnished with tiger-skin rugs, crystal balls, skulls, mummy cases, and other vamp paraphernalia, for the benefit of the press and her fans.

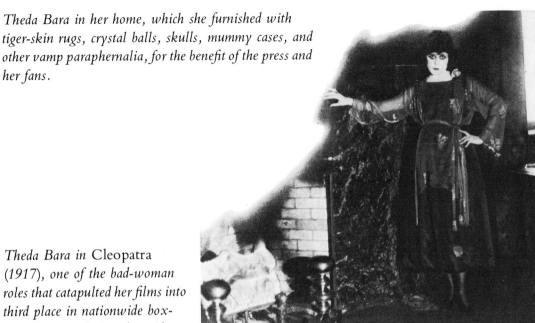

Theda Bara in Cleopatra *(1917), one of the bad-woman roles that catapulted her films into third place in nationwide box-office receipts during the mid-teens.*

It was not an easy act to follow—nor an easy image to live up to. But Theda Bara did her best. To heighten her wicked appearance, the dark-eyed heavy-lidded Theda whitened her face with makeup and wore black dresses. And she turned her large pseudo-Tudor house in downtown Los Angeles into another stage set for her vamp routine, filling it with tiger-skin rugs, crystal balls, skulls, mummy cases, and anything else that looked mysterious and sensual. Here she reportedly practiced her two favorite hobbies: astrology and distilling perfume.

Her fans took this vamp stuff seriously. Once when she was in New York and started talking to a child on the sidewalk, the child's mother recognized the dark-eyed, pale-faced stranger and started screaming, "Save him! Save him! The vampire has my child!" and called the police. And when Theda walked into a New York department store one afternoon, the manager rushed over and begged, "Please don't come in, Miss Bara. We'll send the gowns to your hotel, but we can't stand any more of these riots." Just the day before, Theda had gone to the same store and touched a hat on display. After she left, a mob of women had broken several plate-glass windows and strewn merchandise all over the floor in a desperate attempt to grab the hat and perhaps acquire some of Theda's power.

Theda Bara's hold over the public lasted only a few years. In 1918 audiences started giggling at her onscreen "vamping," and Fox Studios did not renew her contract. Theda's career was over, and she sold her West Adams Boulevard home. In 1921 she married Charles Brabin, who had directed some of her films, and became an eminently respectable Beverly Hills housewife.

Theda Bara had been none too welcome on West Adams Boulevard, for this was Los Angeles' most fashionable street in the two miles between South Figueroa Street and Western Avenue, and oil-rich Edward Laurence Doheny—now the wealthiest man in Los Angeles—lived around the corner from Theda on gated, block-long Chester Place. Theda's "society" neighbors were horrified that she, of all the movie people, had dared to invade their elegant turf. But they were going to get an even greater shock after she moved out and the boisterous, hard-drinking comedian Roscoe "Fatty" Arbuckle moved in.

A native of Smith Center, Kansas, Fatty had been a singing waiter, burlesque comic, and vaudeville performer before he met Mack Sennett in 1913. According to Hollywood legend, Fatty was a plumber's helper at the time and had come to Sennett's home to unclog one of the drains. Sennett took one look at the hefty, baby-faced hulk and promptly hired him—at a salary of three dollars a day.

In the next few years, Fatty made dozens of mayhem-filled comedy shorts for Keystone Studios, and he worked with Charlie Chaplin, Mabel Normand, and the Keystone Kops. His gift for improvisation and his timing were just right, and he accentuated his comic look by wearing a plaid shirt and cuffless pants that were too short and too tight. He even directed some comedy shorts at Keystone. In 1917, Fatty signed with producer Joe Schenck and made more comedy shorts and a few full-length movies for the Comique Film Corporation and later for Paramount. His salary was five thousand dollars a week, and Schenck felt his new star needed—and could afford—a more elaborate setting.

This was one of the first times that a studio executive told one of his stars how to live, and it foretold the "a star has to live like a star" ideal of the 1920s. Moving into Theda Bara's expensive house was only the beginning: Shortly afterward Arbuckle spent twenty-five thousand dollars for a custom Pierce Arrow convertible, and he went through thousands more holding parties, giving presents to his friends, and buying jewelry for his wife, Minta.

Even Fatty's famed practical jokes became more elaborate, and no one was safe from these pranks, not even Paramount Pictures head Adolph Zukor, when he came to dinner at Fatty's West Adams Boulevard house one night in 1919. Buster Keaton was going to play the part of the clumsy butler, and all the guests knew ahead of time, except Zukor. Arbuckle didn't think Zukor would figure out what was happening, because Buster had not appeared in any feature-length pictures yet. But Fatty dimmed the dining-room lights nonetheless.

The first course was shrimp, and this was the start of the trouble. Buster served the shrimp appetizers to the men, then the women, not the other way around. "You stupid numbskull!" shouted Fatty. "Don't you *know* better than to serve the men first?" Buster apologized profusely and removed the shrimp—even the half-eaten ones—from the men's plates and gave them to the women!

Roscoe "Fatty" Arbuckle and his wife, Minta, outside the West Adams Boulevard home that they purchased from Theda Bara in 1918. Hulking, 266-pound Fatty was one of America's favorite slapstick comedians in the late teens. But today he is remembered for the scandal over the mysterious death of actress Virginia Rappe after the raucous several-days-long drinking party that he hosted over Labor Day Weekend, 1921.

Home of the stars. This Tudor mansion at 649 West Adams Boulevard in downtown Los Angeles was, over a ten-year period, the home of Theda Bara, Fatty Arbuckle, actor-director Raoul Walsh and his actress wife, Miriam Cooper, and producer Joe Schenck and his actress wife, Norma Talmadge. Of this star-studded roster, Norma Talmadge was the most flamboyant: She kept her jewelry in the icebox in brown paper bags next to the vegetables. Later she switched to her shoes: rubies in the red shoes, emeralds in the green shoes, and sapphires in the blue shoes.

The next course was soup. Keaton carefully placed empty bowls in front of each guest and returned to the kitchen to get the soup. Suddenly crashing and banging sounds filtered into the dining room. It sounded as if Buster had dropped the soup tureen on the floor, and then some. Actually he had dumped a dozen pots and pans into the kitchen sink, then drenched his uniform with water to look as if he'd spilled the soup on himself. After a suspenseful interval of silence, Buster returned to the dining room and wordlessly removed the empty soup bowls from the table. That brought more screams from Arbuckle.

But Buster's best performance that night was the roast turkey. After walking into the dining room through the swinging double doors, Buster accidentally dropped his white linen service napkin on the floor. So he bent over to pick it up while dexterously holding a twenty-four-pound turkey aloft on a silver serving tray. At just that moment, however, another servant walked through the double doors, pushing Buster and the turkey onto the carpet. The two men struggled to get the greasy turkey back on the tray, and this slapstick took another few minutes, as Zukor watched with a mixture of laughter and horror.

This last episode was the final straw for host Arbuckle. Jumping up from his chair, he grabbed Buster and dragged him into the kitchen. Amid more thuds and smashing dishes, the guests clearly heard Buster's cries for mercy. Suddenly the swinging doors were flung open, and Fatty, yelling and cursing, chased Buster through the dining room, into the living room, and out the front door onto otherwise sedate West Adams Boulevard.

Returning to the dining room, Arbuckle announced that—fortunately—he had another turkey in the oven, and his thoroughly entertained but hungry guests would not starve after all. In the meantime, Buster was upstairs in one of the bedrooms, cleaning up for the final act of this evening's performance. As the guests were finishing their turkey downstairs, he called Arbuckle on the telephone, and Fatty graciously invited his friend to come over for coffee and dessert. Shortly thereafter, Buster appeared at the front door of the house. Zukor didn't recognize Keaton from earlier in the evening, but movie theater owner Sid Grauman—who was in on the practical joke—pointed out the resemblance between Buster and the departed butler. Only then did Adolph Zukor realize that the joke had been on him.

Fatty Arbuckle did not enjoy his fine West Adams Boulevard house for long. His career collapsed when actress Virginia Rappe died after a several-days-long drinking party that he hosted in his twelfth-floor suite at San Francisco's celebrated St. Francis Hotel over Labor Day Weekend, 1921. Her bladder had ruptured after she and Fatty spent a drunken hour together in bed, and she died the next day of peritonitis. Fatty was charged with first-degree murder.

Hollywood's gossipmongers had a field day. Had 266-pound Fatty been too ardent in his lovemaking and literally squashed the twenty-five-year-old blond actress and sheet-music cover girl of "Let Me Call You Sweetheart"? Or had he been too drunk to perform, and tried to satisfy her with an empty champagne bottle instead? The bottle story may well have been true, because Arbuckle had been sexually impotent since 1917. Anyway, newspapers began to refer to the drunken weekend debauch as Fatty's "bottle party."

The same fans who had loved Fatty just a few months earlier now turned on him with a vengeance. Clergymen and women's clubs forced Paramount to withdraw his films from theaters across the nation. One day Arbuckle arrived at the Santa Fe Railway station in Los Angeles to find a seething mob of fifteen hundred men and women screaming, "Murderer!" "Big Fat Slob!" "Beast!" "Degenerate Bastard!" Although after two mistrials a third San Francisco jury finally acquitted Fatty Arbuckle of murder charges on April 12, 1922, the damage had been done. Paramount never released a million dollars' worth of completed films, and they scrapped Fatty's early 1921 contract, which called for him to make twenty-two shorts in the next three years for three million dollars. Fatty's acting career was over, although he occasionally got work in Hollywood under pseudonyms—in 1927 he directed Marion Davies' *The Red Mill* as William Goodrich, and, using the name Will B. Good, he worked with his always loyal buddy Buster Keaton. But even ten years later, when men saw him on the street, they would start whistling the 1927 tune "I'm Coming Virginia."

With his acting career abruptly over, Fatty no longer needed—nor could he afford—the trappings of stardom, and in 1923 he rented the

Norma Talmadge, Buster Keaton, Natalie Talmadge, and Constance Talmadge on Buster and Natalie's wedding day, May 31, 1921. Natalie didn't have the looks or the ambition to become a movie star like her sisters Norma and Constance. So Ma "Peg" Talmadge married her off to Buster Keaton. Is Buster's expression an act—or does he already know what's going to happen in this marriage?

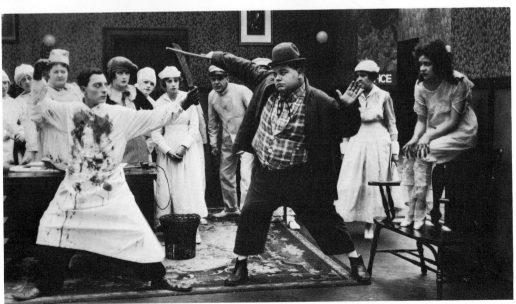

Buster Keaton and his friend Fatty Arbuckle in Good Night, Nurse! (1918).

West Adams Boulevard mansion to director Raoul Walsh and actress Miriam Cooper, who were moving up in the world. Just a few years earlier, they had lived in a thirty-five-dollar-a-month bungalow on North Highland Avenue. But Raoul Walsh and Miriam Cooper lived in the West Adams Boulevard house for less than a year, because they bought a home of their own at 626 South Plymouth Boulevard in 1924.

The next residents at 649 West Adams Boulevard were, ironically, Arbuckle's ex-producer Joe Schenck and his actress wife, Norma Talmadge, who had appeared in over one hundred films since she started acting at Vitagraph Studios in 1911 at the age of thirteen. A devoted husband, Joe Schenck set up a production company just for Norma's films, and he gave her expensive jewelry on birthdays, wedding anniversaries, and Christmas. One day her good friend Miriam Cooper was visiting and noticed that Norma wasn't wearing the ten-carat diamond ring Joe had given her.

"Joe said he can't get it insured," Norma replied. "Insurance companies won't touch picture people."

"Why not?" asked Miriam.

"I don't know," she said. "I guess they think we're a bad risk. And there are all those bums hanging around the studios looking for jobs. Anyway, I can't wear all the beautiful things Joe gave me. I have to keep them put away."

"What do you do—have you a safety deposit box?" Miriam asked.

"Oh, no," Norma said. "I just put them all in a brown paper bag [in the refrigerator], and then I put vegetables on top of them. You know, parsley, lettuce, things like that."

Norma Talmadge had two sisters: Constance, the Vitagraph Tomboy of the teens, who became a popular screen comedienne in the 1920s; and Natalie, a slender, brunette non-actress who married Buster Keaton on May 31, 1921. Keaton had been a vaudeville comedian who got his movie break when Fatty Arbuckle asked him to play a part in the two-reel comedy short, *The Butcher Boy,* in 1917. Audiences loved his sticky bout with a bucket of molasses, and a few years later, he was a leading comedy star. A mournful-looking little man with a "great stone face," Keaton acquired a screen signature that was distinguished by a saucer-brimmed porkpie hat, an oversized suit, and a floppy bow tie.

As his fame and salary increased, Buster moved into bigger and
better houses by the year. After marrying Natalie Talmadge, Buster
rented a big house on fashionable Westchester Place. Still, that proved
unsatisfactory, because Natalie wanted something even more impressive. After all, Buster was a star, and he was making over a hundred
thousand a year. In 1922 they leased a twenty-room, three-story
pseudo-Tudor mansion on Westmoreland Place, an elegant two-block-
long private street, between Olympic and Pico boulevards, just east of
Vermont Avenue. At last Brooklyn-born Natalie felt comfortable.
Buster, however, didn't get carried away by all this rented grandeur.
When the rainy winter weather kept their children indoors, he let them
ride their bicycles around and around the large third-floor ballroom.

One of Keaton's Westmoreland Place neighbors was bachelor
Mack Sennett, the King of Comedy, who directed and developed stars
such as Fatty Arbuckle, Harold Lloyd, Charlie Chaplin, W. C. Fields,
Gloria Swanson, and Keaton himself at the Keystone Studios. The
strapping 6'2", 210-pound, bass-voiced Sennett was earthy, eccentric,
and pleasure-loving—according to Hollywood legend, he invented the
casting couch. The original one was overstuffed, tufted green leather,
and that's where he reputedly discovered most of his Bathing Beauties.
He wore real diamonds and always carried a handful of twenty-dollar
gold pieces in his pants pockets. His favorite dinner was corned beef
and cabbage, washed down with French champagne. Mack was always
chewing tobacco, and his shots seldom missed the spittoons scattered
around his home and office.

In 1920 Sennett bought a twenty-room mansion at 1141 Westmoreland Place, the grounds of which included two acres of landscaping, two tennis courts, and a swimming pool "about the size of Puget
Sound." This lavish playground soon made him one of the social leaders of the movie community, and he frequently held formal dinner parties followed by the screening of a Keystone comedy. Like his friend
Fatty Arbuckle on nearby West Adams Boulevard, Mack Sennett
didn't let these impressive surroundings obscure his sense of fun. "A
very innocent kind of morality, or amorality" prevailed at Sennett's
house, producer Walter Wanger recalled a few years ago. "There were
as yet no gossip columnists . . . and if you didn't take the young lady

OPPOSITE ABOVE: *Plans for Mack Sennett's mansion atop his 304-acre property in the Hollywood Hills. Mack Sennett, the consummate showman, intended to let the public tour his estate—for a small admission fee.*

OPPOSITE BELOW: *Mack Sennett at his studio office, 1925, where he invented the casting couch and often conducted meetings submerged up to the chin in the sudsy water of his eight-by-six-foot bathtub in one corner.*

Dedication of the HOLLYWOODLAND *sign in 1923. Mack Sennett planned to build his mansion on the hilltop just above this landmark.*

on your right upstairs between the soup and the entree, you were considered a homosexual or a lesbian."

That may be an exaggeration, but Mack's parties did have the reputation for lots of sex and drinking. When the servants rang a gong at eleven p.m., it was time for his more prim and proper guests to go home, because the rest of the evening was right out of a Keystone comedy for those guests who weren't busy in the bedrooms or too drunk to stand. "Glistening Haviland china tempted the dexterous jongleurs. The air was filled with costly missiles," recalled Gene Fowler in his floridly written 1934 biography of Mack Sennett, *Father Goose*. "Acrobatic gentlemen used brocaded sofas as springboards. Oriental carpets served instead of sawdust. Sennett laughed uproariously at his butlers' chagrin. Personally, he supervised the grand finale of the evening—a Keystone chase through his own domicile."

The fun and games at Mack Sennett's weren't limited to these spectacular parties. Mack and his friends filled the two-acre estate with animals, particularly ducks. "Mother was partial to ducks," Sennett recalled in his autobiography, "and the studio kept my tennis courts and swimming pool overstocked." One Sunday night, director Thomas Ince dropped by Mack's house. He had a problem. On Friday, he'd told his wife that he was going on a weekend hunting trip. And it wouldn't look right if he returned home empty handed. She might get the wrong idea. Sennett understood. "All you need is ducks," he told Ince. "I am long on ducks and weary of the beasts. Go help yourself."

Ince spent the next hour chasing squawking ducks with a flashlight around the grounds. After he had caught a weekend's worth of ducks, he wrung their necks, hung them over a clothesline, and fired his shotgun. Now he could go home and say that the weekend hunting had been great.

Although millionaire movie people like Mack Sennett were content with their secondhand businessmen's mansions, other Los Angelenos wanted nothing but the best architects and finest styles for their homes. Perhaps the most daring of these trend setters was oil heiress Aline Barnsdall. No one who met Aline Barnsdall ever forgot her, particularly Frank Lloyd Wright, who built her a hilltop residence named Hollyhock House in Hollywood in 1919–1921.

Tired of her husband and Chicago hometown, Aline had moved to Los Angeles by herself in 1916, where she managed the Little Theater on South Figueroa Street. Los Angeles didn't know what to make of this headstrong woman. She smoked in public. She wasn't divorced from her husband but insisted on using her maiden name.

In 1919, Barnsdall bought thirty-six-acre, one hundred-foot-tall Olive Hill, a Hollywood landmark, rising abruptly from the flat coastal plain at Sunset Boulevard and Vermont Avenue. After building her home on top of the hill, Aline Barnsdall planned to rescue Los Angeles from its cultural deprivation by establishing an artists' colony and theater complex on the lower slopes.

Frank Lloyd Wright let his eclectic fantasies run free, and he designed Hollyhock House as a Mayan temple, decorated with the hollyhock motif Aline Barnsdall loved so dearly. He also planned a theater, rehearsal studios, and a lecture hall with a rooftop restaurant overlooking an artificial lake along the Vermont Avenue side of the hill. He laid out the artists' studios and the residences for actors and directors on the hillsides below Hollyhock House.

Aline Barnsdall approved the plans, but translating blueprints into reality was another story. When construction started on the house in 1919, Wright was traveling back and forth to Tokyo to build the Imperial Hotel. He left his architect son, Lloyd, and architect Rudolph Schindler in charge. All probably would have proceeded smoothly if Aline Barnsdall had stayed in Los Angeles. But she, like Wright, was an inveterate traveler: "I would hear from her when wandering about in the maze of the Imperial Hotel in Japan while she was in Hollywood," Wright declared in his autobiography. "She would get my telegrams or letters in Spain when I got to Hollywood. I would hear from her in New York while I was in Chicago or San Francisco. . . . So Hollyhock House had mostly to be built by telegraph so far as client and architect had anything to do with each other."

Perhaps it was better that way, because the two fought bitterly whenever they visited the site at the same time. "She could swear better than any man," recalls Ray Page, a landscape architect who planted dozens of pine and eucalyptus trees on Olive Hill and filled the flat yard near the house with flowers. "One day I was there, trying to get some

Oil heiress Aline Barnsdall, shown here with her daughter in 1922, was just as rich and headstrong as any Hollywood star. And when she built a mansion and artists' colony on her Hollywood estate, she outdid the architectural pretensions of the movie colony by importing Frank Lloyd Wright from Chicago.

The living room of Aline Barnsdall's Hollyhock House, circa 1920, with the furniture designed by Frank Lloyd Wright.

planting done, and Miss Barnsdall and Wright were having another fight. 'How can you put a door there? I don't like it, and I won't have it! Change it!' she'd shout at him. 'No! That's the way it's going to be! I won't change it!' he'd shout back. She'd yell at Wright some more, and he'd listen, and then pay no attention to what she'd said, and do exactly what he wanted all along.''

Somehow Hollyhock House was finished in 1921, but Aline Barnsdall, her daughter, twelve dogs, and several servants only lived in it for a year: In December 1923, Barnsdall offered Hollyhock House and Olive Hill's ten highest acres to the City of Los Angeles as a public park, library, and art center. Why did Aline Barnsdall want to give away such a sumptuous and costly new home? In public, she cited tax considerations and her footloose nature. That may have been partly true. But she didn't mention another reason: The surrounding neighborhood just wasn't what it used to be. In the few short years since she had bought Olive Hill, bungalow subdivisions, neighborhood shops, and traffic-filled streets had replaced the orange groves and barley fields in the flats below. The population and real-estate boom of the early 1920s was in full swing.

After the First World War, Los Angeles had plenty of well-paying jobs, because of expanding movie production, increased manufacturing, and an incredible jump in oil output. Thousands of Americans decided to take advantage of the opportunities there. As if Los Angeles' *reputation* as a Garden of Eden wasn't enough, people had *seen* the city's tidy bungalows and beautiful scenery in the backgrounds of countless movies.

Los Angeles' population more than doubled in the 1920s, from 576,673 in 1920 to 1,238,048 in 1930. Most of this increase actually occurred between 1920 and 1924, with a jump of nearly 400,000 in just five years!

All these newcomers to Los Angeles had to live someplace, and the resulting real-estate boom has never been equaled before or since. In those years, 86,501 building lots totaling 17,300 acres—an area larger than 14,308-acre Manhattan Island—went on sale. Real-estate speculation, in fact, rivaled "the big break" in Hollywood as the way to get rich quick. But the boomtown also had to accommodate those recent arrivals who could not afford to buy homes and needed to rent a room or a small apartment. To meet this demand, thousands of fine homes in older neighborhoods near downtown Los Angeles were converted into apartments or genteel boardinghouses. Even the proud mansions in the vicinity of West Adams Boulevard were not immune to the changes sweeping the city. The neighborhood was a quick trolley ride or drive to downtown Los Angeles, and the twenty- and thirty-year-old houses no longer were new or stylish by the 1920s.

Apartment buildings and cheap subdivisions started filling in the gardens and vacant land that had once made the neighborhood so attractive. As the neighborhood's population density sharply increased, shops and more apartment buildings replaced single-family homes at major intersections and along busy streets like Vermont Avenue. The growing traffic was an additional nuisance. The broad, palm-lined boulevards, which had once provided such an elegant setting for the big homes, now became noisy, exhaust-filled commuter routes for downtown office workers and shoppers. Automobile noise and pollution made its first assault on Los Angeles' extraordinary environment.

As the neighborhoods around West Adams Boulevard and Westmoreland Place declined, rich first-generation Los Angeles residents panicked and sold their homes for whatever they could get—thereby accelerating the change—and moved to new, expensive, and hopefully change-resistant neighborhoods. Some families bought homes in the Hollywood Hills. Others settled in Windsor Square, a twenty-block subdivision five miles west of downtown Los Angeles, bounded by Irving, Wilshire, Rossmore, and Third streets, or equally elegant Hancock Park, a thirty-block subdivision, bounded by Rossmore, Wilshire, Highland, and Beverly boulevards. Windsor Square and Hancock Park still are elegant "old-line" neighborhoods and have a patina of age and taste that is so uncommon in much of present-day Los Angeles.

Movie people, too, sensed the decline of the downtown neighborhoods. In 1923, Buster Keaton left his rented Westmoreland Place mansion and paid fifty-five thousand dollars for a "big red tile-roof deal with lawns and clipped yews" on Ardmore Avenue. Ten months later, the ever-restless Keatons bought a "bigger, better, fancier" house on

Muirfield Road in Hancock Park. But "Muirfield was only a ready-made job, somebody else's hand-me-down," according to Keaton. Shortly after, they started thinking about building a place of their own.

Only a handful of movie people ever lived in Windsor Square and Hancock Park. Middle-class Los Angelenos may have worshiped their favorite stars, but local "society"—oil men, merchants, and real-estate developers who'd made their fortunes ten or twenty years earlier—made them feel uncomfortable in these upper-crust neighborhoods. Los Angeles "society" looked down on movie people, because they usually had humble origins, liked to show off their money, and were foreign-born or Jewish. "They thought we were tramps," Anita Loos recalled recently, and "they saw themselves being invaded and supplanted as elegant ladies and gentlemen. So they ganged up against us." The "society" families refused to invite movie people into their homes and blackballed them from their clubs. The Los Angeles newspapers ran two separate society sections—one for Hollywood and one for the self-appointed "society."

"But you have to realize the awkward position of Los Angeles 'Society' in the 1920s," according to Douglas Fairbanks, Jr. "Some of the so-called prominent families were not that far removed from their relatively humble origins themselves. Even the ones who had risen above that weren't so sure of what they called their position because most of the real local 'Society' lived in Pasadena, not in, but a bit east of, Los Angeles. Then there were the old upper-class Spanish or Mexican families in Los Angeles, who still had considerable land holdings but kept very much in the background. They followed many of their old Spanish customs. The older generation in the families still stubbornly spoke Spanish and the ladies wore their mantillas."

The motion picture people didn't suffer these social snubs silently. Ethel Barrymore once defined a cultured Angeleno as "anyone who hadn't been kicked out of grammar school," and Anita Loos correctly observed that the lineage of the "snobbish families" in Pasadena "had been established by brand names such as Heinz's Pickles, Smith Brothers' Cough Drops, and Chalmers' Underwear."

In the mid-1920s, Mack Sennett started making plans to leave rapidly fading Westmoreland Place. Sennett's net worth was wildly and

Opening day, Midwick View, east downtown, Los Angeles.

variously estimated as between six and fifteen million dollars, so he could easily afford the 304-acre mountaintop east of Cahuenga Pass that he purchased. It was just above a new, twenty-thousand-dollar sign that Sennett, Harry Chandler—the early Hollywood promoter and publisher of the Los Angeles *Times*—and other investors had erected in 1923 to advertise their five-hundred-acre Hollywoodland tract on the hillside below. HOLLYWOODLAND, it read, and each of the thirteen letters was thirty feet wide, fifty feet tall, and built of sheet metal secured to a scaffolding of pipes, wires, and telephone poles. A line of twenty-watt light bulbs ran around the edge of each letter, one every eight inches. The HOLLYWOODLAND sign became an immediate landmark and was visible for miles on clear nights. After the Second World War, the Hollywood Chamber of Commerce removed the LAND from the sign, and the barren hillside has read HOLLYWOOD ever since.

Sennett bought his mountaintop sight-unseen. One day he decided to find out what the view on top looked like, and he started climbing up the weed-choked hillside, because no road led so far up. About halfway to the top, a dusty Mack Sennett changed his mind and returned to his car on the road below. When Sennett got back to Keystone Studios, he called a road-building company. Several months later, Mack returned to his mountain, drove to the top of his seventy-five-thousand-dollar private road, and proclaimed, "That's just about the finest view there is."

Sennett had grand plans for his property. He was "going to build the greatest monument in the world on top of that mountain," he told Jimmy Starr, the Los Angeles *Record* reporter who had become Keystone's publicity director.

"That's biting off quite a bit, don't you think?" Starr asked. "They have some pretty good monuments in Greece and Rome—what's left of 'em. And swell cathedrals all over Europe. And before I forget it, the Taj Mahal in India."

"I don't know what they've got in India," Mack replied, "and I care less. But I know a monument when I see one. I want something like the Pennsylvania Station in New York. Lasting. Made of granite and marble and as big as all outdoors."

"What's it going to be?" asked Starr.

"Wise guys talk of India and monuments, but the greatest monument in the world is a home. I'm going to build a home up there and live in it, and it'll cost two million dollars."

That was a lot of money in the 1920s, even for Mack Sennett. But "I've figured out how to beat the game," the director told Starr. "I'm going to charge admission to the public, and after I'm up in the morning, they can even see my bedroom and bath." Here was a man who understood the public.

By the time architect John de Lario was finished with the plans for Sennett's mansion, it looked more like the Dalai Lama's winter palace at Lhasa or a vast movie set than a film mogul's home. At the top of the mountain, de Lario planned a several-story-tall masonry embankment with terraces, staircases, fountains, waterfalls, and hanging gardens to provide merely the platform to build the house on. The stucco-walled, red-tile-roofed Spanish-style mansion had additional terraces and porches to take advantage of the view, and its fifty rooms sprawled over half a dozen levels.

But Sennett's mountaintop mansion never went past the planning stages. His career declined as he lost his best talent to other studios in the mid-1920s and as the verbal joke replaced the visual gag with the advent of the "talkies" several years later. Mack Sennett was still a rich man, but he lost millions in the 1929 stock market crash. Sennett's corporation declared bankruptcy in 1933, and he lost his three-hundred-acre mountaintop. A junk dealer hauled away the rusting steam shovel that had been waiting several years in vain for construction to begin.

CHAPTER FIVE

Beverly Hills is the classic rags-to-riches story. At the turn of the century, its reputation was premised not on movie stars and their mansions, but on *beans*, acres and acres of beans. The several-hundred-acre tract, separated from the westernmost edge of Los Angeles by six miles of barley fields, orange groves, cattle ranches, and oil fields, was owned by Henry Hammel and Charles Denker. They were also the proprietors of downtown Los Angeles' United States Hotel, "where every bed is a spring bed"—or so their advertisements boasted—and they planted their ranch in beans because that was about the only cash crop that grew in the dusty unirrigated soil.

Only a few dozen people lived in Beverly Hills then—Mexican farm workers in a cluster of shacks along unpaved Santa Monica Boulevard, families like the Benedicts and Willfongs nestled in the hills and canyons above the bean fields, and a Chinese man named Seng, who cultivated a vegetable farm in a little valley called "Chinaman's Canyon" in the hills near present-day Schuyler Road.

Shortly after the turn of the century, big things began to happen in Beverly Hills. Oil had been discovered just to the east in the workingmen's village of Sherman (now West Hollywood), and an oil syndicate headed by Edward Laurence Doheny's sometime partner Charles Canfield, Burton Green, and Max Whittier paid $670,000 for the Hammel-Denker ranch, hoping to find exploitable deposits under the bean fields. In 1905 and the early months of 1906, the syndicate drilled over thirty wells but didn't find appreciable oil except in the south-western edge of the property, near today's Century City office towers.

Canfield, Green, and Whittier had paid too much money for the Hammel-Denker ranch to continue raising beans. So they decided to turn the ranch into a real-estate development. Its boundaries started at Wilshire Boulevard (then Los Angeles Avenue) on the south and ended a mile and a half north in the hills above Sunset Boulevard; it bordered on the east near present-day Doheny Drive and extended two miles west to the vicinity of present-day Whittier Drive.

Despite their property's remote location, Canfield, Green, and Whittier had high hopes for their venture. The Los Angeles real-estate market was thriving, and the ranch occupied a favorable spot, thirty-five minutes from downtown Los Angeles and twenty minutes from beach towns such as Venice and Santa Monica by way of the trolley, which ran along Santa Monica Boulevard and stopped in Beverly Hills at the corner of present-day Canon Drive. The foothills of the Santa Monica Mountains formed a striking backdrop to the beanfield-filled flats and offered fine views of the Pacific Ocean in those pre-smog days.

After forming the Rodeo Land and Water Company to sell off the land, Canfield, Green, and Whittier named their development Beverly Hills after the Massachusetts town of Beverly Farms. Burton Green, so the story goes, was a great admirer of President William Howard Taft, and he thought up the name after reading that Taft had visited Beverly Farms.

Unlike other Los Angeles real-estate developers, Canfield, Green, and Whittier were not out just to make a quick buck. Having paid so much money for the Hammel-Denker ranch, they were now willing to tie up hundreds of thousands of dollars more over several years to en-sure their profits and to ensure that Beverly Hills—unlike the early downtown developments that had gone to seed—would become an at-tractive and fashionable community and remain that way many years into the future.

That vision was in part the brainchild of Wilbur David Cook, Jr., whom they hired in 1906 to design the master plan for the development of Beverly Hills. One of America's foremost landscape architects and

Coldwater Canyon, 1910, before the development of Beverly Hills.

BELOW: *Sunset Boulevard, in 1907, was a dirt road cutting through the dusty bean fields and barren ranchland of Beverly Hills. Twenty years later, Sunset Boulevard was lined with the estates of Hollywood stars and millionaire businessmen.*

INSET: *515 North Canon Drive, one of the original model homes in Beverly Hills.*

community planners, Cook had worked with Frederick Law Olmsted (the designer of New York City's Central Park) on the Columbian Exposition of 1893 in Chicago, the improvement of the White House grounds in 1902, plus parks for Boston and Chicago, and had himself laid out a system of city parks for Oakland, California.

Wilbur Cook convinced Canfield, Green, and Whittier to turn Beverly Hills into an economically balanced community, not just a home for rich men and their families. This sounds remarkably egalitarian for three oil millionaires in turn-of-the-century Los Angeles, but circumstances dictated a heterogeneous approach. The rich families that Canfield, Green, and Whittier hoped to attract to Beverly Hills needed the daily services of shopkeepers, servants, and professional men. Beverly Hills was—and for some time would be—in the middle of nowhere, without a low-rent or middle-income "support community" nearby, where these people might live. So Cook included some not-so-rich neighborhoods in Beverly Hills.

That was easy enough to accomplish, because not all land in Beverly Hills had been created topographically equal. Property in the rolling foothills above Sunset Boulevard, with views of the surrounding countryside and the ocean, obviously was more desirable than land in the flats beneath it. So Cook simply harmonized lot sizes with the buyer's ability to pay for his proximity to the picturesque hills. The result was a three-tiered residential community.

For the less affluent buyer, Cook mapped out a rectangular street grid in the triangular piece of land formed by the already existing angled intersection of Wilshire and Santa Monica boulevards, then divided it into small lots, sometimes no more than 50 feet wide and 100 to 150 feet deep—just the right size for shopowners, servants, and young families to build their modest bungalows on.

The part of Beverly Hills that lay "below the tracks" of the Pacific Electric Railroad along Santa Monica Boulevard may have been set aside for common folk, but Canfield, Green, and Whittier sought only the right kind of common folk. So they inserted restrictive covenants into the property deeds of every Rodeo Land and Water Company lot, forbidding blacks and Orientals from buying or even occupying property, except as live-in servants.

The covenants, however, did not forbid apartments or shops on the property south of Santa Monica Boulevard. Cook wanted a local shopping district to develop south of Santa Monica Boulevard, close— but not too close—to the large houses and estates to the north. Cook's development scheme even included a small industrial zone, just below Santa Monica Boulevard and east of Canon Drive, an area reserved for the unsightly warehouses, laundries, and building supply houses that a prosperous and growing community required. The industrial zone still survives, although smaller than its original size, and even now motorists driving along Santa Monica Boulevard, just east of Rexford Drive, can smell baking Wonder Bread in the evening.

Wilbur Cook next laid out lots north of Santa Monica Boulevard for upper-middle-class and well-to-do families. He divided the one-mile-wide strip of land between Santa Monica and Sunset boulevards into four blocks, with the lots on each block generally getting larger and more expensive as they neared Sunset Boulevard and the hills. The rolling land above Sunset Boulevard was reserved for very rich men's mansions, nestled among the foothills or perched on knolls along winding roads that followed the contours of the land.

In January 1907, Percy Clark, the Rodeo Land and Water Company real-estate agent, set up a desk at the Pacific Electric Railroad station on Santa Monica Boulevard and offered the first Beverly Hills lots for sale. One-acre lots along Sunset Boulevard were $800 to $1,000. The 80-feet-by-200-feet lots in the blocks nearest to Santa Monica cost $300 to $400. For the first few years, Clark offered a 10 percent discount if the purchaser paid cash and another 10 percent if construction on the lot started within six months; the latter discount, Canfield, Green, and Whittier hoped, would encourage families to build homes and give Beverly Hills a settled look that would in turn attract more buyers.

And Beverly Hills did have a barren, almost desolate appearance that first year. The four or five model homes just above Santa Monica Boulevard, including one still surviving at 515 North Canon Drive, stood almost alone in the middle of the dusty bean fields. Only four of the north-to-south streets—Crescent, Canon, Beverly, and Rodeo drives—had been opened and paved in the flats between Santa Monica and Sunset boulevards. Dusty alleys ran down the middle of these blocks, so that tradesmen could enter the so-far nonexistent houses by rear service entrances and their horse-drawn wagons would not mar the serenity of the still-unused streets. But the strangest sight of all was the telephone and electric poles straddling the empty Beverly Hills flats in long rows, without any wires strung between the tops because there weren't any customers yet.

To improve the landscape, Canfield, Green, and Whittier hired horticulturist John J. Reeves, who prepared and implemented a master tree-planting plan. Reeves specified a different kind of tree for the full length of each broad street, and deserves "all the credit for the beautiful trees in Beverly Hills today," according to Ray Page, a landscape architect who came to the community in 1919. "He was stubborn as hell, a typical stubborn Englishman. He picked out the trees, and he fought to keep them properly watered and trimmed to a uniform height and shape. One day Reeves planted sapling pepper trees along Crescent Drive, below the Beverly Hills Hotel, and a strong wind came along and blew the little things down. Reeves was replanting the trees when Burton Green came along and told him that he didn't want pepper trees along Crescent Drive. This infuriated Reeves, and he was one of the few men in Beverly Hills who dared talk back to Green. 'You *are* going to have pepper trees, Mr. Green,' he replied, and went back to work. And that was the end of that. Reeves' pepper trees stood along Crescent Drive until they died off years later and had to be replaced with Southern Magnolias."

In the first year of lot sales, about a dozen modest houses were completed in the Beverly Hills flats, and several mansions were underway along Sunset Boulevard and in the nearby foothills. But after this promising start, a nationwide recession in 1907 virtually stopped lot sales and house construction in Beverly Hills. When the economy returned to normal around 1910, the Los Angeles real-estate market picked up again, but not in outlying Beverly Hills. So Canfield, Green, and Whittier had an idea. They knew that construction of the Hollywood Hotel a few years earlier had spurred real-estate sales in Hollywood, because it provided a focus and morale-booster for the community. Why wouldn't the same tactic work in Beverly Hills?

In 1911, Rodeo Land and Water completed the Beverly Hills Hotel, a rambling Mission-style structure, built of stucco and designed by architects Myron Hunt and Elmer Grey, along the north side of Sunset Boulevard between Crescent Drive and Hartford Way. The land was so dry that swirling clouds of dust raised by workingmen grading the site could be seen in Hollywood, four miles to the east. But the hotel quickly became famous for several acres of fragrant gardens and for the ragged line of little palm trees on each side of the driveway from Sunset Boulevard and the porte cochere that grew into an impressive tropical *allée.*

Margaret Anderson, proprietor of the Hollywood Hotel before the ever-proper Mira Hershey, took over management of the Beverly Hills Hotel despite her friends' warning that the hotel would surely fail because it was so far out of town. But Canfield, Green, and Whittier had offered Mrs. Anderson a deal too irresistible to turn down. They gave her a $250,000 mortgage so that she would own, rather than lease, the hotel, and they threw in the land for free. Margaret Anderson spent another $125,000 furnishing the hotel, and she quickly proved that her pessimistic friends were wrong.

The Beverly Hills Hotel became an immediate landmark and social center for the new community. Tourists spent weeks, even months, at the hotel or in one of the spacious bungalows scattered throughout the gardens. When Los Angelenos visited Beverly Hills to look over property, they, too, often stayed overnight at the hotel. Local residents frequented the hotel dining room—it was the only restaurant in town—and watched the "flickers" in the Venetian Room every Saturday night.

But even the sight of this neo-Spanish pleasure dome rising above the bean fields like a mirage in the desert wasn't enough to get land sales really moving again. So Canfield, Green, and Whittier decided to build mansions and move to Beverly Hills themselves. Theirs was an undeniable show of faith in the town's future, going far beyond the usual Los Angeles subdivision promotional stunts, and it encouraged other families—the rich and the not so rich—to buy land and build homes in Beverly Hills.

Burton Green's mansion, the first one built, set the standard of architectural splendor in early Beverly Hills. In 1911 he paid $14,500 for three and a half acres at the northwest corner of Lexington Road and Crescent Drive, a block above Sunset Boulevard, and started building the twenty-room Tudor mansion that still stands today. It featured a 25-by-30-foot reception hall, a mahogany-paneled 24-by-45-foot living room, and an equally large walnut-paneled dining room. Each one of the five upstairs bedrooms had its own dressing room and marble bathroom.

But Green's Tudor-style mansion was almost eclipsed by the estate's extensive landscaping, particularly the row of full-grown oaks along both sides of the gently curving driveway that set the house well back from the main gate on Lexington Road. Green had not wanted to wait for oak saplings to mature, so he hired the Beverly Hills Nursery to transplant twenty- and twenty-five-foot-high trees from nearby canyons to his driveway.

Charlie Canfield died in 1912 and never lived in the community he had worked so hard to launch and promote. But just a year before Canfield's death, Silsby Spaulding married Canfield's daughter Caroline and started building a thirty-room mansion, called Grayhall, on a fifty-four-acre estate in the hills above Sunset Boulevard. Jack Danziger, the attorney and oil man who married Canfield's other daughter, Daisy, didn't wish to pay several thousand dollars an acre for land in Beverly Hills. So he bought six hundred acres at forty-eight dollars each in the even more remote hills a mile west of Beverly Hills and built a house on top of one of the knolls. This land later became Bel Air.

In 1916, Max Whittier, the third of the original Rodeo Land and Water partners, purchased four and a half acres at the northwest corner of Sunset Boulevard and Alpine Drive, where he constructed a graceful Spanish-style mansion. Sixty years later Whittier's mansion became the much-publicized, much-reviled "Sheik's House," infamous for its stucco walls painted lime-green, its copper roof, its outdoor urns planted with plastic flowers, and its naked statues, complete with realistic pubic hair, standing on the proud terrace overlooking Sunset Boulevard.

The partners' plan was working: By the late teens, Sunset Boulevard and Lexington Road were beginning to get an elegant, settled

The Beverly Hills Hotel, soon after its opening in 1911. The new hotel was so far out of town, Los Angelenos scoffed, that it was sure to fail. But owner-manager Margaret Anderson quickly proved these cynics were wrong, even though the hotel looked out on empty fields for a decade after its completion.

BELOW: *View from the Beverly Hills Hotel, looking east, 1915.*

Entrance to the Beverly Hills Hotel, 1915.

look. The bean fields in the flats were giving way to dozens of large, comfortable homes and more newly opened streets. A neighborhood shopping district was emerging on several streets below Santa Monica Boulevard. Beverly Hills' population had reached 634 in 1920, quite a jump over the 250 residents it claimed in 1914, when Beverly Hills voted to become an independent city.

The foothills above the Sunset Boulevard and Lexington Road estates, however, remained quite wild and unspoiled. When Los Angeles attorney Lee A. Phillips built a weekend hunting lodge on a knoll on Summit Drive overlooking Benedict Canyon in 1911, the few families who lived full-time in the hills might just as well have been living in the country. The unpaved roads were mud troughs in the rainy winter months and choking clouds of dust the rest of the year. The hills teemed with wildlife and with weekend hunters and hikers from the flats. Water, gas, and telephone lines were nonexistent. If homeowners wanted water, they dug a well. If they wanted a telephone, they strung a line down to the Beverly Hills Hotel. Still, some folks gladly made the best of these inconveniences to enjoy a countrified setting that was an easy drive from Hollywood or Los Angeles.

In March 1919, Lee A. Phillips decided to sell his Benedict Canyon retreat. Raoul Walsh and Miriam Cooper were among the first to inspect the property, and Walsh liked the hunting lodge and its rustic setting. But Miriam Cooper heard a coyote howling in the distance, and that did it. She wanted nothing to do with wild animals, and her husband reluctantly agreed to start looking for a house in town. Although no one realized it at the time, that decision was a turning point in the history of Beverly Hills.

Several days later, a friend of Walsh's drove out from Hollywood to see the Phillips lodge. Leaving Benedict Canyon Drive far behind, he proceeded up into the hills along Summit Drive, a twisting dirt road that ended abruptly in the chaparral-covered hills half a mile above the Beverly Hills Hotel and Sunset Boulevard. Accompanied by real-estate man Stanley Anderson, he walked through the hunting lodge, which had only six rooms, lacked electricity and running water, and had the musty, slightly run-down air of a country place that city folk visit only on occasional weekends.

The location, however, was glorious, particularly on an early spring day. Sage and wildflowers scented the air, and the chaparral in the canyons and hillsides was green from the recent winter rains. And the house itself sat on a flat knoll looking out over Benedict Canyon, the nearby mountains, and the distant ocean.

The prospective buyer was Douglas Fairbanks, and he liked the property immediately. On April 22, 1919, Fairbanks took title to the hunting lodge and the surrounding fourteen acres, having paid $35,000 for the privilege, and sedate, somewhat-remote Beverly Hills was never to be the same again.

Fairbanks had come to Hollywood from the Broadway stage in 1915 and quickly become a box-office favorite in satirical comedies like *In Again Out Again* (1917) and *A Modern Musketeer* (1918). Handsome, energetic, and athletic, Fairbanks usually played the clean-living young American male that women dreamed about and men wished they were like. Fairbanks wasn't only acting a part. He radiated good health and a genuine zest for life, both onscreen and off.

Doug was always a favorite with the ladies, and after he and his first wife, Beth, separated in 1918, he resumed his bachelor ways with his typical enthusiasm. "He didn't drink or smoke much," recalled Anita Loos, who wrote the scenario for *His Picture in the Papers* (1916) and several other Fairbanks films, "so he thought he had the right to some kind of vice. He chose women. He went after every girl who crossed the studio lot." And most women couldn't resist Doug's attentions. He was "a real smoothie," according to silent movie actress Lila Lee, "a complete charmer who knew just what to say and do to bend a girl's heart in his direction. And he did it as a matter of course, even when there was no ulterior motive involved. He was just about the best morale-booster I ever ran into."

By 1918, however, Fairbanks was seeing Mary Pickford regularly and wanted to marry her. They had first met in 1915 and fell in love two years later. Mary was then in her mid-twenties but looked like a young girl onscreen with her angelic face and famous golden curls, which she brushed two hundred strokes every night and rolled up in kidskin. But her appeal went far beyond surface appearances. "She was the most feminine female I've ever met in my life," according to Anita

Douglas Fairbanks and the cast of The Good–Bad Man *(1916), including blond actress Bessie Love and director Allan Dwan in a three-piece suit and pith helmet. After leaving the Broadway stage for Hollywood in 1915, Fairbanks (né Douglas Elton Ulman) starred in light romantic comedies and Westerns. His swashbuckling roles—and international fame— came in the 1920s.*

Loos. "She'd flirt with any man—a bellhop or a busboy would do as well as a high-powered producer or the handsomest leading man. I don't like coyness, but with Mary, it wasn't a come-on. It was innocent and absolutely genuine, the one way in which she could not be imitated."

By 1918, Mary Pickford had left her first husband, Owen Moore, for good and was living with her mother, Charlotte, in rented splendor—a twenty-room stucco neoclassical mansion on gated and guarded Fremont Place. But Mary was still legally married, and she and Doug had to see each other on the sly, usually at the end of a day's shooting in her studio bungalow or at the home of his brother-manager, Robert Fairbanks. The Phillips hunting lodge in Beverly Hills, Doug reasoned, would make a good home for himself and the perfect place to court Mary, far from the prying eyes of the press and their fans.

Fairbanks had a definite vision for his new home: large, comfortable, even luxurious, but never ostentatious. It should look like the home of a cultivated, well-to-do country gentleman, and not a Broadway actor who had just struck it rich in the movies.

Doug wasted little time building this stage set for his private life. By June 1919 dozens of workmen swarmed over the old lodge, adding a wing and a second story and ripping down most of the interior walls to make larger rooms and a more spacious layout. Fairbanks rented the thirty-room Silsby Spaulding mansion, Grayhall, just down the road, to follow the progress on his estate. But Doug was actually too busy with his movies to plan and supervise the remodeling. So Robert Fairbanks became the building superintendent, and Max Parker, the art director for many of Fairbanks' films, prepared the architectural plans. This was the first time, but not the last, that a set designer was the architect for a star's home, and it foretold the enormous impact of the motion picture industry on residential architecture in Los Angeles in the 1920s and 1930s.

When Doug moved into his new home at the end of 1919, the original hunting lodge had almost disappeared in all the remodeling. Now the house had an ever-so-proper mock-Tudor facade. It encased two wings, one 95 feet long and the other 125 feet, facing the front lawn with its view of the canyon below. The first floor consisted of a large entrance hall, screening room, living room, and dining room, which led to a glassed-in sun porch, breakfast room, kitchen, and servants' quarters. Doug's bedroom suite and five guest bedrooms occupied the second floor, and a bowling alley and billiard room were on the third floor.

Fairbanks transformed the dry chaparral-covered grounds into a beautifully landscaped setting where he could enjoy his favorite sports and graciously entertain his friends without ever leaving home. Doug liked to swim but usually didn't have time to drive to the Pacific Ocean in the middle of the week when he was shooting a picture. That was no problem. He brought the Pacific Ocean to the estate, or at least a scaled-down version: a 55-by-100-foot swimming pool, with a sandy beach along one side. Because Fairbanks also enjoyed canoeing, he dug a series of small ponds where he and his friends could paddle canoes right in the middle of the arid Santa Monica Mountains. In the canyon just below the house, he built a six-stall stable. Now he could ride through the fourteen acres around the house or up into the nearby mountains.

The Beverly Hills Nursery planted hundreds of trees and shrubs around the house. When the landscaping work remained unfinished a year after he moved in, Doug started complaining that it didn't go more quickly. He was accustomed to getting everything he wanted and getting it right away. At the studio, he had often watched set carpenters build rooms in a matter of hours. One day, Fairbanks spoke to landscape architect Ray Page, who was supervising the work for the nursery.

"Ray, this work is going too slowly," he said.

"What should we do, Mr. Fairbanks?" Page replied.

"Well, I've got an idea," Fairbanks said. "Let's move in some lights from the studio and work three eight-hour shifts."

"That's exactly what we did," Page recalled recently. "But you know, every time I went up to the house at night to check on the progress, I'd find half the workmen asleep under the bushes."

Doug was never alone in his new home. He genuinely liked people but also needed companionship all the time. Sometimes he'd bring technicians or cowboy extras home from the studio for dinner, or he'd

AMERICA'S SWEETHEART

Mary Pickford, circa 1918. When these publicity stills were taken, she was twenty-five years old, earning over a million dollars a year, and married to Owen Moore. And she was secretly seeing Douglas Fairbanks, who was living with his wife, Beth, and young son, Doug, Jr. But the public knew nothing of Mary's double life. Her fans flocked to movie theaters to watch her portray ten- and twelve-year-old girls, and they affectionately nicknamed her "Little Mary" and "America's Sweetheart."

invite friends like Charlie Chaplin, Mabel Normand, or Lillian Gish for the weekend. "It was a beautiful house, nothing within sight, nothing around," Lillian Gish remembers vividly. "Douglas and I would drive up the mud road [Summit Drive], and he'd carry a shotgun. It was unsafe in those roads, a wild place up there. You never knew who you might meet, but the major nuisance was coyotes. Sometimes they would gang up in the middle of the road. Douglas would just shoot up in the air, and they'd run away."

But Doug's favorite guest was Mary. Wearing old clothes and floppy hats, they went horseback riding through the empty hills, drove to the beach, or simply ate dinner at home, sometimes with a few close friends, other times just the two of them. They were very much in love. If anything, their relationship had deepened during the last two years of secret courtship. But Doug and Mary were also quarreling by 1919, because they couldn't agree on marriage plans.

Doug wanted to get married at once. He was a free man. But Mary was still Mrs. Owen Moore, and she feared that a divorce, quickly followed by remarriage, might alienate their fans and ruin both their careers. Fragile appearance and sentimental screen roles aside, "America's Sweetheart" was also a canny businesswoman who was proud of the millions of dollars she earned as a movie star and was intent on making millions more. Besides, Pickford's screen career was her life. She'd gone onstage at the age of five to help support her widowed mother, and she didn't know much else. "The greatest menace" for a star, she believed, "was always the loss of popularity—more than health, more than anything." What would her fans *think*, she agonized over and over again, when they learned that America's Sweetheart had not only made a mess of one marriage but had also assumed the off-screen role of The Other Woman?

Mary was almost certainly remembering the unhappy example of movie idol Francis X. Bushman a few years earlier. Known as "King Romeo," the handsome, square-jawed, muscular star was single and available, according to Essanay studio publicity. That bit of news about being available stirred Bushman's female fans into a frenzy: Essanay hired eight secretaries just to answer his fan mail and three stock boys to carry the "autographed" pictures to the post office. At one particularly tumultuous personal appearance in Chicago, King Romeo's fans rioted and ripped off nearly all his clothing.

But Bushman wasn't single and available at all. He'd been married for ten years, and his wife and five children lived hidden away at Bushmanor, his Maryland country estate. Bushman, in fact, had a second secret leading lady—his blond mistress and co-star, Beverly Bayne. When Mrs. Bushman got tired of hearing rumors about King Romeo's escapades with Miss Bayne in his Manhattan penthouse, she filed for divorce in 1918, and the truth came out.

Bushman's fans were appalled, then angry, to learn that his private life was so different from what they had been told. The same newspapers that had once heaped praise on Bushman now went in for the kill. After running a photograph of a worried-looking Bushman, one newspaper declared, "Oh, see the handsome man. He looks worried. Why should the nice man be worried?" After exposing the facts about King Romeo's double life, the article concluded: "Millions of sweet young girls in America with more affection than good sense have stayed awake mooning over his face. Now is the time to tear up the picture and go to sleep. Francis X. Bushman is a fake."

Bushman's enormous popularity evaporated in a matter of months. His last starring film was ironically titled *Social Quicksand* (1918), with Beverly Bayne as leading lady. By 1919, Bushman and Miss Bayne—they'd gotten married after his divorce—were breeding Great Danes at Bushmanor. Bushman returned to Hollywood to play the wicked Messala in the 1925 silent *Ben-Hur,* but his comeback attempt failed, and for the next forty years he earned a living as a radio announcer and actor in B-pictures. In 1966, the year of his death, he played his last role, a bit part in *The Ghost in the Invisible Bikini.*

This same humiliation, Mary Pickford feared, might await her and Doug if their fans would not accept the unpleasant facts behind their private lives. On the other hand, the public might welcome a Fairbanks-Pickford marriage. What could be more romantic, more exciting than two of America's most popular stars playing the real-life roles of husband and wife?

Mary didn't know what to do. She was really suffering and started losing weight. Her face became pale and drawn. And after Fairbanks

Pickfair, the home of Douglas Fairbanks and Mary Pickford after their March 28, 1920, marriage. The first dream palace.

Aerial view of Pickfair and its fourteen acres of grounds.

finally forced the issue during a long-distance telephone call, delivering a now-or-never ultimatum, she started sobbing uncontrollably in front of her mother, Charlotte, and good friend Frances Marion, the screenwriter.

"Remember, Mary, you're America's Sweetheart," cautioned Charlotte Pickford, now more Mary's business manager than mother.

"I only want to be one man's sweetheart," Mary cried, "and I'm not going to let him go!" She called Doug back.

In March 1920, Mary divorced Owen Moore, paying him one hundred thousand dollars not to contest the suit or name Doug as co-respondent. Even though she suffered the indignity of settling with her husband, Mary had gotten off cheaply. Doug had given Beth five hundred thousand, plus custody of their son, Doug, Jr., as a settlement. All was ready. Doug initiated a very ardent, very public, and very brief courtship. And on Sunday afternoon March 28, 1920, Gladys Mary Smith Moore and Douglas Elton Ulman Fairbanks were secretly married in a simple double-ring ceremony at the suburban Los Angeles home of Baptist minister J. Whitcombe Brougher.

After the ceremony, Doug gave the men-in-attendance seven-inch Havana cigars, which Mary autographed "Mrs. Douglas Fairbanks." Then Doug, Mary, and the wedding party returned to his new Beverly Hills home for dinner. Doug put Mary at the head of the table, then sat at her left, just as they would always eat meals together.

"This house is yours, Mary," declared Doug. "It's my wedding present to you."

"Oh, no, Douglas," she objected. "I want to feel that this is your home, and that I'm sharing it with you."

Two days later, Doug and Mary invited the same group for dinner at the Beverly Hills house, plus several newspapermen. As the reporters arrived, Doug and Mary reputedly answered the front door, flashing happy smiles and their wedding rings. The next morning the whole world heard the news.

At first Doug and Mary attracted some bad publicity over the quick divorce and remarriage, and Mary didn't stray from Doug's estate except to go to the studio. Everything was up in the air. They didn't know what would happen to their careers. They couldn't decide whether to stay in Doug's bachelor house, find something else in Beverly Hills, or build a mansion in Fremont Place near Mary's former home, where Charlotte still lived. Even their honeymoon had to be postponed, because Charlotte Pickford got sick and Mary wouldn't leave her side.

In late May, however, Doug and Mary finally left on their honeymoon, taking the train for New York to board the S.S. *Lapland* on the 29th and sail to England. Now they learned firsthand that their fans still loved them. In New York thousands of people jammed the sidewalks outside the Ritz Carlton Hotel, where they were staying. In Europe the crowds were even larger, and one mob in London dragged Mary out of an open car in their eagerness to see her. Aided by four policemen, Doug carried Mary away on his shoulder, to save her from certain injury.

When the couple returned to New York, a delegation headed by Babe Ruth and Jack Dempsey greeted them at the pier. The pair were more popular than ever before, and the next year *Vogue* dubbed the twice-wed Mary "the patron saint of childhood." Soon after, Mary and Doug announced that they were going to make Doug's Beverly Hills bachelor quarters their permanent home, and the press immediately combined parts of their last names and dubbed the estate "Pickfair."

CHAPTER SIX

Pickfair was Hollywood's first dream palace. A larger and more extravagant house than Douglas Fairbanks and Mary Pickford really needed, or sometimes wanted, Pickfair was more than just a place to live. With its private screening room, acres of carefully landscaped grounds, and canoe ponds, Pickfair was both a grandiose plaything and a compound where the Fairbankses could be themselves. But Pickfair was also a stage set—carefully thought out and frightfully expensive to maintain—and there Doug and Mary played out their well-publicized private-life roles for millions of fans.

Within a few years, other stars' dream palaces would be architecturally more distinguished, more expensive, and even much larger than Pickfair. But no other star's home ever claimed the same feverish public devotion year after year. Douglas Fairbanks and Mary Pickford were two of Hollywood's biggest and most enduring stars, and they were the nation's most popular couple. Working hard to gain and then keep their fans' fascination in themselves and their lives, the couple opened Pickfair to the press and their public—or at least they left everyone with that impression. A small army of publicity people gave the press just enough information and photographs to make fans believe they really knew what Douglas Fairbanks and Mary Pickford were like and how they lived. Newspapers and fan magazines reported who came to dinner, how Mary rearranged the living-room furniture, what Doug gave Mary for her birthday.

Millions of Americans bought this act. They spoke of "Doug and

Mary," using their first names as if they were friends. And Pickfair was the most famous house in America, even more famous than the White House. More Americans cared about what happened there than at Warren G. Harding's or Calvin Coolidge's White House. Fairbanks relished the spotlight; Pickford endured it as an occupational hazard of stardom.

Although Douglas Fairbanks and Mary Pickford lived very well, they never stopped cultivating the common touch that their fans could identify with. In many ways, they were the ideal middle-class couple when they got married: young, attractive, hardworking, clean-living, and very much in love with each other. Their publicity staff played this folksy image for all it was worth. "Offscreen Mary Pickford contents herself with being Mrs. Douglas Fairbanks," reported *Ladies' Home Journal*. "She is the 'little woman' whose sole concern is her husband's happiness." *Ladies' Home Journal* neglected to mention that Mary had sixteen full-time servants to help her achieve this domestic bliss.

Doug and Mary were genuinely devoted to each other and, during the first eight years of their marriage, never spent a night apart—"a tighter knot was never tied," Anita Loos once commented caustically. Their behavior may have been one way they unconsciously atoned for their surreptitious courtship, her settlement-tainted divorce, and their hasty marriage. But Douglas Fairbanks was incredibly possessive of Mary as well. Except for a few good friends, he did not allow any other men near her, unless they were considerably older than he was. In a movie colony filled with young, good-looking men and women, this attitude was bound to create embarrassing incidents.

"One day Rudolph Valentino made an unexpected appearance on the Pickfair lawn, which, in the warm months, was our outdoor living room," recalled Mary in her *Sunshine and Shadow* autobiography. "I never saw Douglas act so fast, and with such painful rudeness, as he did in showing Valentino that he wasn't welcome."

Doug specifically asked Mary never to dance with other men. When she refused to waltz with the Duke of York (later King George VI) on their European honeymoon, British newspapers reproached her for this unintended snub. She sweetly replied that it wasn't right "to meet a man one minute and then the next to go into his arms and dance." Even with her husband, Mary was prim and proper on the

Douglas Fairbanks in The Thief of Baghdad (*1924*).

Mary Pickford drives the last nail into the framework of her studio bungalow, which contained a reception room, a dressing room, an office for her secretary, quarters for her maid, and a kitchen and bath.

dance floor. "Of course, we never dance in public," she once said. "Occasionally we have a few people—six or eight—at Pickfair, but then I dance only with Doug, and then it's only the waltz or two-step. We never 'jazz.' "

Fairbanks' smothering possessiveness extended beyond casual dance partners. "He was jealous of *me*," according to Mary's old friend, screenwriter Frances Marion. "He was jealous of her *mother*! It was so silly, there wasn't any reason for it."

But Mary accepted her husband's demands. When she wasn't working on a picture, she gave him an exact accounting of where she went and what she did every day. "I didn't even go to downtown Beverly Hills without first telling him where I was going and promising to call from there or having him call me," she recounted in her book. "Since it was all as complicated as this, I seldom went anywhere. At the same time I never asked where Douglas himself had been or where he planned to go."

During the first two or three years of their marriage, life at Pickfair was rather tranquil for the two Hollywood deities. If Fairbanks was making a movie, he got up at five a. m. in his light-brown second-floor bedroom. He didn't have to worry about waking Mary, because she slept in her own bedroom down the hall. Regardless of the early morning weather, he put on old clothes, and for the next half hour jogged around the house on a gravel path, high-jumped some hedges, even did handstands on the metal lawn chairs. Then he returned to his bedroom, washed, and put on a suit or a sport jacket and slacks—even though he always changed into an old shirt and pants at the studio. Fairbanks had plenty of expensive, well-tailored clothes in his dressing room at Pickfair to choose from: 70 suits, over 100 shirts, 37 hats, 50 pairs of dress shoes, and 35 camel's hair overcoats.

Mary Pickford awoke shortly after her husband if she was filming a movie at the studio. Her bedroom, painted in soft shades of pale green and pink, was unabashedly feminine and represented the epitome of taste for upper-middle-class women of the 1920s. Her dressing table and bench, bedside table, commode, and side chairs with cane seats were expensive 1920s parodies of eighteenth-century neoclassical French furniture that were sold in sets at fashionable Los Angeles

At home with Doug and Mary. We can tell that these publicity stills were shot on the same day, in the early 1920s, because Doug is wearing the same sport jacket and Mary the same dress, with sagging trim on the hem. And what wonderful shoes!

Inside Pickfair in the early 1920s, when most of Douglas Fairbanks and Mary Pickford's guests were old Hollywood friends, business associates, even extras that Doug brought home from the studio.

department stores. The wall-to-wall carpeting was pale green, as were the silk window curtains and the yards of silk that cascaded down the wall to the floor from a princess-like coronet—which had a light for soft nighttime illumination—on the ceiling above the head of her double bed. The bed itself was littered with several embroidered flossy pillows with taffeta ruching, and covered by a simple but elegant Italian lace bedspread, the one truly good thing in the entire room. And—as befitted America's Sweetheart—Little Mary had placed some representatives of her collection of dolls on the dressing table next to the silver-framed photographs of husband Douglas and her cherished mother.

After checking her makeup and clothes in the full-length mirror on the back of the bedroom door, Mary joined Doug in their cheerful first-floor breakfast room. An oval bay window looked out over the hills to the east of Pickfair, and a handsome silver tea service sat on the sideboard. But this piece of furniture, like the breakfast table and chairs, was part of an expensive department-store set. She particularly liked the chairs, which had flowers—each blossom hand-painted a different color—growing out of vase-shaped trelliswork in the oval chair backs.

After breakfast the Fairbankses drove—or were driven—to the studio and usually started shooting around nine a. m. Beginning in 1922, they worked at the same lot, the ten-acre Pickford-Fairbanks Studio at 7200 Santa Monica Boulevard in Hollywood, later the Goldwyn Studio. But the two of them were each busy with his or her own films, and they did not see each other until they ate lunch together in her five-room studio bungalow. Then Doug and Mary returned to the cameras until late afternoon, when they looked at the previous day's rushes and conferred with their directors about the following morning's schedule.

Douglas Fairbanks and Mary Pickford usually returned to Pickfair in time for dinner at seven p. m. Sometimes they were too tired to take off their costumes before dinner, and Little Lord Fauntleroy and D'Artagnan sat down together at the table. Douglas Fairbanks had decorated the dining room before the marriage, and it reflected that baronial well-to-do country-gentleman look that he originally favored at Pickfair. The room was comfortable, even a little elegant, with its beamed ceiling painted a light color, watered silk wallpaper, a fine sterling silver tea service on the sideboard, and an antique Persian carpet. But the furniture was yet another 1920s department-store set, made from a dark wood, heavily carved, in the Jacobean style.

Dinners for just the Fairbankses were the exception rather than the rule at Pickfair, particularly on weekends or when one of them was between pictures. Continuing a habit from his brief "bachelor" days at Pickfair in 1920, Doug frequently dragged co-workers or friends home from the studio on the spur of the moment, and Mary instructed the staff to set the table for fifteen every night. "Imagine my surprise," she once said, "when I came to dinner and saw three stock-car drivers and a bunch of dirty cowpunchers sitting around the table."

Millions of fans were eager to know what Douglas Fairbanks and Mary Pickford served at Pickfair, and one fan magazine obligingly published this menu for a "Typical Family Dinner" in 1928:

BOILED HALIBUT WITH HOT TARTAR SAUCE
FRENCH FRIED POTATOES

FILET OF CHICKEN À LA POULET
SWEET POTATO CROQUETTES
SPINACH WITH EGG SAUCE

HEARTS OF LETTUCE WITH FRENCH DRESSING

NEAPOLITAN BASKETS
WITH HOT CHOCOLATE SAUCE

COFFEE

Often Mary was the only woman at these casual weekday dinners in the early 1920s. At other times her mother, Charlotte, childhood friend Lillian Gish, or Frances Marion balanced the table-seating a little. But the presence of ladies did not stop Doug from playing his practical jokes. Sometimes he crawled under the table and grabbed—or bit—guests' ankles. Occasionally he insisted that someone sit down in a chair that had been wired to give a mild electric shock. Or he set one place at the table with a flexible fork and a dribble glass.

Douglas Fairbanks and Mary Pickford rarely went out to a restaurant or a nightclub because adoring fans never gave them a moment's peace in public places, and Mary didn't want to be seen wearing one of the fine gowns or the jewelry that did not match her wholesome "Little Mary" screen image. Once in a while they accepted an invitation to dinner at a friend's home, but their secretary always sent the hostess the following notice:

Mr. and Mrs. Douglas Fairbanks
beg to inform ——————————
that it is their desire to be placed
next to each other at the table.

On most weekends, Douglas Fairbanks and Mary Pickford preferred to entertain at home, and hardly anyone in the movie colony ever turned down an invitation to Pickfair. A typical formal dinner menu consisted of:

CAVIAR CANAPÉS

ICED CELERY HEARTS   SALTED NUTS

CONSOMMÉ WITH EGGBALLS

LOBSTER IN CASES

FILET OF BEEF À LA JARDINIÈRE
POTATO RINGS   PEAS À LA FRANÇAISE

ROAST WILD DUCK
BUTTERED WILD RICE
ORANGE CREAM SHERBET

ROMAINE SALAD

CUSTARD SOUFFLÉ WITH FOAM SAUCE
PETITS FOURS

CRACKERS AND CHEESE

CAFÉ NOIR

---

*The hall out-
side the living
room, where
Doug, Mary,
and their guests
sometimes
danced after
dinner parties.*

*The living
room.*

The breakfast room, furnished with an expensive department-store set.

The dining room, furnished in the country-gentleman look that Douglas Fairbanks so dearly loved in the early 1920s.

To loosen up these dinner parties, where often the only conversation was the movies, Douglas Fairbanks played more practical jokes, such as feigning anger at his Japanese valet and twirling the man in a circle by his heels. But most guests felt that something was missing at the Pickfair dinners. "We'd go there all dressed up," recalled Miriam Cooper, "and sit down at this huge table with lovely china and servants falling all over themselves serving you, and not even get one lousy drop of wine." Douglas Fairbanks had a phobia about alcoholic beverages because his father had been a drunkard. Consequently, he did not serve any liquor at Pickfair, not even beer and wine, during the early 1920s.

On some evenings after dinner, the servants removed the furniture from the hall next to the living room, and Doug, Mary, and the guests danced on the gleaming terra-cotta tile floor. At other times everyone played bridge at tables set up in this hall or in the pale-green living room, which was furnished in an eighteenth-century French mode, with a down-filled silk damask upholstered sofa, several rococo-style armchairs, yellow drapes, two antique vases converted into lamps, and a fine Oriental rug over the dark-stained hardwood floor. But on most occasions, the hosts showed a movie in their screening room after dinner, then served fresh fruit and Ovaltine, and bid an early good-night to their company.

Many guests thought that this dinner-then-movies routine was a little boring, and a few had some fun on their own. One night John Barrymore never got to the screening room. After dinner he took one of the women guests upstairs to the wide hallway that doubled as an informal sitting room and made love to her on the sofa outside Mary's bedroom door.

Barrymore got away with that because he was an old friend of Douglas Fairbanks' and was only living up to his well-known reputation as one of Hollywood's great lechers. Although his was the sort of prank that was routine fare at Mack Sennett's mansion, for instance, Doug and Mary usually did not abide such willful breaches of etiquette, particularly once they started entertaining European royalty, after 1923.

Alfonso XIII, the last King of Spain, was the first titled guest at Pickfair, and, according to Anita Loos, "Doug was never the same

Mary Pickford's bedroom looked more like an upper-middle-class matron's than an internationally acclaimed screen star's, with its pale-green and pink walls, pale-green wall-to-wall carpeting, and pseudoclassical furniture set.

again." In the next eight to ten years, he and Mary entertained much of the world's remaining nobility for dinner or a several nights' stay, including Lord and Lady Mountbatten, the Earl and Countess of Lanesborough, the Duke and Duchess of Sutherland, the Duke of York, the King and Queen of Siam, the Crown Prince of Japan, Crown Princess Frederica of Prussia, and the Duke and Duchess of Alba.

The prosperous country-gentleman look that Doug had favored at Pickfair only a few years earlier no longer seemed appropriate for such exalted guests or, for that matter, for the "King and Queen of Hollywood," as some newspapers now described Douglas Fairbanks and Mary Pickford. Rather than build a larger home, Doug and Mary started to redecorate their beloved Pickfair in 1925. For the living room, they bought several more eighteenth-century French-inspired chairs, placed a white grand piano in one corner, and purchased some "important" nineteenth-century genre paintings. But their most prized acquisition cost nothing and occupied a place of honor on a small French-style table in one corner. This was a framed picture of Lord and Lady Mountbatten, inscribed "To Doug and Mary, from Edwina and Dickie."

Mary did not change her pink-and-pale-green second-floor bedroom, except to move the cage of her pet canary, Nugget, into the dressing room. Nicknamed "Baby," the little bird whistled "Yankee Doodle" and "Over There," or so Mary told reporters, and he even accompanied her on trips to New York and Europe. Doug's light-brown bedroom often served as guest quarters, and it was totally redecorated in 1925 and 1926. Hereafter the virile and athletic Douglas Fairbanks slept in a canopied satinwood bed, and the rest of the delicate bedroom furniture looked as if it might have been part of the boudoir set in a Hollywood film about Madame Du Barry.

Doug and Mary devoted their greatest care to upgrading the dining room. The store-bought Jacobean dining-room furniture and the well-worn antique Persian carpet were banished to their beach house at Pacific Terrace and Appian Way in Santa Monica. Out went the baronial-looking beamed ceiling. The mood they sought was eighteenth-century French, but they again bought costly reproduction chairs, a dining table, and a sideboard, rather than the real things. The hardwood floor was wall-to-wall carpeted in the familiar pale green, and built-in illuminated china closets with mirrored backs showed off their porcelain collection in each corner of the room.

This was only the beginning of the changes in the dining room. Doug splurged on crystal place-card holders, a gold dinner service, and a set of china that Napoleon had given Josephine. For formal dinners, a footman stood behind each chair, and the master of the house even relaxed his no-liquor rule. Now the housemen served weak mixed drinks before dinner—no more than two per guest—and some wine during the meal.

Having created the perfect stage-set home with his movie millions and with the help of Albert, the tireless majordomo, Douglas Fairbanks began to believe his own publicity about being the King of Hollywood. "He'd kowtow to a duke and a duchess," Frances Marion recalled, but "when some nice ordinary people . . . were expected, he'd say, 'Why are those people coming?' and turn up his nose. But then they'd arrive and he'd swagger up, shoulders back, and put on his act."

Hollywood wits began to tell the following joke:

> Question: "Why does Doug go to Europe each year?"
> Answer: "To book his royal visitors for the coming year."

Even Doug's good friend Charlie Chaplin couldn't resist kidding him a little. One day, Chaplin came up to Doug and said:

> "Hello, Doug. How's the duke?"
> "What duke?" asked Fairbanks.
> "Oh . . . any duke," Chaplin replied.

Douglas Fairbanks would do anything to please his titled visitors. When Prince George of England, the youngest son of King George V and Duke of Kent, who later died during the Second World War, visited Doug at his studio, the guards at the gate thought that the royal entourage was a group of unemployed extras and brusquely turned them away. After Prince George got into the studio, Douglas Fairbanks apologized for the case of mistaken identity, and he invited the Prince

Harold and Mildred Lloyd leaving a party at Pickfair, 1932.

Once Doug and Mary started to entertain, even seek out, royalty and celebrities after 1923, Pickfair's relaxed country-gentleman look no longer seemed quite right, and they redecorated the house in the more stylish eighteenth-century French mode, beginning with the dining room in 1925.

to watch him film the next sequence of *The Iron Mask* (1929), the story of an aging D'Artagnan. The Prince was delighted to see a movie being made, never realizing that the scene had been shot earlier in the day. Douglas Fairbanks, the other actors, the director, and the cameramen faked the entire scene, running the cameras without film, just to give the Prince a good time.

Doug and Mary didn't limit their celebrity guests only to royalty. Any big name would do. At various times, they entertained Jack Dempsey, Albert Einstein, Amelia Earhart, F. Scott Fitzgerald, Henry Ford, Walter Johnson, Babe Ruth, and H. G. Wells. Doug particularly enjoyed meeting famous sports heroes. Once studio executive Adolph Zukor came to Pickfair to discuss some business with Doug. The servants told him that Doug was at the swimming pool. When Zukor reached the pool, he didn't see anyone, at least not for a moment. Suddenly one head rose out of the water, gasping for breath, followed by another, then another. Doug, Babe Ruth, and Walter Johnson had been holding a contest to see who could stay underwater the longest. Later that day Doug threw a few baseballs for Babe Ruth to hit. Ruth's bat sent one ball hurtling toward an upstairs window, but, unfortunately for Doug, the ball hit the side of the house, and he couldn't show everyone the window that Babe Ruth had broken.

Mary Pickford wasn't always enthusiastic about receiving company at Pickfair, particularly those people Anita Loos has described as "men of genius, the writers, poets, painters, who were fascinated with the movies and wanted to see Hollywood for themselves. When they showed up, it threw the movie colony into a panic. The big stars would say, 'I'll have them over for dinner, but what *can* we talk about?' What *would* Mary have to say to H. G. Wells, by any chance? But there he was sitting at her right at the dinner table one night. We were rushed through our meals, I remember, and then Mary turned to H. G. Wells and said, 'Let's all watch a new movie.' That way, nobody had to talk. We could sit and look at the movie, and, as soon as it was over, we all went home. There was no opportunity for conversation."

Hardly a week passed without out-of-town guests at Pickfair, because the invitations were made quite casually. "My father and stepmother," recalls Douglas Fairbanks, Jr., "used to get telegrams or letters of introduction saying, 'Dear Mary, Dear Doug, My old friend Fred and his wife are coming out to California, and we'd be awfully grateful if you would have them out to the studio and to the house for dinner.' Or some of their friends from Europe or New York would invite themselves. 'Dear Mary, Dear Doug, Would you put me up for a few days? I'm going through California on my way to the Orient.' And, of course, they would be delighted to have their friends as house-guests, although they didn't entertain as much as their fans were led to believe.''

Sometimes Doug and Mary's spur-of-the-moment invitations stretched their hospitality to disconcerting limits. A British countess, Lady Millicent Haas, came for a weekend and stayed over a year! Then there was the visit, probably apocryphal, of the Princess Vera Roma-noff. The Princess was staying at the Biltmore Hotel in downtown Los Angeles and called Pickfair to ask if she could meet Doug and Mary. They couldn't have been more flattered and sent one of their Rolls-Royces to bring the Princess for the weekend. The Princess enjoyed every minute of her stay, thanked Doug and Mary for their hospitality Sunday night, and returned to her secretary's job in Santa Monica the next morning.

Occasionally Mary Pickford got tired of the endless guests and of spending almost every waking hour in the spotlight. Lillian Gish recalls that "one day, around 1930, Mary called me from a hotel in New York, not far from where I was living then. She hadn't told me she was coming to New York for a visit, and I said, 'What in the wide world are you doing here?' She replied, 'Oh, I just couldn't take it any longer, the house, the servants, the company. I'm here in a little hotel room, just for the quiet.' ''

Mary Pickford had a right to be tired. Besides reigning over Pick-fair and keeping up with Douglas's near-manic pace—she always called him Douglas—Mary was involved in running United Artists, the stu-dio that Charlie Chaplin, Fairbanks, D. W. Griffith, and she had formed in 1919 to gain artistic control of their films and to get all the profits from the smash hits. And Pickford had a busy movie career of her own. Beyond the physical demands of completing thirteen feature-

Joe Schenck's dinner to celebrate Valentino's signing with United Artists, early 1926: Natalie Talmadge Keaton, William S. Hart, Norma Talmadge, B. P. Schulberg, Douglas Fairbanks, Peg Talmadge, unknown, Buster Keaton, unknown, Mary Pickford, Charlie Chaplin, Charlotte Pickford, Joe Schenck, Natasha Rambova, unknown, Rudolph Valentino, Constance Talmadge, John Considine, unknown, unknown.

length films in the 1920s, she was trying to guide her career, not always with success.

In 1925, Mary Pickford was thirty-two years old, but she had just convincingly portrayed a twelve-year-old girl in *Little Annie Rooney,* one of her most popular films. The following year she played a fifteen-year-old girl in *Sparrows,* also a highly regarded movie, if not a big hit at the box office. But she'd been portraying these juvenile characters for over ten years now, and knew that she couldn't continue to play little girls much longer. Yet Pickford's fans were so wrapped up in their screen fantasies about golden-curled Little Mary that they deserted the box office when she attempted to take new, adult roles in *Rosita* (1923) and *Dorothy Vernon of Haddon Hall* (1924). When, in fact, a 1925 magazine polled her fans, asking what roles they'd most like to see her play, they responded with those staples of childhood and goodness: Anne of Green Gables, Alice in Wonderland, and Heidi. Exasperated, Mary Pickford knew that the American public had issued a warning.

Fairbanks, conversely, had been able to change *his* screen image around the time of his marriage to Mary. After having played perfect young men in light comedies of the late teens, Doug made *The Mark of Zorro* in 1920. It was a hit, and he went on to achieve his greatest popularity starring in action spectaculars such as *Robin Hood* (1922), *The Thief of Baghdad* (1924), and *The Black Pirate* (1926).

Yet for all his devotion to his career and to Mary, Douglas Fairbanks' least successful role may have been as father to Doug, Jr., his only child from his first marriage. Doug, Jr., didn't get invited to many Pickfair parties or even the quiet middle-of-the-week dinners. "I would go over to Pickfair and just hang around, hoping to be asked to dinner," Douglas Fairbanks, Jr., once recalled. But most of the time, no one invited him to stay, and he left alone. Perhaps Doug, Sr., was too self-engrossed to be a good father, and he unquestionably perceived his son as a threat to his ego and career. By 1925, Doug, Jr., had grown into a handsome seventeen-year-old, several inches taller than his five-foot-eight father. Doug, Sr. did not want to be reminded—or remind his fans—that he was now in his early forties and still playing athletic swashbucklers.

Douglas Fairbanks, Sr., on the other hand, was devoted to other,

Doug and Mary plant a tree
at Pickfair—using that
trowel? and wearing that
dress?

less threatening members of his family, lavishing expensive presents and planning surprise junkets to local toy shops for his four young nieces. One day he drove the children's parents, Robert and Lorie, to Laurel Canyon on the pretext of visiting some of his friends. When they arrived at the house, no one was there. The front door, however, was open, and Doug led Robert and Lorie into the new, handsomely furnished house.

"It's just what I'd like to have someday," said Lorie Fairbanks.

"Then why don't you move in?" Doug replied. "It's yours!"

Douglas Fairbanks enjoyed spending money—collecting Frederic Remington paintings of the Old West, purchasing a prized hundred-pound German shepherd for a purported five thousand dollars, or outfitting friends who accompanied him on his frequent clothes-buying sprees. In 1922, Doug invited Charlie Chaplin, Pola Negri, and fifty other of his closest friends on a six-month round-the-world cruise. He planned to charter a steamer for $250,000. This was just like Fairbanks, but eventually he dropped the idea, because it was just too expensive—even for him.

Although Mary's movies earned more money some years than his did, Douglas Fairbanks paid for the day-to-day expenses at Pickfair. That was a husband's duty, he believed, and it proved to be an expensive one. The staff was the greatest single outlay. Albert, the major-domo, received $300 a month to supervise the help, look after Doug's wardrobe, and organize luncheons for important visitors at Mary's studio bungalow. Two housemen cleaned the downstairs rooms, served meals, and tended fires for $150 a month each. Mary's $125-a-month personal maid cleaned her bedroom suite and tended her clothes, while the $90-a-month upstairs maid was responsible for the other second-floor rooms.

The Fairbankses' cook received $200 a month. Doug always insisted that a woman fill this job. A woman, he believed, bought provisions more carefully than a man, and, incidentally, could be hired for $50 a month less. The $90-a-month kitchen maid did all the scullery work and prepared the staff's meals. The $80-a-month laundress did all the washing, including Mary's delicate finery.

Outside the house, Douglas Fairbanks hired a $200-a-month head gardener, several $4-a-day laborers, and a $140-a-month watchman. One chauffeur received $150 a month for driving and automobile maintenance and another earned $200 for the same duties, plus operating the motion picture projector after dinner. Charlie Daugherty, the Pickfair handyman, was also responsible for fetching the evening movies from various Hollywood studios, a mission he undertook in his wheezing black jalopy. This long "downstairs" list was only the permanent staff at Pickfair. For formal dinner parties and large receptions, Albert hired additional help to prepare food, serve the meals, and clean up afterward.

Mary Pickford however, held a different attitude about money than Doug. Always more fatalistic about the vicissitudes of Hollywood life and stardom than her husband, she was frugal, even to the point of being cheap. "Mary always pinched her pennies," Anita Loos said recently. "She never paid for anything if she could get out of it." More than once Mary bought a dress, wore it one time, then returned it to the shop saying that it didn't fit.

But Mary did not deny herself certain luxuries, though. She bought dozens of exquisite Paris gowns and owned a glass-enclosed custom-made 1924 Rolls-Royce roadster that sat only two. The roadster was "the last word in daintiness," according to Mary, and only two others had been built: one for the Prince of Wales, the other for Lady Mountbatten. Mary had to obtain their permission before Rolls-Royce agreed to make a third car.

Mary Pickford could easily afford these indulgences. Because of Doug's gallant upkeep of Pickfair, she invested most of her earnings in real estate and bonds, with the help of her mother. As one of Douglas Fairbanks' nieces once remarked, "Doug paid the bills; Mary bought corner lots."

CHAPTER SEVEN

Not long after Douglas Fairbanks moved to Beverly Hills in 1919 and started remodeling the Phillips hunting lodge into the estate that became Pickfair, Gloria Swanson bought razor-blade millionaire King C. Gillette's three-year-old mansion at 904 North Crescent Drive, just above Sunset Boulevard and opposite the main entrance to the Beverly Hills Hotel. A restrained Southern California adaptation of the Italian Renaissance style, with cream-color stucco walls and a red tile roof, Swanson's two-story home was one of the largest in Beverly Hills: 115 feet wide and 100 feet deep, with twenty-two rooms, five baths, and one automatic electric elevator, built around three sides of a thousand-foot-square terrace overlooking sweeping lawns and full-grown palms and acacias.

Swanson's new home was one of the great showplaces of Beverly Hills. The five-foot-two-inch star, who played leads in sophisticated and naughty Cecil B. De Mille comedies such as *Male and Female* (1919) and *Why Change Your Wife?* (1920), followed her neighbor Douglas Fairbanks' lead and turned her home into a dream palace—an extravagant, sometimes eccentric, and always inspired stage set for her well-publicized private life. And to reinforce her glamorous screen image, Swanson made unabashed luxury the theme of her Beverly Hills estate.

She draped the enormous reception room in peacock silk, hung tapestries and paintings on the walls of the elegantly furnished living and dining rooms, painted the breakfast room cream and gold, turned

Gloria Swanson and Lew Cody in Don't Change Your Husband *(1919), one of Cecil B. De Mille's naughty postwar comedies.*

Gloria Swanson in the bedroom of her Beverly Hills home, 1923. This room, with its open drawers and piles of books, is surprisingly untidy for that of a glamorous screen goddess who had a dozen servants.

ABOVE: *Gloria Swanson and her Russian wolfhound, Ivan, in front of her Beverly Hills estate, where she was the first star to live like a star, 1923.*

BELOW: *Gloria Swanson's estate, the rear grounds.*

one room into an intimate movie theater, and installed a black marble bathroom with a golden tub next to her bedroom.

Just twenty-three years old when she bought her Beverly Hills estate, Gloria Swanson shrewdly took her elegant and somewhat haughty screen image seriously. "I have decided," she once proclaimed, "that while I am a star, I will be every inch and every moment a star. Everyone from the studio gatemen to the highest executive will know it."

A Beverly Hills mansion, no matter how richly furnished, could be nothing more than a deity's backdrop. Stars must live like stars in their own homes, Swanson believed, and in this belief she was several years ahead of everyone else in the movie colony. While Douglas Fairbanks and Mary Pickford were entertaining stock-car drivers at Pickfair in the early twenties and Norma Talmadge was hiding her jewelry with the lettuce in her West Adams Boulevard icebox, Gloria Swanson hired four butlers for her Beverly Hills mansion and staged dinner parties with liveried footmen stationed behind each guest's chair. She bought three Rolls-Royces—one white, one maroon, one black—and her two chauffeurs wore matching uniforms. For less formal occasions, Gloria drove her own leopard-skin-upholstered Lancia sports car.

Gloria Swanson's fans were captivated by her innovative "a star should live like a star" existence. "There is no star in Hollywood who lives in such gilded luxury as Gloria Swanson," gushed Adela Rogers St. Johns in the September 1923 *Photoplay*. "Gloria's home is the home of a great lady. Her manner of life belongs usually to women of wealth and fashion and enormous social prestige."

Not loath to dress as well as act the part, Gloria Swanson was the height of 1920s wardrobe chic. One year her clothing bill reportedly was $25,000 for fur coats, $50,000 for gowns, $9,000 for stockings, $5,000 for shoes, $10,000 for lingerie, $5,000 for purses, $5,000 for headdresses, and $6,000 for perfume. "In those days, the public wanted us to live like kings and queens," she later recalled. "So we did—and why not? We were in love with life. We were making more money than we ever dreamed existed, and there was no reason to believe it would ever stop."

Perhaps Swanson's greatest coup was her 1925 marriage to her third husband, Henri, Marquis de la Falaise de la Coudraye, whom she met while making *Madame Sans-Gène* on location in France. This was the first marriage between Hollywood royalty and authentic European nobility, and Gloria's fans were beside themselves with joy. When Swanson, now the Marquise, returned from Europe with her new husband, the Los Angeles police roped off Vine Street near Paramount Studios, and a huge platform in the middle of the street opposite the studio gate carried the banner "Welcome Home, Gloria!" Hollywood schools were closed for the day, and thousands of cheering fans packed the streets in all directions, even climbing on top of cars or up telephone poles to watch the open car carry Swanson and her husband slowly down the street and under the studio gate in a blizzard of rose petals. The scene was right out of the movies.

When Swanson's contract expired in 1926, Paramount offered to raise her salary from $6,500 to $15,000 a week. But Swanson knew what her name on a theater marquee meant for ticket sales—hadn't the press reported that her "popularity has been sweeping the country like wildfire"?—and she held out for a better deal. So Paramount upped their salary offer to $18,000 a week, plus 50 percent of the film's profits. Swanson still wanted more. But when Paramount said no, she formed Gloria Swanson, Inc., which was financed by Joseph P. Kennedy and became a part of United Artists.

With prim Little Mary and the worldly Marquise on the same studio lot, some tension between the two stars was inevitable. Years later, Swanson remembered one incident concerning *Sadie Thompson,* her steamy 1928 melodrama about a repentant South Seas prostitute. "Mary'd come over to my bungalow with her little bee-stung lips and pout, 'I want to do Sadie Thompson.' I'm exactly the same height as she is, maybe just a half inch taller, but she affected being a child, with her little Mary Janes and those damned curls, and I'd wear these enormous high heels and act like I towered over her. I'd say very imperiously, 'Get out of here, you little shrimp, I'm Sadie Thompson. You can be Sadie Thompson if you let me play Little Annie Rooney—give me your wig!' She'd get furious and say 'These are my own curls.' "

Sometimes Gloria Swanson and Mary Pickford's professional differences spilled into purely social occasions. Swanson was a frequent guest at Pickfair, even though she thought that most of Mary's parties were "deadly," an opinion shared by other stars. One evening in 1928 madcap Gloria managed to liven up the party a little and one-up Mary at the same time. The occasion was one of Douglas Fairbanks and Mary Pickford's social triumphs: a formal dinner-dance that Mary had organized on a day's notice for Prince George, youngest son of King George V of England.

The guest list for the dinner, which preceded the arrival of more company for the dance, read like the Social Register of late-1920s Hollywood: Mary Astor, Walter Byron, Charlie Chaplin, June Collier, Ronald Colman, Lily Damita, Ralph Forbes, Greta Garbo, Jack Gilbert, Jeta Goudal, Marie Gray, Dorothy Gulliver, Kenneth Hawks, John Loder, Bessie Love, Tom Mix, Ramon Novarro, Norma Shearer, Irving Thalberg, Lupe Velez, Irvin Willat, and Claire Windsor, plus Gloria Swanson.

During dinner, Prince George told Swanson that he hoped to see more than just Pickfair during his one-day visit to Los Angeles. He specifically asked about Fatty Arbuckle's popular nightclub at the beach. That was all Gloria needed to hear, and she devised a wonderful scheme. Calling home, she instructed her butler to send some champagne to her Rolls-Royce parked outside Pickfair. As Swanson danced with Prince George, he told her whom he'd like to have join them at Fatty Arbuckle's club later. Then the Prince said good-bye to Doug and Mary, and the eight guests he had chosen sneaked out the back door. The revelers headed for the beach.

Fatty Arbuckle wasn't there, Swanson recalls, "but they had an orchestra, and we danced and sang until three a.m., when we went back to my house in a whole string of cars. We brought the orchestra back to my house with us. We woke up the butler and cook, but they were English and delighted to see the Prince. We served breakfast, and for three solid hours Chaplin entertained us with all the acts he ever did, every impersonation, every character, before we took the Prince to the airport. If Mary ever found out about it, she never let on."

About the same time that Gloria Swanson moved into her Beverly Hills mansion, Will Rogers bought a several-acre estate less than a block away at 925 North Beverly Drive. The two neighbors couldn't

have been more different in personal styles. A cowboy and circus performer before coming to Hollywood in 1918 to make his first silent
film, *Laughing Bill Hyde,* Rogers was rapidly becoming the nation's
favorite comedian and pop philosopher. His wry expressions and carefully cultivated drawl lent a simple country-boy flavor to his otherwise
sophisticated observations.

Before moving into their new home, Betty Rogers decided to ex-
pand the large bungalow that stood on a hill at the end of the estate's
long driveway. That house, Rogers quipped, "oughta been made of
rubber . . . the way she went round there, pushin' out this wall and
then pushin' out another."

After Betty Rogers had finished the remodeling, their Spanish-
style house was large and comfortable, but it did not look like the pretentious mansion of a rising star. The exterior stucco walls were cream
color, and the roof was red tile. A large columned porch ran across the
front of the building at the first floor. Will had definite ideas of what
the estate's grounds should be like. To ensure privacy, he constructed
an eight-foot-tall red brick wall around the property. Just below the
house he added a stable, a riding ring, and a swimming pool. Then he
built two log cabins: a small one for daughter Mary, and a larger one
for the family, complete with an open fireplace and five bunk beds
along the wall. Rogers and his family often ate dinners and even spent
weekends and holidays in the rudely furnished bunkhouses. "Formal
Christmas Day callers could never find our hideout, concealed by trees
and shrubs," Betty Rogers once wrote. "We could hear one motorcar
after another roll up to our front door and roll away again."

Within a few years, Will Rogers' bunkhouses and riding ring had
become rural anachronisms, for Beverly Hills was again sharing in the
fantastic Los Angeles real-estate boom of the early 1920s. The small
town's construction activity increased 1,000 percent in just five years.
And yet, Beverly Hills was still much like an island in the middle of
nowhere in 1920, separated from the western edge of Los Angeles by
barley fields, oil wells, and the drab workingman's village of Sherman.
Nor did it have the uniformly prosperous and manicured look that
would attract development ahead of the usual early twentieth-century
pattern of contiguous urban growth.

Indeed, "Beverly Hills looked like an abandoned real-estate development" around 1920, recalled Charlie Chaplin, a bit dramatically, in his autobiography. "Sidewalks ran along and disappeared into open fields, and lampposts with white globes adorned empty streets; most of the globes were missing, shot off by passing revelers from roadhouses." The hills above Sunset Boulevard were "scrubby" and "barren," and "the alkali and the sagebrush gave off an odorous, sour tang that made the throat dry and nostrils smart." Coyotes were everywhere, according to Chaplin, who was probably remembering many evenings at Pickfair. As a houseguest there, "I would listen to the coyotes howling, packs of them invading the garbage cans."

Despite Chaplin's unromantic description, Beverly Hills' building boom benefited from the incalculable advantage of its four glamorous new residents: Douglas Fairbanks, Mary Pickford, Gloria Swanson, and Will Rogers. Their combined presence gave Beverly Hills an exciting image of wealth and prestige. When Los Angeles residents got off the Pacific Electric train in Beverly Hills, they didn't notice the unpaved roads above Sunset Boulevard, or the acres of bean fields in the flats, or the modest shopping district just below Santa Monica Boulevard. Instead they were mesmerized by their proximity to these four stars and by the sight of their homes. Dozens of wealthy businessmen and their families moved from slowly decaying downtown Los Angeles neighborhoods like West Adams Boulevard into suddenly chic Beverly Hills.

Many other stars and studio chiefs also built homes in Beverly Hills. Now the movie colony had a town all its own, free from the lingering hostility toward motion picture people which permeated "society" neighborhoods such as Windsor Square and Hancock Park and even tainted the fashionable palm-lined boulevards of Hollywood itself.

Few stars regretted leaving Hollywood. Its days as a charming suburb of business titans' estates and retired Midwestern farmers' bungalows were quickly ending. In the Los Angeles boom, Hollywood's population jumped from 36,000 in 1920 to 157,000 in 1930. Although winding hillside roads and restricted subdivisions like Laughlin Park remained desirable throughout the 1920s and 1930s, shops and middle-

A new house under construction. A publicity still for the Beverly Ridge tract, 1928.

OPPOSITE ABOVE: *Will Rogers on the set of* Doubling for Romeo (*1921*).

OPPOSITE BELOW: *Beverly Hills, 1922, looking north from Wilshire Boulevard.*

class apartments were replacing the attractive homes along streets in the flats or on the edge of the foothills.

Hollywood Boulevard had become one of America's busiest, and most celebrated streets. Lined with shops, office buildings, restaurants, and theaters, it was filled with crowds all day long and far into the night. Once respectable Hollywood had given way to speakeasies, gambling dens, marijuana smoking, and call girls, who evaded prosecution under vagrancy laws by claiming to be movie extras. This bustling, almost honky-tonk atmosphere was exactly the sort of thing that drove sturdy middle- and upper-class families from their homes on nearby side streets.

Movie stars, of course, wanted to live as far away from their fans as possible. But just as important, stars and studio chiefs certainly did not want to live in a community with an increasingly questionable reputation, because some ugly and still-fresh scandals rocked the movie colony in the early 1920s.

On September 10, 1920, pretty Olive Thomas, ex–Ziegfeld girl, rising comedy star, and sister-in-law of Mary Pickford, committed suicide in her Paris hotel room. Olive, it turned out, was a heroin addict; she killed herself after she failed to score a large supply of smack for herself and her husband, Jack, who was also an addict. In the ensuing uproar, Jack was exposed as a hopeless philanderer as well. He went into a hospital for nervous exhaustion and offered no comment on these charges, but his sister, Mary, denied these "sickening aspersions" on his good name.

That same month Robert Harron, a member of D. W. Griffith's stock company since the early teens, committed suicide in his New York hotel room just before the premiere of *Way Down East*. Harron had appeared in *The Birth of a Nation* and *Intolerance,* and he was despondent that Griffith had selected Richard Barthelmess over himself to play the farmer's son in the film.

A year later Fatty Arbuckle held his infamous bottle party in San Francisco's St. Francis Hotel. That story was still front-page news when Paramount director William Desmond Taylor was shot to death in his Alvarado Street bungalow on the night of February 1, 1922. Taylor had directed *Tom Sawyer* (1919) and the much-acclaimed *Huck-*

leberry Finn (1920); he was a handsome, educated, and courtly fifty-year-old bachelor, who enjoyed his reputation as a ladies' man.

But Taylor had several secrets. Detectives investigating his murder discovered that he, like Francis X. Bushman, was no bachelor. Taylor had, in fact, abandoned a wife and child in New York in 1908. One thing about Taylor was true, however: He was a favorite with the ladies. At his bungalow detectives uncovered a collection of women's underwear, each one labeled with initials and the date of conquest. According to one story, he had been juggling three affairs simultaneously at the time of his death, the first with Keystone comedienne Mabel Normand, the second with Paramount's curly-headed Mary Miles Minter (a Mary Pickford look-alike), and the third with Minter's mother, Charlotte Selby!

Taylor's murder was never solved, but the scandal severely damaged Mabel Normand's career. She had a $2,000-a-month cocaine habit, or so many people said. And to make matters worse, Mack Sennett withdrew her latest film, *Susanna* (1922), after *Good Housekeeping* magazine pronounced Normand too "adulterated" for the screen. Mary Miles Minter's film days were over too when detectives found her passionate love letters to Taylor, and some underwear in his collection monogrammed MMM. Her last film was *Drums of Fate* (1923).

As if Taylor's murder wasn't enough to give Hollywood a bad name, fans learned in March 1922 that boyish, six-foot three-inch blue-eyed Wallace Reid, the King of Paramount, was a morphine addict. Like many stars before and after him, Wally—his nickname was "Good Time" Wally—started using drugs to get through day after grueling day of picture-making. When Good Time Wally died in a sanitarium on January 18, 1923, at the age of thirty-two, his wife, Florence, who was a featured player at Universal under the name Dorothy Davenport, moved to capitalize on the tragedy. Now billed as Mrs. Wallace Reid, she starred in an anti-drug film titled *Human Wreckage*—"the Greatest Production in the History of Motion Pictures," claimed its shrill advertisements.

The exodus from Hollywood was on, and one of the first stars to leave was Charlie Chaplin. In 1922 he broke ground on a large Spanish-style home at 1085 Summit Drive, just down the road from

Fatty Arbuckle was tried for murder, not once, but three times, for the death of actress Virginia Rappe following his Labor Day Weekend "bottle party." After two mistrials, a third jury finally acquitted Fatty of murder charges, but Arbuckle's career was over, although he occasionally got work as a director using the name Will B. Good.

"Good Time" Wallace Reid and his wife, Dorothy Davenport, at home. At the height of his career, blue-eyed, six-foot-three Reid became a morphine addict, and he died in a sanatorium in 1923 at the age of thirty.

Pickfair. Even though Chaplin was still married to Mildred Harris, this was going to be a bachelor's home, because their marriage was all but over. Mildred had been sixteen years old—and several months pregnant—when they were married in 1918 and moved into the large, somber-looking house at 2010 De Mille Drive in Hollywood's Laughlin Park. Their child lived only three days, and they drifted apart in less than a year. "Although we lived in the same house, we seldom saw each other," Chaplin wistfully recalled in his autobiography. "It became a sad house. I would come home to find the dinner table laid for one, and would eat alone. Occasionally she was away for a week without leaving word, and I would only know by seeing the open door of her empty bedroom."

His were memories dry-cleaned for posterity. Actually Charlie had all but deserted Mildred and the De Mille Drive house by 1920. He lived at his LaBrea Avenue studio bungalow, frequented his brother Sydney's white-frame colonial-style home at Sunset Boulevard and La Brea Avenue, and even rented an East Indian–style house at 6147 Temple Hill Drive in the Hollywood Hills, just east of Cahuenga Pass. In 1920, Chaplin often stayed with good friend Douglas Fairbanks at his new Beverly Hills estate. Even after the Fairbanks-Pickford marriage, Charlie was such a frequent guest at Pickfair that Mary set aside an upstairs bedroom for his use, even though she considered him an "obstinate, suspicious, egocentric, maddening, and lovable genius of a problem child."

When they were together, Doug and Charlie loved to play practical jokes. Once Doug wore a trick shirt under his dinner jacket to a formal party. During the evening, he and Charlie pretended to have a violent argument. Once they had attracted everyone's attention, Charlie shouted, "If you don't shut up, I'll rip your shirt off!"

"Go ahead, try it!" Doug roared back. That was Charlie's cue. He walked up to Doug and grabbed the front of his shirt. The shirt came apart, and Charlie was left holding the tattered remnants, while Doug stood there wearing only the cuffs.

At other times, Doug and Charlie got into an open car and drove around Beverly Hills looking for tourists. Here was a switch. Usually it was the tourists who came looking for stars. When the pair found some unsuspecting victims, Charlie stopped the car, raised his voice to a falsetto, and asked, "I say, would you tell me where Sunset Boulevard and Benedict Canyon meet?"

The tourists were flabbergasted. They were standing next to two of Hollywood's biggest silent-picture stars, and Doug and Charlie's voices were so *high*. Most of the time, the tourists mumbled the directions, forgetting to whip out their autograph books, never stopping to wonder why Doug and Charlie needed directions to a major intersection less than a mile from each of their homes. "Charlie, shall we go now?" Doug squeaked, as they started to drive off.

Occasionally the joke was on Chaplin. One day Doug and his reporter friend Tom Geraghty dropped over to Charlie's estate while the house was still under construction. The afternoon was hot, and the two men found Chaplin cooling off at the bottom of a hole that was going to be a well. Fairbanks and Geraghty jumped into the hole with him. While they were sitting at the bottom, Doug turned and said, "Fellows, did you feel that?"

"Yes, I did," replied Geraghty.

"Feel what?" asked Charlie.

"Must have been an earthquake," Doug replied. Charlie didn't wait to hear how Geraghty responded. He had already scrambled out of the hole as fast as he could, while Fairbanks and Geraghty stayed behind, convulsed with laughter.

Unlike Gloria Swanson on the one hand or Will Rogers on the other, comedian Chaplin was not trying to reinforce a screen image by arranging and decorating his home in a particular way. But he did know what his Summit Drive mansion should look like and the kind of ambience it should project. Born in a London slum, bounced in and out of gloomy orphanages and workhouses as a child, the grown-up Chaplin hoped that his estate would reflect comfort, success, and money, and it did—at least on first impression.

Sitting on a hillside above Summit Drive, Chaplin's two-story, four-bedroom Spanish-style mansion had the customary yellow stucco walls and red tile roof, and it was large enough to be impressive yet not so large that it looked ostentatious. The simple iron gate on Summit Drive was rarely closed. A narrow driveway ran up the hill and stopped at the thick oak front door, which opened onto a small vestibule with a tile floor and pots of ferns. Another oak door led directly into the two-story-tall hall, which ran through the house to French doors that overlooked the back lawn.

Charlie Chaplin took several years to furnish his new home, but when it was completed, the great hall was easily the most sumptuous room in the house. It was decorated with two thick strawberry-color Oriental-style carpets and velvet curtains in the same hue at the French doors, and it contained a huge fireplace, built-in bookcases, a pipe organ, and a beamed oak ceiling. In the center of the room was a large, richly carved, hand-painted table with cigar and cigarette boxes, match holders, and ashtrays sitting on a gold tray. One cigarette box, when opened, played a tune. A toy bird pecked at the table when it was wound up. The one really jarring note in this otherwise splendid room was the almost bare white plaster walls.

This two-story hall was the busiest room in the house. Here Charlie sometimes curled up with a book in one of the softly padded window seats. He usually favored dime novels over the impressive-looking books on the shelves, which included several encyclopedias, all of Shakespeare's plays, classic authors such as Dickens and Rabelais, even a three-volume *History of Modern Marriage*.

Chaplin liked to sit down at the pipe organ and pick out a tune, usually his own composition. If any of his guests knew how to play the organ, he'd insist that they try a few tunes together. As with all Hollywood stars, Chaplin loved to show his own films at home, and this hallway doubled as a screening room. Two small square holes in the wall near the stairway to the second floor revealed the location of the projection booth. At the push of a button, a movie screen dropped down in front of the pipe organ, where one of his studio employees or occasionally a guest performed the music to accompany the films.

To the left of the two-story hall was the living room, with paneled walls painted white, dove-gray wall-to-wall carpeting, a large fireplace, built-in bookshelves, and a Steinway grand piano in one corner. The ponderous-looking overstuffed oak sofa and easy chairs were upholstered in pale terra-cotta-colored brocade, the same shade as the Oriental throw rugs over the carpeting and the brocade floor-to-ceiling drapes at the bay window. Chaplin's furniture was comfortable and not unattractive for this period, but the entire room looked as if it had been arranged piece by piece without much thought for harmonized beauty or easy socializing.

In this stiff, decidedly masculine room, Charlie Chaplin acted out the role of the English gentleman by hanging prints of London in the fog, by filling the bookshelves with more good books (and his movie awards), and by burning coal, not wood, in the fireplace on chilly evenings. Whether he was alone or entertaining friends, Charlie was quite fussy that the coal be arranged just right. Many evenings he took over the task from his Japanese butler, Frank, and spent ten minutes making a perfectly symmetrical pile of coal in the fireplace grate.

Across the two-story hall from the living room was the large, mahogany-paneled, rarely used dining room. The Louis XIV-inspired mahogany table sat eight, but the orange velvet upholstered chairs of a similar style were so large that just six comfortably fit around the table. Charlie's own chair had a high throne-like back. A sideboard sat along one wall with a lovely English tea set and candlesticks that were reflected in a mirror hung on the wall. A second sideboard usually held a silver platter overflowing with fruit.

A swinging door in one wall of the dining room discreetly opened into the servants' hall and butler's pantry, which was stocked with fine white Haviland china with plain gold rims, sterling service for thirty-six that Charlie brought back from a visit to Berlin, plain linen tablecloths and napkins, and cheap domestic glassware instead of imported crystal. A little farther down the hall was the kitchen, equipped with three iceboxes and a Japanese cook named Harry, who prepared Charlie's favorite dinner of lamb stew, a vegetable, and a rich pudding.

Charlie Chaplin furnished his upstairs master bedroom with a simple three-quarters bed, a dressing table, a chest of drawers hand-painted in old gold, and an overstuffed settee upholstered in the same shade of old gold. The wall-to-wall carpeting was green-gray in an unobtrusive pattern, and the window drapes were a soft green. More bookshelves lined the walls, and a desk and a large telescope stood near one window. On a nearby table was his framed photograph of neighbor Mary's royal favorites, Lord and Lady Mountbatten, inscribed "To Charlie, from Dickie and Edwina Mountbatten."

For all of his bedroom's simplicity, Charlie Chaplin wanted certain things done just so. Every afternoon, the Japanese upstairs man put Charlie's soft brown leather bedroom slippers at the exact same spot on the carpet near the bed where they would receive his feet when he got up the next morning but not intrude too far into the room. And Chaplin insisted that a fancy silver toilette set be kept on the yellow dressing table in the bedroom, even though he always used an old ebony brush and comb—the first good ones he ever owned—at a simple table in his largely empty dressing room. Charlie Chaplin did not care to wear fashionable clothes at home, except for several pair of pale green Japanese silk pajamas.

Despite its overstuffed furniture and cheery fires, the genteel look of Charlie Chaplin's mansion was no more real than a Hollywood set. For the first year after Chaplin moved in alone in 1923, the large house was almost bare, except for a few motley pieces of furniture here and there, carried over from the cheap rooms Chaplin had rented in downtown Los Angeles six or eight years earlier. Rather than spend more money, he called one of the big department stores in Los Angeles and asked them to send beds, dressers, and tables to fill the other second-floor bedroom suites. The store did that, but Charlie never paid the bill. Six months later, the store repossessed the furniture. That created a problem. Charlie needed furniture for the guest rooms again. So he called another store, and they sent the beds, dressers, and tables. He didn't pay this bill either, and six months later the second store came to the house and took all the furniture back.

Shortly thereafter, Mary Pickford called Charlie to ask a small favor. A British lord was arriving at Pickfair with an entourage of ten, and she didn't have that many guest rooms. Could he put up six visitors? Certainly, Charlie replied, forgetting that the "borrowed" bedroom furniture was gone. When the high-toned British guests arrived at Charlie's home, they found their rooms furnished in worse-than-secondhand chests of drawers and old mattresses on the floors instead of beds. After one night of Charlie's hospitality, the six headed for a hotel.

Charlie's house reflected his well-developed sense of economy in other ways as well. One day director King Vidor was getting ready to take a shower in Charlie's bathroom, and he noticed a short piece of pipe poking through the tile wall of the shower stall instead of the usual spray attachment.

"How's a fellow supposed to take a shower here?" Vidor called out.

"Cup your hands and splash the water over you" was Charlie's answer.

On a later visit, Vidor saw a small pan in the shower. This was Charlie's answer to guests who complained about the cup-your-hands method. Even though Charlie was a millionaire many times over, he simply wasn't about to pay a plumber to come to the house and install a proper shower head.

Chaplin's greatest false economy, however, was the house itself. To save money on its construction, he used his studio carpenters when they weren't busy making sets. This seemed like a sensible plan, but it turned out to be a mistake. His carpenters had become so accustomed to putting together temporary sets that they had forgotten how to build a permanent structure. No sooner had Charlie moved into his new house than little things began to go wrong. Paneling split. Ornamental trim fell off the walls. Doors came loose on their hinges. Floors started to squeak. To Charlie's chagrin, his friends and neighbors began calling his Summit Drive dream palace "Breakaway House."

Chaplin had moved into the house alone, but already he was headed for another marriage—to Lillita McMurray, also known as Lita Grey. In 1915, Charlie met Lillita at the prophetically named Kitty's Come-On Inn restaurant near his studio. She was eight years old, and her mother Nana worked as a waitress at Kitty's. Charlie immediately liked the little girl and later hired her as an extra in some of his films. Lillita appeared as a flirting angel in *The Kid* (1920) and a maid in *The Idle Class* (1920). Mrs. McMurray quit her waitress job to manage her daughter's budding career, and she landed an occasional extra part for herself.

By the time Lillita turned fifteen in 1923, she was old enough to play grown-up parts. Charlie had become infatuated with Lillita and even though she couldn't act, signed her under the name Lita Grey to

Charlie Chaplin's Beverly Hills estate, better known as "Breakaway House."

Charlie Chaplin.

play the dance-hall girl in *The Gold Rush* (1924). At the contract sign-ing, the ever-present Mrs. McMurray stood by beaming while Lita reportedly jumped up and down shouting, "Goody! Goody!"

But Lita never completed her role in *The Gold Rush*. She became pregnant instead. Apparently her evening coaching sessions with Char-lie had included more than dramatic technique. Now the McMurrays had Charlie in a tight spot. Lita's uncle, Edwin McMurray, was an attorney, and he solemnly informed Charlie that premarital sex with an underage female was statutory rape. Having seen one star after an-other's career destroyed in the scandals of the early 1920s, Charlie didn't want to be hauled into court for that offense, and so he married sixteen-year-old Lita on November 24, 1924.

Lita and her mother Nana moved into Charlie's Summit Drive mansion and started counting the months until the baby's birth. And the rest of Hollywood also started counting when Charlie announced the birth of Charles Spencer Chaplin, Jr., on June 28, 1925, just seven months after his marriage. That was compromising enough, but Hol-lywood gossipmongers whispered that Charlie had secluded Lita in a rented house and the boy had actually been born on May 5, 1925, after only five and a half months of marriage. According to the rumors, Charlie had paid the attending physician twenty-five thousand dollars to change the birth certificate to the less embarrassing June 28 date.

By the time their second son, Sydney Earle Chaplin, was born on March 30, 1926—just nine months and two days after his brother's reported birth—Charlie and Lita's marriage was in trouble. Mrs. McMurray was still living at the Summit Drive house, and whenever Charlie didn't come home at night, she or Lita invited some of their family and friends over for a drunken revel. On December 1, 1926, Charlie returned from the studio unexpectedly, found the house empty, and went straight to bed. When Lita, her mother, and their drunken friends returned home, they didn't know Charlie was in bed upstairs, and they started another one of their parties. The noise woke Charlie from a deep sleep. Standing on the balcony at the head of the stairs, he thundered, "What do you think this is, a whorehouse?" and ordered the guests out of the house.

Lita, her mother, and the two babies departed as well, and Edwin

McMurray filed a divorce suit on January 10, 1927. The McMurrays hoped to reap as much of Charlie's estimated sixteen-million-dollar fortune in the settlement as they could, and Uncle Edwin's fifty-two-page Bill of Divorcement detailed every bit of trouble in the Chaplin marriage—and then some. A public document, it could be read by anyone, and the day after Uncle Edwin filed the papers, a line stretched out of the County Clerk's office, out of the building, and around the corner.

These sensation-seekers, however, need not have waited on line. Within a day, Los Angeles newsstands were selling twenty-five-cent copies of the Bill of Divorcement, titled *Complaint by Lita Grey,* which accused Charlie of cheapness, spying on her, asking her to have an abortion, changing all the house locks, extreme cruelty, and carrying on an affair with "a certain prominent moving picture actress." Who could that be? everyone wondered. But they quickly forgot about that juicy item when they reached the part in the complaint where Lita charged that Charlie forced her to gratify his "degenerate sexual desires." These "acts" were "too revolting, indecent, and immoral to set forth in this complaint . . . the act of sex perversion defined by Section 288a of the Penal Code of California." That law made oral sex punishable by fifteen years in jail. "Relax, dear, all married people do it," Chaplin had reportedly told his child bride.

The *Complaint by Lita Grey* went still further. Charlie reportedly had read pornography to his innocent bride to excite her passions, even suggested that "they could have some fun" with another young woman known for her sado-masochistic tastes. Only a few stars, like the unfortunate Fatty Arbuckle, ever endured such a thorough public humiliation, and thousands of Chaplin's fans turned on him in the months before the trial. During this hellish year, his hair turned gray.

Charlie, nonetheless, fought back against Lita's accusations, that is, until Uncle Edwin threatened to reveal the names of five actresses with whom Charlie had supposedly carried on affairs during his marriage. According to Uncle Edwin, the five were Marion Davies, Peggy Hopkins Joyce, Pola Negri, Edna Purviance, and Claire Windsor. Not wanting to drag these women's names into the scandal, Charlie agreed to settle with Lita, provided she change her Bill of Divorcement to a single charge of Cruelty. On August 22, 1927, Lita made a ten-minute appearance on the witness stand—her best acting performance yet—and the judge awarded her a $625,000 settlement and custody of the two boys, each of whom received a $100,000 trust fund. After Charlie paid the attorney's fees, this divorce had cost him over a million dollars.

Having contended with a scandal like this and the McMurrays occupying his home long before it, it's not surprising that Chaplin rarely entertained at 1085 Summit Drive in the 1920s. Besides, he didn't share his neighbors' obsession with turning their homes into glittering showplaces, and more importantly, he didn't have the personality of a good host. Errol Flynn frequently played tennis with Charlie at Summit Drive in the 1930s, and he later observed that Chaplin was "gay and witty and charming," but "unless every bit of conversation centered around him, he was deadly bored." Another occasional guest, David Niven, would add that Chaplin was "allergic to laying out large sums of money for food and drink to be guzzled by those reckoned to be passengers and noncontributors."

Just down the hill from Charlie Chaplin's lonely Breakaway House was cowboy Tom Mix's six-acre estate at 1018 Summit Drive. Protected by a wall along the road and surrounded by formal gardens, Mix's stucco mansion looked deceptively sedate—except for the large neon sign with the initials TM on the roof. That sign was only a clue to Mix's rather extreme tastes in architecture.

Extravagant, vulgar, sometimes intentionally comic, Tom Mix's dream palace was designed for entertaining and for showing off his wealth. Just as a cowboy brands his cattle, Mix put his initials almost anywhere he could find the space: on the gates to the driveway, on the front door of the house, over every fireplace. When Tom's favorite horse, Tony, died, he turned its tail into a bellpull. In the dining room an illuminated fountain sprayed water in a variety of different colors.

The mansion's *pièces de résistance,* however, were the his and hers parlors on either side of the entrance hall. One parlor obviously belonged to the King of the Cowboys: a twenty-foot-high room with a beamed ceiling, silver-embossed saddles resting on sawhorses, a small arsenal of rifles and guns on display, and a collection of medals and trophies. The other parlor, furnished in Louis XVI-cum-1920s style,

Cowboy Tom Mix and his fourth wife, Vicki, had his and hers living rooms at their Beverly Hills estate. His was filled with trophies, dozens of rifles and guns, and several silver- embossed saddles resting on sawhorses. Vicki's was decorated in garish reproduction Louis XVI furniture.

Tom Mix, family man, outside the modest Hollywood bungalow where he lived before moving to Beverly Hills in the early 1920s.

The master bedroom. What would Cowboy Tom's fans have thought if they had seen this bedroom, obviously decorated by Vicki Mix, the former cowgirl who now fancied herself a French duchess?

had been set aside for Vicki, the fourth Mrs. Mix, a former cowgirl and actress who now fancied herself a French duchess.

Tom Mix's sumptuous estate was quite a step up for someone who had been a rootless cowboy and adventurer in his youth. Tom's actual life was almost as fantastic as the Fox Studio publicity releases. Mix was born in Clearfield County, Pennsylvania, in 1880 and not a log cabin north of El Paso, as the studio insisted. He joined the U.S. Army during the Spanish-American War, fought in the Philippines, and later served as a member of the American Expeditionary Force, which put down the Boxer Rebellion in Peking in 1900. After being badly wounded in the chest at Peking, he was sent back to America and mustered out of the Army. Never one to sit still for long, Mix broke horses for the British forces fighting the Boer War in 1899–1902 and even accompanied one shipment to South Africa.

After returning to America, Tom Mix worked as a cowboy for a few years, served as sheriff in several Oklahoma and Kansas towns, and eventually became a performer in the Miller Brothers' 101 Ranch, a traveling Wild West show, where he met Will Rogers. In 1908, Mix bought a ranch, married for the third time, and started to settle down. But not for long.

In 1909 pioneer filmmaker Colonel William N. Selig used Mix's ranch to shoot *Ranch Life in the Great South West* (1910), a modest documentary about cattle being rounded up for shipment to slaughterhouses. Tom Mix supervised the cowboy extras and the cattle during filming, and less than a year later he was working full-time for Selig in Chicago and California—but not before he went to Mexico for a few months, fought for the revolutionary leader Francisco Madero, and barely escaped execution by a firing squad.

Between 1910 and 1917, Mix appeared in about one hundred one- and two-reelers for Selig, sometimes writing the scenarios and directing the films as well. But Tom did not become a star until he signed with Fox Studios in 1917, where he made his memorable feature-length films. Rather than copy reigning Western idol William S. Hart's ride-'em-hard, shoot-'em-up style, Mix developed another image altogether: the wholesome hero, who never drank, smoked, or fought without provocation. Tom Mix even included comic scenes and parts for child stars in his films to attract youthful fans.

When audiences tired of William S. Hart's "good badman" character around 1920, Tom Mix emerged as the nation's top cowboy star. Over six feet tall and ruggedly handsome, even in his forties and fifties, Tom had found a screen role that suited his personality and pleased his audiences as well—and he stuck with that. Nearly all his films had the same basic plot: "I ride into a place owning my own horse, saddle, and bridle," Mix once declared. "It wasn't my quarrel, but I get into trouble doing the right thing for somebody else. When it's all ironed out, I never get any money reward. I may be made foreman of the ranch, and I get the girl, but there is never a fervid love scene."

By 1925, Tom Mix was earning seventeen thousand dollars a week and spending most of it. One room at his Summit Drive mansion was given over to his silver-studded saddle collection, while another held dozens of pairs of boots. Wearing one of his many Stetsons, Tom drove a white Rolls-Royce sedan or a white Packard convertible, the doors of each embossed with the gold initials TM. Mix owned a ninety-six-foot yacht, the *Miss Mix-It,* but preferred to spend his leisure time at his Arizona ranch. For Hollywood parties, Tom often wore a white or purple tuxedo with matching boots and a Stetson, plus a blaze of diamond stickpins, rings, and wristwatch. Sometimes he wore his cowboy garb, dressing it up with a pair of diamond-encrusted spurs and one of his diamond and platinum belt buckles.

Yet when it came to jewelry, Tom Mix was just a piker compared to his wife, Vicki. With the possible exception of Mrs. Cecil B. De Mille, Vicki Mix owned the most valuable jewelry collection in the movie colony in the 1920s, and she had very particular taste. She didn't care for rubies and emeralds; she was superstitious about pearls. But she did like diamonds and sapphires. Besides owning several dozen diamond and sapphire rings, Vicki Mix's jewel box contained 8- and 11-carat diamond solitaires, a wristwatch with a large diamond face, a 10-carat diamond drop on a platinum chain, and a platinum, diamond, and sapphire anklet.

Vicki Mix liked to wear her favorite jewels to breakfast at the Summit Drive estate. And while the habit didn't start a new fashion in the movie colony, Vicki became a trendsetter in another way. She got a nose job in 1924. "I didn't do this because I'm contemplating a return to the screen," commented the ex-actress, "but I felt that my nose could be improved and I believe a woman should look her best for her husband." That's what Vicki Mix told a fan magazine. Actually, she had changed her mind about the operation on her Roman nose, but Tom made her go ahead with it anyway.

Tom Mix was "just an ordinary cowboy with a cowboy's mentality," according to Anita Loos, but he did enjoy his fame and his money more spontaneously and more genuinely than many other stars who calculated their every move and every statement. When the movie cameras stopped rolling at the end of the day, Mix abandoned his wholesome never-drinking, never-fighting screen personality. During one party at his Summit Drive home, Tom got roaring drunk, had a knockdown drag-out fight in the finest Wild West tradition with cowboy actor Art Accord, and then rode his beloved horse Tony up the main stairs to the second floor, hollering and firing his gun into the ceiling all the way.

CHAPTER EIGHT

Despite its garish rooftop neon sign and the improbable his and hers parlors, Tom Mix's home was not so unusual a sight in the architectural landscape of Southern California during the 1920s and 1930s. Some stars and studio executives, like *nouveaux riches* everywhere, did try to emulate social respectability by building California approximations of centuries-old Italian palazzos, secluded Spanish villas, or half-timbered Elizabethan country houses. But architectural purity was not an important consideration in Los Angeles at the time. Nor has it ever been. What really mattered in the 1920s was to achieve a romantic, faraway look, and most architects freely mixed different national, historic, and aesthetic styles on the same house to picturesque, often baffling effect.

Nobody batted a purist's eye, for instance, when director Fred Niblo added a several-hundred-years-old paneled English drawing room to his very Spanish mansion at 1330 Angelo Drive, high above Beverly Hills—or when John Barrymore installed a seven hundred-year-old Scottish fireplace, Italian stained-glass windows, and two two-thousand-year-old doors from India in his Spanish home, Belle Vista, overlooking Benedict Canyon.

Domestic architecture did not always synchronize with its resi-dent's screen personality. During the mid-1920s, pretty, auburn-haired, All-American Mary Astor lived on Hollywood's Temple Hill Drive in an East Indian fantasy, complete with ogee doorways and lotus-flower domes. During those same years, Clara Bow rented a large red brick Georgian-style house on Fairholme Drive in the Hollywood Hills above Fairfax Avenue that looked more like the home of a Main Line society matron than the residence of the frenetic, sexy, twenty-year-old "It" Girl. Exotic Polish-born vamp Pola Negri owned a Mount Vernon knockoff in Beverly Hills.

Perhaps the most bizarre coupling of occupant and architectural style was actor Julian Eltinge's tasteful Spanish-style mansion on a beautifully landscaped hillside at 2329 Baxter Street, east of Hollywood in the Silverlake district. If any star would have been expected to live in an outrageous house, it was Eltinge, a nationally beloved female impersonator. A lifelong bachelor, Eltinge had been a favorite on the Broadway stage in the teens, starring in *The Fascinating Widow* (1911) and *The Crinoline Girl* (1914). Eltinge came to Hollywood in the late teens, built his Silverlake home, and made several movies for Famous Players–Lasky Corporation, such as *The Countess Charming* (1917) and *The Clever Mrs. Carfax* (1917). "He could put Mae Murray, Gloria Swanson, and all the rest of our glamor girls to shame with the way he modeled women's clothing," Jesse Lasky wrote about Eltinge in his autobiography. "When he made an entrance at a Hollywood party, wearing a wig and a Lady Duff Gordon evening gown, neither men nor women could take their eyes off him." A contralto during his popular performances and a baritone in real life, Eltinge did not like to be kidded about his female impersonations, and he punched out more than one man on the studio lot who made teasing passes at him.

Sometimes, even in the world's capital of make-believe, where anything was architecturally possible, the end result went far afield from a client's original plan. In 1929, George Fitzmaurice, director of Valentino's *Son of the Sheik*, started building a Spanish-style mansion on a three-acre estate in Benedict Canyon. When Fitzmaurice became engaged to actress Florence Vidor, she told him that that look wouldn't suit her. Although Fitzmaurice had his heart set on the Spanish style, he changed the now half-completed house to a mock-Tudor design to please Florence. But Florence never moved in. She met violinist Jascha Heifetz and married him before Fitzmaurice finished the house. That left Fitzmaurice without Florence, with an English-style house he didn't want, and feeling more than a little schizophrenic.

Female impersonator Julian Eltinge outshone Gloria Swanson, Mae Murray, and all the other Holly-wood glamour girls—or so claimed Jesse L. Lasky, who starred Eltinge in light comedies like The Countess Charming *(1917), shown here.*

All Los Angeles, not just the movie colony, was suffering from this architectural identity crisis. When Los Angeles' population more than doubled in the 1920s, it didn't have any strong local architectural tradition to guide the accompanying building boom, except for the nearly vanished remnants of Spanish California. The result was an architectural free-for-all from which no Los Angeles neighborhood escaped unscathed. Builders lined block after block with a jumble of Spanish haciendas-in-miniature, "Olde English" cottages, shrunken French châteaus, scaled-down Arabian mosques, or Aztec and Pueblo-inspired homes. The lush Southern California landscape only compounded the architectural confusion. The most proper slate-roofed, half-timbered Tudor mansions sometimes stood beneath distinctly un-Tudor palm trees.

In 1934, Frank Lloyd Wright declared that "the eclectic procession to and fro in the rag-tag and cast-off of the ages was never going to stop" in Southern California. Wright shouldn't have spoken so harshly, because he too had loosed his eclectic fantasies when he worked in Los Angeles for several months each year during the early 1920s. After completing Aline Barnsdall's Hollyhock House, he designed three concrete-block neo-Mayan houses that still stand in the Hollywood Hills: John Storer's residence at 8161 Hollywood Boulevard (1923), Charles Ennis's at 2607 Glendower Road (1924), and Samuel Freeman's at 1962 Glencoe Way (1924). The largest of the three, the Ennis house, looks like some forbidding ancient monument, topping a prominent hillside at the head of Vermont Avenue near Griffith Park.

The confusion in residential architecture inevitably spilled out into the commercial district. During the 1920s and 1930s, Los Angeles embarked on a binge of "programmatic architecture," so named because the buildings actually signified their functions through their forms. A building that imitated a ten-foot-tall orange, for instance, denoted an orange-juice stand; an overscaled doughnut indicated a doughnut shop. Often these programmatic buildings took on the physical characteristics of the restaurant or shop inside. The Frog ice-cream stand resembled a big green frog with a walk-up window for its belly. A hot-dog stand, called the Tail of the Pup, looked like a hot-dog in a bun. But the most famous and enduring programmatic building was the Brown

Derby restaurant, where a sign on top of the enormous stucco derby invited passersby to "Eat in the Hat."

Programmatic architecture was perhaps the ultimate expression of a tradition-free Los Angeles. All these oversized oranges, frogs, and derbies were familiar, reassuring sights for newcomers to the area, and these buildings became overnight landmarks in a city that was too new to have the traditional kind. Besides, programmatic buildings were fun to look at—and Los Angelenos didn't have to read street signs to find their destinations. If you wanted to dine at the Green Dragon Chinese restaurant, you weren't going to end up at the Coffee Pot by mistake.

The motion picture industry encouraged this trend toward architectural exotica. Elaborately ornate movie palaces in downtown Hollywood, like the Spanish Baroque Million Dollar Theater, the Egyptian Theater, and the Chinese Theater prepared the public's appetite for the architecturally fantastic, as did the romantic vistas presented on the screens of these theaters.

But it was the studio complexes themselves that provided the strongest and most immediate inspirations for Los Angeles' architectural eclecticism. Impressive stage sets of ancient Babylon for D. W. Griffith's *Intolerance* (1916) and the wood-and-plaster Roman Colosseum for the first *Ben-Hur* (1925) loomed over Los Angeles' squat bungalows and dusty suburban streets years after the films were completed. For over a decade, the Middle Eastern domes and minarets from Douglas Fairbanks' *The Thief of Baghdad* (1924) graced the otherwise dreary Culver City landscape.

Studio offices often emulated the movie sets. At his La Brea Avenue studio in Hollywood, Charlie Chaplin built a street of mock-Tudor cottages. The administration building at Thomas Ince's Culver City studio was a copy of Mount Vernon, with liveried receptionists at the front door and hallways inexplicably decorated with portraits of U.S. Presidents and movie stars. When Cecil B. De Mille bought the Ince Studio, he went Thomas Ince one better and remodeled his office in the Mount Vernon building into an exact replica of George Washington's own study, down to the last inkwell.

The most fantastic studio building of all was the combination of offices and dressing rooms for Irvin Willat Productions at 6509 Washington Boulevard in Culver City. Designed and built by Willat's art director, Harry Oliver, this studio building was a replica of Hansel and Gretel's cottage, and it stood in front of a picturesque rock-edged artificial pond. The walls and sharply pitched roof were purposely built to look old and sagging as was the exterior woodwork, which was burned, charred, scraped—and left unpainted. Roof shingles were all different shapes, sizes, and colors. No two leaded-glass windows were alike, and the shutters were hung askew.

Not surprisingly, Irvin Willat made B-pictures, usually mysteries, adventures, and dramas, and occasionally he used his studio headquarters as a stage set. But the Willat studio closed in the mid 1920s, and Willat joined Famous Players–Lasky. Harry Oliver left art directing entirely and designed fanciful apartment buildings throughout Southern California, plus the original Van de Kamp's bakery windmill logo. In 1931 his Hansel and Gretel studio building was moved to Beverly Hills, where it still stands amid fashionable residences at the southeast corner of Carmelita and Walden drives.

Hollywood's architectural eclecticism was so pervasive, so influential, that some otherwise conservative Los Angeles businessmen built dream palaces of their own. In 1927, Earle C. Anthony, the rich and cultivated Packard dealer, hired talented San Francisco architect Bernard Maybeck to design a Medieval castle on an eight-acre hilltop overlooking Los Feliz Boulevard and Griffith Park. Anthony had already visited Europe seven times in the previous ten years to photograph dozens of castles and to bring thirty-five thousand dollars' worth of Caen stone, tons of roof tile, and yards and yards of fabric back to Los Angeles.

By the time Bernard Maybeck completed Anthony's Medieval stage-set-cum-residence at 3412 Waverly Drive, he had spent over half a million dollars, more than the cost of any other house in Hollywood at the time. But Anthony was satisfied: The exterior structure incorporated an improbable but attractive mix of Spanish, Norman, and Italian styles, accented with gargoyles, portcullis spikes, and balustrades copied from Anthony's photographs. The castle's interior—with its twenty-one different changes in levels—included an enormous living room with five-foot-thick Caen stone walls and a thirty-five-foot-high

Middle Eastern domes and minarets from the set for Douglas Fairbanks' The Thief of Baghdad (*1924*).

Miss Gwen Lee at Barkies Sandwich Shop. Don't miss the dog paws on either side of the front door.

OPPOSITE: *Van de Kamp's Bakery-as-windmill.*

carved wood ceiling, a Gothic chapel, and massive doors weighing as much as 1,500 pounds. And the driveway into the sprawling estate was planted with cypress and olive trees to duplicate the entrance to Hadrian's villa outside Rome. The Medieval-style garage held seven distinctly un-Medieval Packards.

This spectacular architectural hodgepodge was entirely international. The variety of styles, according to one of Anthony's assistants, "reflect the changes, additions, and variances which would have been wrought by dozens of succeeding generations. This tower might have been added by the hand of a conqueror, that one by some gentler baron so that his chatelaine might view the countryside. This section seems the work of some wandering Spanish mason, while only a Tudor craftsman would have designed these leaded windows."

Earle C. Anthony wasn't the only Hollywood resident to act out his neo-Medieval fantasies on a grand scale. In 1924, Patrick Longden, a seventy-year-old prospector who'd struck it rich in South America, built his own castle, a stucco and red tile roof Southern California version of mad Ludwig of Bavaria's Neuschwanstein. The architect was John de Lario, who prepared the plans for Mack Sennett's never-completed palace above the HOLLYWOODLAND sign.

Longden's Spanish-mode Tower Hill castle at 6342 Mulholland Highway marched nine stories up a steep hillside, and measured 106 feet tall from its front door to the top of its tower. The house, with its panoramic view of the entire city, had 20,000 square feet of space, but only 8,000 square feet of it was actually livable space because of the castle's several towers and winding staircases. Seventeen gravity furnaces took the chill off winter nights, including two just for the 25-by-40-foot living room with its 25-foot-high ceiling.

All that Longden's Tower Hill castle lacked was a moat and a drawbridge. But that oversight did not prevent mobster Bugsey Siegel from operating a gambling casino in the mansion during the 1930s. Tower Hill fit Bugsey's needs perfectly. Because of the unobstructed views, Bugsey's boys could see the police approach in any direction, and storming Tower Hill would have been foolhardy. The only entrance to it was in the courtyard at the bottom of the house, at the end of a long, narrow, winding driveway.

The romantic allure of old California captivated Los Angelenos during the 1920s, and thousands of Los Angeles buildings incorporated the Spanish style's characteristic white stucco walls, red tile roofs, and round arches, including Patrick Longden's Neuschwanstein-inspired castle on a hillside above Lake Hollywood (ABOVE) and William Fox's studio at 1845 Allesandro Street (BELOW).

Los Angeles' freewheeling architectural spirit during the 1920s also made itself felt in styles of interior decoration. Even middle-class bungalows boasted sunken living rooms, colorfully painted fake ceiling beams, oversized baronial fireplaces, and Spanish shawls draped over obligatory pianos. For all their decorative falsehoods, some of these bungalows looked quite charming. Inevitably, others were downright dreadful. When Lillian Hellman was a script reader at MGM around 1930, she rented a pseudo-Spanish house in Hollywood's Beachwood Canyon. A built-in picture of a lion above the living-room fireplace had eyes that lit up with the flip of a nearby switch.

Middle-class Los Angelenos usually did not have the money, the space at home, or the daring to exploit the 1920s eclecticism to its fullest potential. But movie stars and studio chiefs did. Beginning with Douglas Fairbanks and Mary Pickford's Pickfair, studio art directors and set designers built many of the stars' dream palaces that the public worshiped, with several stars actually furnishing parts of their homes with the help of studio prop and furniture departments. The decorative requirements of some stars, though, far exceeded the inventories of their own studios' technical departments. So Pola Negri installed her very own "Roman plunge" in her Mount Vernon–style mansion in Beverly Hills. Beautiful vamp Barbara La Marr, who married six times, had a sunken onyx bathtub with gold fixtures in her onyx-walled bathroom. Nothing less would do for "The Girl Who Was Too Beautiful," who died in 1926 at the age of twenty-nine because of "overdieting," or so said the newspapers. Actually Barbara La Marr had died of a drug overdose.

Well-known Westerns director Thomas Ince, however, went further than anyone else into the realm of 1920s decorative kitsch when he built his twenty-five-room Spanish mansion, named Dias Dorados, on a thirty-acre estate at 1051 Benedict Canyon Drive in 1923–1924. With the help of his architect, Roy Selden Price, Ince turned his basement screening room into a romantic version of a pirate ship's deck, complete with caulked floors, sails, and rigging. Regulation red and green lanterns lit the room, and through the rigging was a view of a tropical island the ship was sailing past.

A large stained-glass door, depicting a grizzled pirate, led from the

Irvin Willat Studio Headquarters, Culver City, 1923, now moved to Beverly Hills and known as "the witches' house."

Thomas Ince's "peephole house," 1051 Benedict Canyon Drive, Beverly Hills, 1924.

Thomas Ince, the famous director of Westerns, decorated one room of his Benedict Canyon mansion with Indian rugs, feathered headdresses, and a buffalo head.

Ince residence, the dining room, with a chandelier that looked like a bunch of grapes over the table.

screening room into the stone-walled, circular billiards room. The windows, fireplace, and ceiling carried out the circular motif, and a totem pole in the center of the room was decorated with grinning gargoyles and triangular pieces of colored silk radiating from the top in all directions.

Thomas Ince's death was just as confused and improvised as his architecture. Just a few months after moving into Dias Dorados, Ince died in his bedroom on November 19, 1924, shortly after his celebrity-filled forty-third birthday party on board William Randolph Hearst's two hundred-eighty-foot yacht, *The Oneida*. On the day of Tom's death, an early edition of the Los Angeles *Times* ran the headline "Movie Producer Shot on Hearst Yacht," but that story was pulled in later editions.

The Hearst newspapers published a different version of Ince's death. At first he reportedly suffered an attack of acute indigestion at Hearst's San Simeon estate near San Luis Obispo, and had been rushed home to Dias Dorados, where he died of a heart attack. But that story didn't hold up, because witnesses had seen Tom board *The Oneida*. So Hearst changed his story. According to the second official version, Tom had eaten too much at his birthday party on board *The Oneida*, been taken sick, and had been rushed home to Beverly Hills where he died.

But what really happened in this much-repeated Hollywood tale? Charlie Chaplin had been on board *The Oneida*. He wasn't saying anything, but his Japanese chauffeur, Kono, told friends that he'd seen Ince carried off the yacht with a bullet wound in his head. That lent some credibility to the rumor that Hearst had caught Tom playing around with Marion Davies, Hearst's movie-star mistress, on a lower deck and shot him in a fit of rage. "W.R." was known as a good marksman, and he liked to shoot seagulls from *The Oneida*'s deck. If that story wasn't enough fuel for Hollywood's rumor mills, another equally intriguing version of Ince's death began to circulate quietly. Hearst had found *Charlie Chaplin* and Marion together on the lower deck, had attempted to shoot him, but hit Ince by mistake in the ensuing struggle.

Immediately following Thomas Ince's November 21 funeral, his body was cremated without an autopsy having been performed; that fanned suspicions of a cover-up. Even the official investigation into the causes of Tom's death raised more questions than it answered. The San Diego district attorney interviewed none of the guests on board *The Oneida* that weekend, except for Dr. Daniel Carson Goodman, the production director for Hearst's Cosmopolitan Pictures. But Mr. Goodman's testimony was enough for District Attorney Charles Kemply, and he closed the investigation with the statement that Ince died "from ordinary causes."

Still the rumors would not die. "All you have to do to make Hearst turn white as a ghost is mention Ince's name," D. W. Griffith declared a few years later. "There's plenty of wrong there, but Hearst is too big to touch." Hollywood wits had their fun anyway and started calling *The Oneida* "William Randolph's Hearse."

Throughout the investigation into his death, Thomas Ince's good name remained respectfully free of any scandal. But Tom had his secret, and it was discovered after his widow, Nell, sold Dias Dorados to producer Carl Laemmle for six hundred fifty thousand dollars in 1927. After Laemmle moved in, he found a special feature in Ince's house: a locked secret hallway above the guest bedrooms with peepholes strategically placed for full views of the beds. Thomas Ince should have been called "Peeping Tom" all along.

CHAPTER NINE

Thomas Ince's houseguests weren't the only members of the movie colony to lose their privacy in the 1920s. By then all Hollywood resembled one big goldfish bowl. Watchful studio chiefs told their stars what kind of houses to buy and what cars to drive. Movie magazines began to publish, even solicit, unflattering stories about some stars rather than accept studio press releases almost verbatim. But it was the fans who were the most prying of all. The word *fan* comes from *fanatic,* and that is the only word to describe their behavior accurately.

Otherwise ordinary-living men and women waited for hours outside studio gates to see their favorite stars come and go; they loitered around restaurants the stars patronized, even lurked outside their homes. The fans' actions, though extreme, were understandable. Movies were an exciting new medium and America's leading form of mass entertainment. By 1927 sixty million Americans paid their way into darkened movie theaters every week to live out their fantasies about wealth, fame, and good looks through celluloid images on the screen.

Studio publicity departments and movie magazines preyed upon fans' devotion to their favorite stars. "Even European nobility angles for invitations to Pickfair," gushed *Photoplay* in 1929. "An aura of glamour surrounds it—even for the neighbors. One can cut no end of a dash by having been a guest of Doug and Mary. One then has a popular subject of conversation forever after." This breathless kind of reportage only made moviegoers want to see Pickfair for themselves

Guides to Movie Stars' Homes, 1935.

and some, indeed, sneaked into the estate. After this happened several dozen times, Douglas Fairbanks and Mary Pickford hired a watchman and built the masonry wall around the property. But that didn't prevent the "rubberneck buses" from climbing Summit Drive for a glimpse of Pickfair or stop a hot-dog vendor from setting up his stand outside the gates.

Even Greta Garbo, always one of the most reclusive of stars, could not elude her determined admirers. When she was living at the Beverly Hills Hotel in the late 1920s, about a dozen fans gathered every morning in the lobby to watch her leave for the studio. Garbo marched through the lobby to her chauffeur-driven secondhand Packard limousine, determined to look through her fans and ignore their pleas for autographs.

One young woman figured out a surefire way to attract the divine Garbo's attention. She waited until Garbo had gotten into her limousine and then threw herself onto the driveway in front of the approaching car. The chauffeur slammed on the brakes, narrowly missing her. In the ensuing confusion, the young woman got up off the pavement and ran back to the limousine's passenger compartment. The window was open.

"Please, Miss Garbo!" she shouted breathlessly. "May I have your autograph?" and she pushed a pen and a piece of paper at the flabbergasted Swedish actress.

"Gott!" Garbo gasped. "Are you all right?" The young woman assured Garbo that she was unharmed and only wanted an autograph. "Drive on," Garbo instructed the chauffeur, leaving the disappointed fan behind without her autograph.

Stardom was such a mixed blessing that some actors and actresses even had trouble finding suitable homes. Movie people knew that conservative neighborhoods like Hancock Park and Windsor Square were virtually off-limits. But they were surprised to learn that some realtors in the Hollywood Hills and in Beverly Hills jacked up the price of a house if they knew that a rich star was looking at it.

John Barrymore knew about this kind of price gouging, and he asked his manager, Henry Hotchener, to act as his front man when he wanted to buy a new house in the late 1920s. Originally a favorite on the Broadway stage, Barrymore had become a star with his dual performance in *Dr. Jekyll and Mr. Hyde* (1920). Thereafter, he alternated between the legitimate theater and Hollywood, where he played swashbucklers in the popular *Don Juan* (1926) and *The Beloved Rogue* (1927). Barrymore was best known for his profile—which he allowed to be photographed only from the left side.

In 1927, John Barrymore was happily living in a suite at the stylish Ambassador Hotel on Wilshire Boulevard, near downtown Los Angeles, with his pet monkey, Clementine. But Barrymore was courting the lovely blond actress Dolores Costello, and he was so confident that they would be married that he decided to buy a honeymoon estate ahead of time. When director King Vidor's five-room Spanish-style home on Tower Road (now 1400 Seabright Place) in Beverly Hills came onto the market, Barrymore called Henry Hotchener to ask for help.

"Clementine spoke to me in my dreams last night," Barrymore told Hotchener. "She wants a home in the country where she can play." But Hotchener wasn't fooled. He knew about Barrymore's interest in Dolores, and he coyly asked, "Is it to be a bachelor house, or . . . ?"

"A house for two," Barrymore interrupted, "meaning Clementine and myself, of course. All the swells live in Beverly Hills. Why should Clementine reside in a lower social environment?"

Hotchener agreed to look at the Vidor property later that day, and Barrymore asked to come along. According to Hollywood legend, to conceal his identity he wore the leftover makeup and costume from his role as Mr. Hyde in *Dr. Jekyll and Mr. Hyde*. By the time Hotchener arrived for him at the Ambassador Hotel, Barrymore had a twisted face, long curling fingernails, and protruding, wolflike teeth, and he was wearing a fright wig and an old hat. "I don't think the real-estate harpies will mistake Mr. Hyde for a man of means," Barrymore said as he and Harry Hotchener drove off for Beverly Hills.

When they reached King Vidor's estate, Barrymore waited in the car with Clementine while Hotchener spoke to the real-estate agent. The asking price was sixty thousand dollars, and Hotchener and the realtor started to negotiate in the garden, within sight of the car. After some time had passed, an anxious Barrymore wanted to know what was happening, and he stuck his head out of the window to signal Hotchener. The real-estate agent caught a glimpse of something horrible-looking, turned pale, and became speechless. Hotchener played it cool. "A friend," he said. "A somewhat peculiar fellow. You see, I take care of him."

The agent resumed his spiel. The price was high, he admitted, "but the property has many advantages. Large acreage, permitting no end of improvements."

"No! No!" Hotchener shouted. "We don't wish to make improvements. We lead simple lives."

The realtor—the legend goes—knocked a thousand dollars off the price. Then he heard Clementine's screams from the car. She had crawled out an open window and had gotten tangled up in her leash. Hotchener and the agent saw a hairy hand with long curling fingernails reach out of the window and pull Clementine back into the car. "Have to humor him with pets," said Hotchener, quite matter-of-factly.

"I see," said the real-estate man, who paused briefly and returned to his pitch. "Think of the beauties of this location. You have an excellent view of the sea, the mountains. At night, millions of lights of Los Angeles twinkling like a jewelry store. You can have, as you see, an extensive tennis court."

"We don't play tennis," replied Hotchener, and another thousand came off the asking price.

"But that space can easily be turned into a swimming pool," continued the realtor.

"Unfortunately, we don't swim," said Hotchener, and the price dropped another thousand.

"Well, you can have extensive walks, gardens, fountains—even an orchard." The realtor wouldn't give up.

None of this interested his client, Hotchener explained. "You see, we entertain *very* seldom. Except for the physicians."

Barrymore wanted again to know what was taking so long, and he stuck his head out of the car window. The agent saw the ghastly-looking face and inexplicably took another three thousand off the price. Now it was fifty-four thousand. Wouldn't that be all right? he asked Hotchener.

"No, we do not feel justified in investing in such a great sum. You have been very kind. Good day." Hotchener started walking back to the parked car where John Barrymore, alias Mr. Hyde, was shamelessly kissing Clementine in the open window.

"Wait!" the realtor shouted, and started running toward Hotchener. "How about fifty-two?"

The right price was fifty thousand, Hotchener replied. The real-estate agent hemmed and hawed, took another look at Barrymore and Clementine, and drew up a purchase agreement for fifty thousand. Because of his Mr. Hyde performance and Hotchener's agile negotiation, Barrymore saved ten thousand dollars that day, but this was the only time he was financially practical with his new home.

As soon as King Vidor and his family moved out, in December 1927, Barrymore started to transform the estate into his private vision of a dream palace. And although he never turned it, like Pickfair, into a social center for the movie colony, Belle Vista—as he called the property because of its spectacular city and ocean views—most certainly came to reflect Barrymore's fertile imagination and high spirits, not some studio executive's notions of how a star should live.

After taking title to the property, Barrymore promptly bought the adjacent four acres, thereby enlarging the estate to seven acres. Then he decorated the house with heavy masculine furniture and turned one of the two bedrooms into a library for his several thousand books. At the same time, Barrymore built another Spanish-style hacienda just up the hill and joined the two houses with a grape-covered arbor. When Barrymore married Dolores Costello on November 24, 1928, he named the second building the Marriage House and the former Vidor home became Liberty Hall.

The Marriage House was an attractive Spanish home, with oak doors, whitewashed walls hung with old prints, and tile floors covered with Oriental rugs. The upstairs drawing room was particularly handsome. Several mulberry-colored rugs lay on the pegged wood floors. Paintings and tapestries decorated the oak-paneled walls. The fireplace

ABOVE: *John Barrymore in the library of his Belle Vista estate, which grew from a simple five-room house in the late 1920s to sixteen separate buildings, totaling fifty-five rooms, scattered around seven acres on Beverly Hills' Tower Road in the late 1930s.*

Skeet shooting at Belle Vista, circa 1940. Clark Gable has the gun; Barrymore is seated to his right.

mantel was marble, the drapes were gold brocade, and the furniture was a mixture of tasteful antiques. The adjacent dining room was octagonal, and a pink Dresden china chandelier that reputedly had belonged to the Austrian Archduke Francis Ferdinand hung from the ceiling. The six-room, two-story-tall Marriage House looked like "a castle out of fairyland hanging from the crest of a precipitous mountain," recalled Barrymore's first child, Diana.

Yet for all this good taste, the Marriage House also reflected Barrymore's eccentricities. Barrymore had a secret hideaway for when he wanted to get away from his family, his friends, and the ringing of the telephone. Above his bedroom in the Marriage House, he built a small tower with a trap door and a ladder he could pull up after himself. Even though the ceiling was low and the room got hot on sunny days, Barrymore loved his tower hideaway. "This was my sanctum sanctorum," he once said, "my monastic retreat, my blessed hideaway from the world of idiocy."

The Marriage House was just the beginning of Barrymore's construction activity at Belle Vista. He was earning lots of money—$430,000 in 1929 alone—and he now had over seven acres of land to invest it in. But once Barrymore started to transform Belle Vista in 1927, he never stopped. Marriage House grew to over a dozen rooms and, before the birth of his second child, John Blythe, Jr., Barrymore even added a Children's Wing. Ten years and over a million dollars later, the estate had grown to sixteen separate buildings, totaling fifty-five rooms, with several more buildings under construction. Diana Barrymore described the whole effect as "a little village, a hacienda of buildings with red tiled roofs, iron grilled windows, and gardens."

Belle Vista's gardens and grounds *were* beautiful. After leaving the floor of Benedict Canyon and driving up narrow, winding Tower Road, the first part of Belle Vista that visitors came upon was a water tower and a garish red and yellow totem pole, with a fern growing out of the top, like a mass of unruly green hair. Then the road turned a corner, and the rest of the estate came into view.

John Barrymore, quite characteristically, spared no expense transforming the grounds exactly to his liking. Workmen hauled tons of topsoil to the estate's barren hillsides, then dug a well and installed an extensive irrigation system. Barrymore's gifted gardener, Nishimura, and his assistants planted flowers, shrubs, and rare trees such as dwarf Japanese cedars and hundred-year-old Palestinian olive trees. To keep himself amused, Barrymore built a bowling green, a skeet range, several fountains and fish ponds, an artificial waterfall down one rocky hillside, and six pools, one with a several-hundred-years-old English sundial standing in the middle of the water atop a stone plinth.

But John Barrymore's greatest loves at his home were his animals, and in many ways Belle Vista was more a zoo than a movie star's estate. Besides the monkey, Clementine, he owned opossums, South American kinkajous, mouse deer, dozens of Siamese cats, and nineteen dogs, including eleven greyhounds, several Saint Bernards, and several Kerry blue terriers.

For his three hundred different birds, Barrymore built a large aviary complete with natural and artificial trees, leaf patterns on the glass walls, birdbaths, fountains, and nesting places. A partition inside the aviary separated the carnivorous from the herbivorous species. When the aviary was finished, Barrymore put a granite bench and two cast-iron cemetery chairs under a tree, where he sat for hours watching his birds. This was the one place that he didn't smoke cigarettes or his pipe, and he didn't mind the droppings that inevitably fell on his hair and clothing when birds perched on the branches above.

Barrymore's favorite bird was a vulture named Maloney. Even though Maloney feasted on rotten meat, Barrymore insisted that the bird "had a breath like a kitten's." But Maloney had a tiger's big appetite, and sometimes Barrymore's zoo keeper ran out of aged meat. When this happened, Barrymore peered into garbage cans during his evening walks through Beverly Hills to see if he could find something really choice for Maloney. One evening, Barrymore took his walk without bothering to shave or to change out of his old bird-dropping-stained clothes. Passing one garbage can, he opened the lid, found a piece of rotten meat for Maloney, and put it in his pocket. As Barrymore continued to search for more, a well-dressed middle-aged man walked by. Thinking that he was some starving derelict—in the middle of Beverly Hills?—the passerby stopped, pulled a shiny dime from his pocket, and handed it to Barrymore.

"Here, my man," said the Good Samaritan. "Here you are. But be sure to spend it only for food."

Barrymore was startled, but only for a moment. He reached out, took the dime, and replied humbly, "God bless you, sir!"

Usually other pedestrians recognized the famous Barrymore profile during his evening walks, regardless of what he was wearing. Comedy star Harold Lloyd, however, could go almost anywhere without attracting attention. Only Lloyd's family and friends knew what he really looked like, because he wore his trademark—lensless horn-rimmed glasses—in every film and at all public appearances.

Harold Lloyd had become one of America's favorite comedians in films such as *Grandma's Boy* (1922), *Safety Last* (1923)—where he climbed up the side of a building and dangled from the hands of a giant clock—*Girl Shy* (1924), *The Freshman* (1925), and *Speedy* (1928), in which Babe Ruth made one of his few movie appearances. Playing the quiet, fumbling, but sympathetic adolescent, Harold Lloyd usually won material success and the girl of his dreams at the end of each film. But he was anything but fumbling offscreen. A natural athlete, he performed many of his hair-raising stunts without a double, but he did resemble his screen character by marrying his leading lady, petite, blond Mildred Davis, on February 10, 1923.

With his movie millions, Harold and Mildred Lloyd left their home on Irving Boulevard, west of downtown Los Angeles, in 1928 and moved into Greenacres, their forty-room mansion set on twenty-two acres at 1225 Benedict Canyon Drive in Beverly Hills. Harold Lloyd was the last of the big silent stars to move to Beverly Hills, but he more than made up for his late arrival. Greenacres cost well over two million dollars, and it was the most expensive and most impressive Beverly Hills movie star's estate of the 1920s—or ever, for that matter.

Few guests ever forgot the housewarming party in 1929. The Lloyds built a dance floor on the lawn outside the house and piled tables high with food and drink. The party started on a Friday night and lasted until Monday morning, with a series of bands providing continuous music. Apparently these four days were not enough for some

Harold Lloyd, age three.

Harold Lloyd, wearing his trademark horn-rimmed glasses, dressed as the quiet, well-meaning adolescent that he portrayed in so many films.

Home movies at the Harold Lloyds'. Mildred with Gloria on her lap, and Harold wearing a cap.

Harold Lloyd, Jr., on Peggy's shoulders and Gloria on Harold Sr.'s back, 1935, outside the children's four-room playhouse, which had plumbing, electricity, and custom-made child-size furniture.

partygoers, because the Lloyds still found guests wandering through the house and sleeping on the grounds in the middle of the week.

As befitted his grand estate, Lloyd built a guardhouse at the start of the driveway, where visitors announced themselves before the gateman let them pass. Then they drove up the long palm-lined driveway, past the seven-car garage and servants' quarters, past the greenhouses, and into the courtyard with a fountain before reaching the main entrance to the house.

Built on a knoll a hundred and twenty feet above Benedict Canyon Drive, this rambling Spanish-style mansion had pink stucco walls and a red tile roof, and it had been designed by John de Lario, who built silver prospector Patrick Longden's Neuschwanstein above Lake Hollywood and prepared the plans for Mack Sennett's never-started mountaintop palace. With forty rooms and twenty-six bathrooms arranged around a central courtyard, Lloyd's house occupied over thirty-six thousand square feet, not counting all the covered porches and patios. Unlike rival comedian Charlie Chaplin's Breakaway House, Greenacres was more than cheaply constructed stage-set glamour. The mansion's foot-and-a-half-thick foundation rested on a rocky formation beneath the hill, and the walls were steel-reinforced against earthquakes.

The front door opened into an entrance hall with a sixteen-foot-high ceiling and a circular oak staircase attached to the wall on one side but without any supports underneath the risers. The sunken living room had a gold-leaf coffered ceiling, elaborate paneling, a stone fireplace, and a theater-size, forty-rank pipe organ. Nearby were the formal dining room capable of seating twenty-four guests, a hundred-seat private theater, a music room where the Lloyds never played music, and a library with yards of rarely read leatherbound books. A paneled elevator ascended to the ten bedrooms on the second floor.

Rather than purchasing department-store sets like other stars, Harold Lloyd ordered custom-made furniture for his Greenacres mansion. Even the Oriental-style rugs and the silk drapes were expressly woven to his specifications. In the midst of this finely calibrated stage set, Harold Lloyd's guests did notice one flaw: a scratch on the big refectory table behind one of the living room sofas. But this was no oversight, and no ordinary scratch. Evelyn Walsh McLean, the socialite who owned the Hope Diamond, had visited the Lloyds and had dramatically tossed the diamond on the table, thereby marring its pristine surface. Harold Lloyd liked to tell the story, and he left the table that way.

Harold Lloyd permitted a few other imperfections at Greenacres. Shortly after moving into the house, he hired an artist to paint vines on the walls of the sun room. At first Lloyd took great pride in the man's work. The vines looked so elegant and lifelike, he bragged to guests, and the leaves were so small and delicate. But his pride turned into disgust when the painter had worked on the room for several years, off and on, and the job still wasn't finished. Harold Lloyd did have limits on what he would spend at Greenacres, and one day he told the man to complete the room within three weeks and to get out. That explained why the tiny, carefully wrought leaves suddenly exploded to nearly ten times their former size in one corner of the room.

To keep Greenacres functioning smoothly, the Lloyds hired a staff of thirty-two, including a butler, several maids, a cook, a kitchen staff, a valet for Harold, a lady's maid for Mildred, and two nannies for the children, Gloria, Peggy, and Harold, Jr. They cared for the main house. Then there were the chauffeurs for the automobiles, several men in the workshops, plus guards at the gatehouse. An operator ran the estate's very own telephone system from a switchboard near the kitchen.

As many as sixteen gardeners grew flowers and shrubs in the greenhouses, tended the twelve formal gardens—each one with a different theme—and maintained the nine-hole golf course in the flat canyon floor beneath the main house. Jack Warner, one of the Warner brothers, also had a nine-hole golf course at his estate next door, and sometimes he and Lloyd erected a temporary walkway over the fence so their guests could play all eighteen holes.

If Lloyd's guests didn't want to play golf, they could swim in the Olympic-size pool, play handball and tennis, or paddle around the eight hundred-foot-long canoe lake near the golf course. Indeed no spot on the grounds was far from the sound of water: Greenacres boasted twelve fountains, and a hundred and twenty-foot-high waterfall, which was lit at night, tumbled down the steep hillside from a terrace near the house to one end of the canoe lake. Harold Lloyd turned Greenacres into a plaything, a consuming hobby—but he didn't always get his way. Mildred vetoed his plans to build a bowling alley in the house. Too noisy and too plebeian, she said. So Harold bought a bowling alley in Hollywood. Now he bowled whenever he wanted, and the purchase incidentally proved to be a good investment as well.

In order that Gloria, Peggy, and Harold, Jr., played in the manner befitting a star's children, Harold and Mildred Lloyd built them their own miniature dream palace in one of the gardens: a child-size four-room thatched-roof cottage, with plumbing, electricity, and exquisite miniature furniture. Like the furniture in the main house, it, too, was custom-made. But daughter Gloria apparently saw the cottage more as a responsibility than a place for children to play. When Harold and Mildred Lloyd first showed her through the little house, she didn't say anything.

"What's wrong?" her parents asked.

"Oh, nothing," Gloria replied. "But where's the keyhole? How can I lock it up at night?"

Just as daughter Gloria seems not to have known how to enjoy her playhouse, Harold and Mildred Lloyd did not take advantage of Greenacres. Although they had devoted three years and several million dollars to building the greatest showplace in the movie colony, they lacked the driving social ambition to turn Greenacres into another Pickfair. Nor did Harold and Mildred Lloyd have the personalities to make Greenacres into a comfortable family home.

Harold Lloyd usually worked at the studio from early morning to late at night. When he did come home or wasn't busy with a picture, he didn't show much affection or parental concern for the three children and preferred to play hours of golf with his buddies or immerse himself in his hobbies in the cavelike basement recreation room. Mildred Lloyd, even more than her husband, was not a social person. Even though she was now retired from the screen and had more than enough help at Greenacres, she, too, did not spend much of her considerable free time with Gloria, Peggy, and Harold, Jr. Nor were her energies poured into organizing dinner parties or receptions, because she rarely entertained except for her husband's celebrity golf and tennis

Greenacres, the living room.

No other movie star's estate ever surpassed Greenacres in its size (a 36,000-square-foot, 40-room mansion on 22 acres of grounds), its cost (over $2,000,000 in 1920s dollars), or its extravagant features (a nine-hole golf course, an 800-foot-long canoe pond, and its own telephone system with a full-time operator).

OPPOSITE: *Harold Lloyd in one of the twelve different formal gardens at Greenacres.*

tournaments. At home Mildred Lloyd liked to do needlework and collect Dresden china. She never learned how to drive.

But the reasons for Greenacres' failure as a star's dream palace and as a family home went far beyond Harold and Mildred Lloyd's self-absorption. By building the movie colony's finest architectural dream palace, the Lloyds had become trapped by the formidable physical perfection of their enormous estate and by the "a star has to live like a star" ideal. And the Lloyds understood this from the beginning. "What are we—damn fools?" they asked each other on moving day in 1928. "What did we do? This place is overpowering." On their first day at Greenacres, Harold and Mildred Lloyd rode up and down in one of the mansion's two elevators for over an hour. As Mildred later confided to gossip columnist Hedda Hopper, "It was the only cozy place in the house."

CHAPTER TEN

Although Harold Lloyd did not make the most of Greenacres, at least he earned over two million a year and could afford to build and maintain the kind of home that his position demanded. However, dozens of successful but less-than-top-rank performers faced a terrible dilemma: As stars, they were expected to live as luxuriously as Lloyd or Gloria Swanson, but they could not afford the requisite homes, automobiles, clothes, jewels, and parties on their salaries.

For example, take Buster Keaton, the "great stone face." By the early 1920s, he had become a popular comedian in shorts such as *The Boat* (1921) and *Cops* (1922), but he was financially hard pressed to satisfy his wife Natalie's ambitions to live on the scale of her movie-star sisters, Norma and Constance Talmadge. He spent his entire two-thousand-dollars-a-week salary just to keep the "cars, house, and parties running," and he didn't have any money in the bank. Only periodic bonuses from the Metro studio and some advantageous real-estate deals saved Keaton from falling deeply into debt.

In 1925, Buster Keaton tried to extricate himself from his financial treadmill. Once again the Keatons had traded up, this time from the Westmoreland Place mansion with the third-floor ballroom. Now Buster was paying a large part of his income on rent for an even larger residence on South Plymouth Boulevard, a house Natalie called "a cabin." Believing that "rent was money down the drain," Keaton designed a "real little ranch house and not *that* small" with his technical

Although this is a scene from Buster Keaton's two-reel comedy One Week *(1920), it shows what his wife, Natalie, thought of the surprise house that he built for her in 1925.*

Buster Keaton.

man, Fred Gabourie, during their spare moments at the studio. "Then I built it, all on the Q. T. on . . . a nice hillside plot" in Beverly Hills, Keaton later remembered. "It had to be all done, with every stick of furniture in place and ready down to the last light bulb, before I'd casually drive by with Natalie, and stop. She'd say, 'What a dream of a house.' And I'd say, 'Nat, it's yours.' Final sequence. Fade."

Keaton's "dream of a house" cost thirty-four thousand dollars, including the lot and landscaping. Better yet, everything was paid for. One day, Buster proudly showed Natalie his surprise. As they wandered through the fully furnished new house, she didn't say anything. When the tour was over, Natalie remarked wearily, "Where would we put the servants?"

That wasn't all she said. She announced that they were going to build a house fit for a star. One year and three hundred thousand dollars later, the Keatons moved into their twenty-room Italian villa on a hilly three-acre estate at 1004 Hartford Way, behind the Beverly Hills Hotel. Those twenty rooms were just reserved for the family; another eight were for the servants required to run such a large establishment. "Do the two boys have to have their own butler?" Buster once asked Natalie sarcastically.

Natalie Talmadge Keaton finally had a home in which she could properly entertain her sisters, Norma and Constance, and their shrewd, strong-willed mother, Peg. Always a close-knit family, the Talmadges were together even more after Buster and Natalie began to drift apart in the mid-1920s. Norma and Constance Talmadge were partly to blame for the Keatons' rift. Shortly after the birth of Buster and Natalie's second son, Robert, in 1924, they advised Natalie to give up her "animalistic behavior," specifically, sleeping with her husband. Naive little Natalie should have known that Norma and Constance hardly practiced what they preached. Between the two of them, they had seven husbands and many lovers, yet no children. Natalie, nonetheless, dutifully followed their instructions, and before long Buster was sleeping in another bedroom and staying away from home more and more to play bridge, drink, and chase other women.

When Keaton showed guests around his new Beverly Hills home, he sometimes said, "It took a lot of pratfalls, my friends, to build this

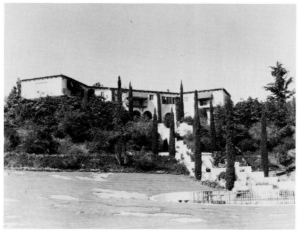

Buster Keaton built his "Italian villa" on a hillock behind the Beverly Hills Hotel, because Natalie wanted to live as grandly as her movie star sisters, Norma and Constance Talmadge. Natalie, however, sold the estate at the time of their 1933 divorce.

Buster and Natalie Keaton, playing the happily married young couple in a publicity still.

RIGHT: A reflective Buster Keaton in the bedroom of his Beverly Hills "Italian villa," 1929.

dump." That was true, and he resented the constant financial drain of maintaining the estate, even though his salary had increased to thirty-five hundred a week after the success of feature-length films such as *The Navigator* (1924) and *Sherlock, Jr.* (1924). But Keaton genuinely liked his new home as well, and probably still loved Natalie. At their Sunday barbecues, he cooked delicious Chinese spareribs and mutton chops for fifty or sixty guests and tested new gags on a few friends. He bought pet raccoons for sons Bobby and Jimmy and even built his boys a playhouse that looked like a miniature version of the main house.

On these spacious grounds, Keaton could also indulge himself. An animal lover, he set quail free on the estate, kept trout in a babbling brook that turned on and off with a switch, and purchased several dogs, including Trotsky, the Irish wolfhound, who on hot days sat in one of the garden pools submerged up to his neck. Inside the house Keaton installed an elaborate electric train set and hung extra-strong drapes at one window so that he could swing from the top of the stairs to the living room below. "Buster's whole life then was a movie," actress Louise Brooks has wisely observed. "His house was a set, the swimming pool was a set, the barbecue pit was a set."

If keeping up appearances was difficult for a star of Buster Keaton's stature, it was next to impossible for those up-and-coming actors and actresses whose salaries had not caught up with their increasing fame and living expenses. Jean Harlow discovered this when she became a star in *Hell's Angels* (1930). To fulfill her fans' expectations of her offscreen life, she bought an expensive home at 1353 Clubview Drive, just west of Beverly Hills, wore fine clothing, hired a day maid, and tipped studio personnel generously. All the while, Harlow was still working under her old several-hundred-dollars-a-week starlet's contract, and she was falling into debt at the rate of fifteen hundred a month, until her agent bought out the old contract and negotiated a new one at a much higher salary with another studio.

Most studios helped their young talent to put up the right front. Publicity departments loaned expensive automobiles for movie premieres, provided fabulous clothing for photography sessions, and sometimes paid for parties at an actor's or actress's mansion. Some stars even bought their homes with the studio's assistance. When Rudolph

Valentino became Hollywood's biggest sensation in 1922, Paramount advanced him forty thousand dollars to build a suitably fine residence at 6776 Wedgewood Place, in the Whitley Heights section of Hollywood. Three years later, Valentino asked his new studio, United Artists, for help to buy Falcon Lair. Valentino could afford to make the down payment, but the owner, Beverly Hills realtor George B. Read, was reluctant to accept Valentino's personal note for the balance due on the sale. Joe Schenck, then chairman of the board at United Artists, obligingly co-signed the note, and the deal went through.

Studio chiefs willingly made these loans in order to perpetuate the myth of stardom. The few thousand dollars that Louis B. Mayer lent Joan Crawford to buy a bungalow on North Roxbury Drive in Beverly Hills in 1927 was nothing compared to the money he hoped the ambitious young actress might earn for herself and MGM in future years. Mayer's hunch was right. A year later, Joan Crawford Charlestoned her way to stardom as a flapper in *Our Dancing Daughters* (1928). But now that she was an established star, Crawford needed a grander home, and Louis B. Mayer obligingly advanced her forty thousand dollars to buy a ten-room mansion at 426 North Bristol Circle in Brentwood, a fashionable new community between Beverly Hills and the Pacific Ocean.

Parading in her sudden prosperity, Joan Crawford furnished the living room with curved gold brocade upholstered settees, window drapes of the same material, reproduction eighteenth-century French chairs, tiny Italian occasional tables, and green wall-to-wall carpeting. A grand piano, covered with a rich Burmese throw, stood in one corner. For the dining room, Crawford bought a matched Spanish-style set with a table, twelve chairs, a sideboard, and a china closet. By the breakfast-room window she hung a gilded cage with a pair of twittering mechanical birds. Her new home "seemed the apotheosis of taste," according to Joan Crawford, and it was, for 1929.

Her favorite room was the sun porch, with windows on three sides and shelves filled with several dozen of her two thousand dolls. "You never saw such a wonderful collection of toys," declared *Photoplay* in its August 1929 issue. "One precious doll, with lovely long hair, used to belong to Joan's grandmother—but most of the toys are modern,

Joan Crawford at the wrought-iron gates of her dining room, 1929. Joan Crawford, after becoming a star in Our Dancing Daughters *(1929), quickly began to live like a star. She bought a ten-room mansion in Brentwood, thanks to a loan from Louis B. Mayer. And several months later, she married Douglas Fairbanks, Jr., thereby gaining entree into Pickfair's exalted circle.*

Joan Crawford collected over two thousand dolls, by her own count, before she started adopting children.

diabolically clever, irresistibly funny. A life-size hen that cackles and lays an egg! A life-size baby pig, that walks and grunts! Teddy bears of every shape and size—with provocative expressions! Rag dogs, rag dolls, gorgeous lady dolls, clowns that sing—and at the end of the porch, a little table about two feet high, with four chairs, and four funny dolls seated in them—with the table laid for dinner!"

And yet even with these two thousand dolls, "I was still collecting like mad," Joan Crawford later recalled. "For the children I dreamed of? What a headshrinker could do with this phase of my life!"

After moving into her North Bristol Circle house, Crawford showed Hollywood that she was more than just another overnight star with a large mortgage and high hopes. On June 3, 1929, she married Douglas Fairbanks, Jr., over the objections of Doug, Sr., and Mary Pickford. This marriage brought the ex-Broadway chorus girl into Hollywood's royal family and into Pickfair's charmed circle, at least to outward appearances. Douglas Fairbanks, Jr., and Joan Crawford never quite fit in at Pickfair, but they copied its mystique by combining parts of their first names and calling their Brentwood home "El Jodo."

After the success of *Our Dancing Daughters,* Joan Crawford made a number of popular flapper spin-offs, like *Our Modern Maidens* (1929) and *Laughing Sinners* (1931) before making an enduring name for herself playing shopgirls, playgirls, and working women in the 1930s. But dozens of other actors and actresses weren't as lucky or as talented as Joan. They enjoyed a brief flash of popularity, started earning big money, and went into debt trying to emulate the tastes and style of the established stars, never dreaming that their comfortable incomes might one day vanish. Most of these newcomers quickly dropped out of sight. Unless they had shrewdly scaled their expenses, bearing this possibility in mind, they lost their heavily mortgaged homes and credit-bought automobiles.

And there were many such unhappy endings. Charles Ray had become a star in the late teens playing "country boy" parts. But he wanted to appear in costume epics and put up his own money to make *The Courtship of Miles Standish* (1923). The film bombed; Ray went bankrupt and lost his mansion at 901 North Camden Drive in Beverly Hills, with its solid-gold doorknobs, gold dinner service, and crystal

Even child stars traveled in style. This is Baby Peggy arriving for another day's work at Century Studios in 1921 or 1922.

Milton Sills and the death car.

bathtub. By the 1930s, the only film work Ray found was as an extra.

When leading man Milton Sills' star began to fade in the late 1920s, he could not endure the humiliation of losing his popularity, his home, or his cars. Before the bank took away his Rolls-Royce, he killed himself by crashing the car into a treacherous curve along Sunset Boulevard.

Flaming red-haired "It Girl" Clara Bow was one of the few stars to live below her means in the 1920s. With her expressive eyes, Cupid's-bow lips, and busy, almost frantic vitality, Bow had become a favorite sex symbol in films such as *Mantrap* (1926), *It* (1927), and *The Wild Party* (1929). High spirited and earthy, Clara Bow actually scorned other stars' grand delusions. One morning, she was having breakfast with MGM's romantic lead, John Gilbert, at his lavish Tower Grove Road mansion. Looking at the silver service on the table, Clara Bow asked, "Do you really like all this crap?"

Clara Bow drove her own automobile, a fire-engine red Kiesel convertible. She might have hired a chauffeur, but, she explained, "I can't get one who'll drive fast enough." She bought a beach house, but it was little more than a shack in then remote and distinctly unfashionable Malibu. Her real home was a one-story seven-room bungalow at 512 North Bedford Drive in Beverly Hills.

Rather than follow prevailing decorative tastes, Clara Bow acted on her own instincts, and the results were outrageous. The exterior stucco walls of the bungalow were painted a traditional pink, but the canvas awnings and the garage doors had vertical orange and black stripes. The Chinese-style front door—on a Spanish-style house?—opened into a small entrance hall just large enough to hold a Chinese throne, a Sarouk rug over the tile floor, and an Italian metal console table and a lamp whose shade resembled a peacock's tail.

Clara Bow filled her living room with a large sofa, a carved and cushioned love seat, several Chinese-style chairs and rugs, and French needlepoint tapestries. Scattered around the room were several art objects: a model of the *Mayflower*, a Grecian screen, Chinese plaques, warrior shields, velvet batik wall panels, smoking paraphernalia, and several French dolls sitting in Chinese chairs.

Clara's social skills were not much better developed than her eye

Silent star Charles Ray had to sell his eclectically decorated Beverly Hills home—including this piano—when his career fizzled out in the 1920s.

Jean Harlow, plagued by money problems in 1935, was forced to sell her three-year-old Beverly Glen estate. And the advertisements read: "Glamour Star's New Ancestral Mansion for Sale."

for interior decoration. Shortly after moving into her North Bedford Drive home, she decided to have a dinner party for some friends from the studio. Newspaper reporter Adela Rogers St. Johns explained how to set the table and how to serve the meal. When she mentioned that the plates should be cleared from the table after the main course, Clara balked. "Oh, no," she said. "That would be pretentious. We'll just push our plates into the middle of the table when we're through with dinner." And that's exactly what they did.

On the night of the dinner, Adela Rogers St. Johns arrived early to help Clara with any last-minute details. When she saw the place cards, she cried out, "Clara, you shouldn't sit husbands and wives next to each other!"

"Nothin' doin'!" she replied. "I ain't getting in no hot water. Everyone thinks I'm trying to steal their husbands. The husbands and wives will sit with each other, and that's that."

Known as "The Hottest Jazz Baby in Films," Clara Bow lived up to her image offscreen. In her dark-red Chinese den, she entertained dozens of men, among them Eddie Cantor, Gary Cooper, Bela Lugosi, and the eleven-man starting lineup of the University of Southern California football team, including tackle Marion Morrison, later named John Wayne. Some of Clara's beaux were a little too smitten with her. She spent several evenings with Robert Savage, a football player from Yale and the son of a millionaire steel manufacturer, but she quickly tired of the young man and didn't want to see him any more. Savage was heartbroken. In a dramatic but unsuccessful suicide attempt, he slashed his wrists and dripped his blue blood on a photograph that she had inscribed to him.

Clara was appalled. "Men don't slash their wrists," she told the press. "They use a gun!"

Another evening, Beverly Hills police started receiving telephone calls about a commotion at Clara Bow's house. When Clinton Anderson, then a patrolman and later chief of police, arrived at her house, he found an enormous man pounding on the front door, bellowing, "Clara! Clara!"

"Look, mister," said Anderson. "What's this all about? What are you doing here this time of night? Do you know whose house this is?"

"It Girl" Clara Bow, unsatisfied with romantic conquests like Eddie Cantor, Gary Cooper, and Bela Lugosi, reportedly entertained the starting lineup of the University of Southern California football team one weekend.

Clara Bow. Is the helmet a souvenir from her USC football players?

Clara Bow in her bedroom.

"Of course, I know whose house this is!" the man shouted. "Clara Bow's! I came all the way out here from Iowa to propose to her, only she won't open the door. Where I come from, when somebody comes to the door, we invite them inside!" As Patrolman Anderson removed the overzealous fan from the doorstep, he saw Clara's "frightened brown eyes peering through the peephole in the front door."

Even before the police started pulling Clara Bow's fans away from her front door, Beverly Hills residents realized their community's quiet, countrified days were over. In 1923, Beverly Hills became an incorporated city, surrounded by Los Angeles on all four sides, and three years later Will Rogers was named honorary mayor. At Rogers' December 2, 1926, "inauguration," Douglas Fairbanks, Sr., made the introductory speech and the Los Angeles Fire Department Band played "The Old Gray Mare." Then Rogers spoke briefly. "I am for the common people," he said, "and as Beverly Hills has no common people, I'll be sure to make good." Rogers promised to give the city's poor bigger and better swimming pools and miles of new bridle paths to ride their horses on before dinner.

Less than two years later Rogers resigned his post, sold his North Beverly Drive estate, and moved his family out to a several-hundred-acre ranch at 14243 Sunset Boulevard in Pacific Palisades, several miles from the ocean. Beverly Hills had become too developed for Will Rogers' taste. The population had jumped from 634 in 1920 to 17,428 in 1930. The dusty bean fields were gone, and the last of the new streets in the flats were open. The one-room schoolhouse at Sunset Boulevard and Alpine Drive had been torn down, and the one-car trolley on Rodeo Drive had been removed. Beverly Hills was becoming awfully pretentious as well. One year, a controversy raged over whether or not a five-and-dime store should be allowed to open on one of the shopping streets south of Santa Monica Boulevard. It did.

By the 1920s, rich non-movie-colony families who might have settled in Beverly Hills five or ten years earlier started looking for property elsewhere. In their genteel eyes, Beverly Hills was becoming a Hollywood circus, where young women clambered over the walls of Falcon Lair and young men hovered around Clara Bow's house like cats in heat.

CHAPTER ELEVEN

Some fashionable Los Angelenos settled in Bel Air, a neighborhood of princely estates in the hills above Sunset Boulevard, about a mile west of Beverly Hills. Other well-to-do families headed even farther west out Sunset Boulevard to Brentwood, or to even more remote Pacific Palisades, the last community before the ocean and the site of Will Rogers' ranch.

Will Rogers' new home, however, was not Hollywood's westernmost outpost on the vast Los Angeles landscape. During the 1920s and 1930s, movie stars and studio executives built a mile-long row of beach houses along the ocean in the nearby town of Santa Monica. Almost all the big names were there, including Douglas Fairbanks and Mary Pickford, Joe Schenck and Norma Talmadge, Louis B. Mayer, Mae West, Sam Goldwyn, Ben Lyon and Bebe Daniels, Jesse Lasky, Cary Grant, Harold Lloyd, and even Will Rogers.

In theory, the beach houses were simple hideaways where stars and studio chiefs could get away from the high-pressured, status-conscious movie colony on weekends. But it didn't turn out that way. Actually, most movie people partied the weekends away with other movie people. And the beach houses—cottages, initially—soon became a new Hollywood status symbol: the seaside mansion.

Louis B. Mayer's beach house was one of the finest. Designed by MGM art director Cedric Gibbons in the Spanish style, it had foot-thick walls as insulation against summer heat, twenty rooms, and thirteen onyx-and-marble bathrooms. Mayer imported a crew of

Douglas Fairbanks and Mary Pickford's Santa Monica beach house, though architecturally charming, was surprisingly modest for the King and Queen of Hollywood, and it was furnished with castoffs from Pickfair.

The dining room.

The living room.

workmen from Greece just to install the bathroom tiles. Mrs. Mayer loved flowers, and the Beverly Hills Nursery brought in tons of topsoil and planted several gardens around the house. But Mrs. Mayer didn't want to wait for the shrubs to grow and flower. So every few months, the Beverly Hills Nursery ripped out the gardens and planted new flowers and shrubs that were ready to bloom.

Yet compared to actress Marion Davies' seaside mansion, all these Santa Monica beach houses—including Louis B. Mayer's—were little more than shacks. As William Randolph Hearst's mistress and confidante, Davies owned nothing but the finest in houses, cars, clothes, and jewels, and her San Simeon-by-the-Sea at Santa Monica was the only rival to Harold Lloyd's Greenacres as the movie colony's most extravagant dream palace.

By Marion's own estimates, Hearst spent several million dollars building and furnishing the beach house in the late 1920s, and several million more in running and continually redecorating the place over the next fifteen years. Marion Davies' beach-house compound was so large that some unsuspecting tourists assumed that it was a resort hotel and stopped at the guard house to ask about rooms.

Marion's property occupied seven hundred fifty feet of prime oceanfront real estate, in an area where anything over fifty feet frontage was regarded as extravagant. But William Randolph Hearst had some trouble acquiring this much beach property, even though he hired Brentwood realtor George S. Merritt to assemble the land under various names. "When I try to buy anything," he told Merritt, "the price has a habit of going up and up." The news that Hearst was behind the purchases leaked out before Merritt could buy the last parcel, a small piece that was just right for a tennis court. Will Rogers owned this land, worth about five thousand dollars, and he wasn't going to let Hearst get off cheaply. Rogers named an outrageous price. When Hearst agreed to pay the figure, Rogers backed out of the deal and raised his asking price. Hearst was determined to have a tennis court at exactly that spot, and Will Rogers finally let him buy the land for one hundred thousand dollars.

Marion Davies' neocolonial-style frame beach house stretched several hundred feet along the ocean; it had a maze of huge public rooms on the first floor, a ballroom, a private theater, and dozens of bedrooms on the second floor, and a grand total of fifty-five bathrooms. To furnish the beach house, W.R. bought dozens of rare Oriental rugs, hundreds of thousands of dollars' worth of china and silver, truckloads of antique furniture, and thirty-seven antique fireplaces. The basement "tavern," which sat fifty, had been a real Elizabethan British public house. Several rooms contained priceless late-seventeenth-century Grinling Gibbons English paneling. A marble Venetian-style bridge crossed over the middle of the extra-long swimming pool. And, as another sign of his devotion, W.R. commissioned a series of life-size portraits of Marion in her various screen roles to hang in the one long hallway.

Whatever Hearst desired for the beach house, he usually got, no matter what it cost. While the house was still under construction, he bought an entire paneled room from an English castle. He wanted to install it in the beach house, but it didn't fit anywhere. So he told the architects to change the half-completed building to accommodate the room.

Marion Davies shared Hearst's spendthrift attitude. Once she ordered an extra-thick 24-by-100-foot custom-made rug for the second-floor movie theater. When the rug arrived in Los Angeles from the factory in New Jersey, Homer Watters, a Los Angeles *Examiner* employee and one of Hearst's "go-fers" asked him what to do with the delivery. Hearst didn't know anything about a rug and told Watters to send it back. Two days later, Marion Davies learned that her rug had come and gone, and now Watters frantically located the shipment in Albuquerque. When the rug was finally delivered, it was too large to bring into the beach house by any of the doors. No problem. Marion had part of the theater wall removed, and the rug was lifted into the house by a crane.

Blond, blue-eyed, and delicately beautiful, Marion Davies had done all right for herself. Only ten years before moving into the beach house, she had been a chorine in Florenz Ziegfeld's *Follies of 1917* in New York City. Marion's life changed the night Hearst wandered into the show and promptly fell in love with her. For the next eight weeks,

Marion Davies' home, Beverly Hills, from the early 1920s to 1946.

BELOW: *Marion Davies in the garden of her Beverly Hills home.*

he attended every show just to gaze at her. Hearst was fifty-four years old, and she was twenty. By 1919 they were living together.

Hearst was determined to turn his former chorus girl into a movie star, specifically a great dramatic actress appearing in showy costume epics. After forming Cosmopolitan Pictures in 1919 to make Marion's films, he hired Frances Marion at two thousand a week to write scenarios and employed the finest directors, public-relations people, and dramatic coaches. Marion Davies did become a star, but she never attained the epic popularity of Mary Pickford or Gloria Swanson. She did have acting talent and more than enough personal magnetism, but Hearst promoted her too aggressively through his publishing empire. "Marion Davies' bizarre publicity hit one full in the face *ad nauseam*," according to her friend Charlie Chaplin. "One could not open a Hearst magazine or newspaper without a large picture of Marion. All this only kept the public away from the box office."

Hearst's personal fondness for romance and sentimentality also obscured his judgment about what roles were best for Marion—or "Muggins," as he called her. She had a natural gift for mimicry and pantomime, as demonstrated by the critical and commercial success of *The Patsy* (1928) and *Show People* (1928). But Hearst usually insisted that Marion keep making the unsuccessful costume pictures, even though she was not a good dramatic actress, no matter how hard she tried.

William Randolph Hearst didn't care what the critics thought. "Never read any of the bad reviews about yourself," he once told her. "Read only the good ones." But Marion Davies took her career very seriously, and this advice didn't make her feel any better. "What if there are no good ones?" she thought. "Then I'm really in the dumps. I'd rather read the bad ones than the good ones anyway, because at least there are more of them."

Hearst was still guiding Marion Davies' film career in the 1930s. Anita Loos remembers a meeting with him after she'd been hired to supply dialogue for one of Frances Marion's stories, *Blondie of the Follies* (1932). "W.R. focused his pale, liquid eyes on me and a faint voice rose from his great bulk, like the squeak of Minnie Mouse coming out of a mountain, 'Now, Nita,' he started off, 'I want you to curb your inclination toward humor, because I see this story as a great romance.' "

Although Anita Loos used all the "soothing syrup" at her command, she still couldn't satisfy Hearst. One day the two of them were sitting in a projection room watching one of the few scenes from the daily rushes where Marion Davies did not appear. Hearst rang the buzzer to stop the film. "Why wasn't Muggins in that scene?" he demanded.

" 'Well, you see, Mr. Hearst, we've got to explain an element of the plot that our heroine mustn't know about.'

" 'But that scene is nothing but wasted footage. Just throw it out and write one that shows Muggins doing something.'

"So I had to abandon the plot for a sequence of Marion picking rosebuds."

Hearst lost an estimated seven million dollars on Marion's career, but that didn't daunt a man who spent fifteen million *a year* on himself. He loved to sit for hours in his darkened screening room and watch her movies over and over again. But Hearst's love of romantic films proved tragic for Marion Davies, who never found out how far her real talent for comedy could have taken her. "I'm convinced that if W.R. had let Marion be herself, she would have ranked as a super box-office attraction," declares Anita Loos. "A pretty girl who can be a clown is rare, and Marion's offscreen antics were hilarious."

Sometimes Marion Davies' jokes were unintentional, such as the evening she attended a party for the King of Siam at Pickfair. Arriving a little late, she ran up the stairs and saw Mary standing on the landing with a man in a white coat. Thinking that he was a butler, Marion Davies handed him her ermine coat, then said to Mary, "I'm sorry I'm late." Mary Pickford's smile froze. The "butler" turned out to be the King.

Mary Pickford soon forgave Marion for this gaffe, just as she forgave her for being Hearst's mistress. W.R. wanted to marry Marion, but his wife, Millicent, refused to divorce him. Marion Davies was well aware of her awkward social position. Raoul Walsh and Miriam Cooper never accepted her dinner or party invitations, because Walsh

Marion Davies' Santa Monica beach house, built by the devoted William Randolph Hearst, was a sprawling 80-room, 55-bathroom compound where Marion could—and often did—entertain two thousand guests. The Gold Room.

The dining room.

OPPOSITE: *Marion Davies, 1929, the glamorous hostess, in the glamorous setting provided by William Randolph Hearst's millions.*

wouldn't let his wife enter a "kept woman's" house. These snubs hurt Marion Davies more than most people realized. Once Anita Loos invited Marion to attend a party with her and her husband, John Emerson. "I'm n-n-not going," Marion Davies replied. She stammered all her life, but it wasn't perceptible in her silent or talking films. "But, why not?" Anita asked. Marion explained that she rarely attended parties outside of her home and a small circle of genuine friends, where she knew she was welcome. "You see N-N-Nita, when I get among st-st-strangers, I never know."

Marion Davies liked to invite close friends, including Charlie Chaplin and Rudolph Valentino, to her Spanish-style mansion at 1700 Lexington Road in Beverly Hills for dinner and an evening of charades. A week later, Valentino would invite the group to Falcon Lair; next time it would be Chaplin's turn; and so on. Other evenings, Marion Davies hired a bus, filled it with food and drink, hired a concertina player, and took ten or twenty friends to Malibu beach, where they built bonfires and had late-night picnics.

Hearst newspaper columnist Louella Parsons often came along with director Harry Crocker, even though W.R. didn't approve of Marion or his employees staying out late when he was out of town, even if it were only innocent fun. Early one morning, about five a.m., the group of revelers was returning to Beverly Hills from one of these Malibu picnics, and Marion turned to Louella and said, "If W.R. hears about this, one of us is going to lose his job, and it won't be me."

When Marion Davies wasn't working full-time on a movie, she held formal dinner parties for one hundred guests two and three times a week at her Lexington Road home. Once Davies wanted to welcome W.R. back to Los Angeles with an extra-special party, but her dining room couldn't seat more than one hundred. So in just two days, she built a banquet room on the back of her house for a hundred and sixty guests, and following the party, it was torn down and carted away.

After her Santa Monica beach house was completed in 1928, Marion Davies never had to worry about being short on room to entertain again. The beach house could—and often did—accommodate two thousand guests. As Douglas Fairbanks and Mary Pickford's marriage began to cool around 1930, William Randolph Hearst and Marion

Marion Davies posing for one of her film role portraits.

The upstairs hall, lined with larger-than-life portraits of Marion Davies in her various film roles on the walls.

The library.

The entrance hall.

Davies became the movie colony's unofficial social leaders, thanks to his ever available wealth and her warmth and vitality. Marion gave no thought to hiring a hundred-twenty-five-piece orchestra from the Ambassador Hotel for dances—or spending ten thousand dollars for fireworks one Fourth of July.

For a circus costume party, Marion wanted to install a merry-go-round on the tennis court. That was easier said than done, but it was done. A part of the service wing and a wall around the tennis court had to be torn down to bring in the merry-go-round. After the party, the merry-go-round was removed, and the service wing and wall were rebuilt. But Marion had enjoyed the circus party so much that she held another one a month later, and the service wing and tennis court wall were torn down and rebuilt a second time!

William Randolph Hearst and Marion Davies loved costume parties, and no theme was too farfetched: Early America, A Midsummer Night's Dream, Germany, the Wild West, even Babies. For those guests without time to locate the right costume, Marion always had several hundred rented costumes, in all different sizes, for them to choose from when they arrived at the beach house. A hulking six feet four inches tall and seventy years old, William Randolph Hearst was an unforgettable sight at some costume parties, but he refused to dress for the Baby party and attended in an evening jacket with simple striped pants.

Despite their extravagance and enormous guest lists, Marion Davies' beach-house parties never became rowdy. With the help of his private detectives, Hearst kept a careful eye on his youthful guests. "If you got caught necking in the corner," Douglas Fairbanks, Jr., remembered recently, "Hearst would see to it that you were thrown out and never asked again. He was very strict. . . . That didn't mean it didn't go on, of course, but you had to sneak."

Marion Davies served wine, mixed drinks, and champagne at her parties, but Hearst frowned on drunkenness, and he expressly asked her to stay away from the hard stuff at all times. Marion, however, liked an occasional drink and went into her bathroom stash or into a corner with a friend who would watch for Hearst or his spies. Joan Crawford was a convenient cover, because she didn't drink in the late 1920s, and Marion could give her the glass if W.R. entered the room. One night he found the two women together, and Joan had Marion's drink in her hand.

"I've never seen you take a drink before, Joan," he said.

"I thought I'd try it," she said, blushing.

"Well, try it!" And he watched Joan choke down Marion's drink.

The only thing that could spoil one of Marion Davies' parties was one of Hearst's occasional bad moods, because guests unconsciously took their cues from him. One night some of her friends had gathered at the Lexington Road estate for a dinner party. She looked particularly beautiful that night, dressed like Madame Récamier and reclining on a settee. But Hearst sat gloomily in a high-backed chair, talking business with several editors gathered around him. Marion Davies grew more and more irritable, because he was ignoring her, the guests, and the party, and she finally shouted out, "Hey! You!"

"Are you referring to me?" Hearst asked indignantly.

"Yes, you! Come here!" she shouted, fixing her blue eyes on him. Hearst's editors dissolved into the crowd, and the room grew silent.

Hearst sat in his chair, tapping his fingers on the arm, his eyes narrowing, his mood growing darker by the moment. Guests began to stir nervously and look for the door. Hearst stood up.

"Well, I suppose I shall have to go," he said quietly, and he walked over to Marion. "And what does my lady want?"

"Do your business downtown. Not in my house," she snapped. "My guests are waiting for a drink, so hurry up and get them one."

"All right. All right," he replied meekly, and headed for the kitchen.

Only Marion Davies could get away with talking to Hearst like that. Thirty-four years her senior, he felt young again dressing up for one of their costume parties, dancing a clumsy but enthusiastic Charleston, or going to Europe together. Hearst loved Marion very much, and she was the kind of person who was easy to love: warm, generous, fun-loving, gamin-like.

Marion Davies was incredibly generous as well. During the Depression, her staff regularly set out tables of food at the service entrance to the beach house for out-of-work movie people or anyone who was hungry. Marion Davies invited actors and actresses whose careers were in trouble to weekends at the beach house or San Simeon, where they could mingle with the big producers and directors who would not see them at their offices back in Hollywood during the week.

Marion also helped dozens of friends through tight financial spots, and she was always ready to lend her best dresses, furs, or jewels to an actress who needed to make just the right appearance. Even Marion's houseguests got to help themselves to her fabulous clothes. She was a night person, often the last in the house to get up. By then, some of her best things had been borrowed. But she didn't mind. "In this house," she once said, "the f-f-first girl up is the best d-d-dressed."

For all its splendor, though, Marion Davies' beach house was not the most expensive or even the largest house in Los Angeles in the 1920s. Nor was Harold Lloyd's opulent Greenacres. Rather, that honor belonged to Greystone, built by Edward Laurence Doheny, Sr., who made the first oil strike in Los Angeles in 1892, and then proceeded to dominate California's rapidly growing petroleum industry. By 1920 his oil empire extended across America and into Mexico, and it was worth over a hundred million dollars.

That fortune evidently was intended to serve as the springboard for more. In 1922, Doheny's son, Edward Laurence, Jr., known as Ned, gave Secretary of the Interior Albert Fall a hundred thousand dollars in a black satchel in return for secret leases to government oil reserves at Elk Hills and Buena Vista in California. But word of the deal soon leaked out, and in the ensuing Teapot Dome scandal, the leases were canceled. Later, Albert Fall served a brief jail sentence for accepting Doheny's bribe. Doheny was tried for making the bribe, but was acquitted.

Hardheaded, greedy, disposed to manipulate the federal government at its highest levels for his own benefit, Edward Laurence Doheny, Sr., did not seem like the kind of man to build Los Angeles' ultimate dream palace. But Doheny, like other Los Angeles businessmen, had gotten caught up in the Hollywood mystique, had in fact, in an act of sublime egotism, melded it into his own image. In the mid-1920s, Doheny invited Cecil B. De Mille for lunch and then suggested his own life story as a suitable movie vehicle!

THE BABY PARTY

Natalie, Constance, and Norma Talmadge, dressed as little girls but still wearing silk stockings.

Norma Shearer, Irving Thalberg, and Constance Bennett.

Marion Davies, Clark Gable, and Eileen Percy.

Joan Crawford and Douglas Fairbanks, Jr.

De Mille declined the suggestion, but Doheny, nonetheless, went ahead with the construction of a real-life stage set against which to act out this instructive life. The result was Greystone, a four-million-dollar mansion on his four hundred and fifteen-acre ranch in the hills above Sunset Boulevard in the eastern reaches of Beverly Hills. As befitted his thirst for wealth and power, Doheny ran this ranch like a principality, complete with its own watchmen, water supply, and fire department. And the enormous neo-Gothic-style Greystone was built on a prominent hillside, looking out over the red tile roofs of Beverly Hills and the town's *mere* millionaires, just as Medieval castles triumphantly loomed over the huts of the lord's lowly serfs.

And the 46,054-square-foot, fifty-five-room mansion was fortress-like. Its gray Arizona stone facade—which gave the house its name—was merely a veneer for thick, steel-framed concrete walls. Even the slate roof was reinforced with concrete. Greystone was the center of an almost completely self-contained compound. The twenty-five acres that immediately surrounded the mansion included a 15,666-square-foot stable, a seven-room gate house, water lines, sewers, and gas lines, as well as vintage dream-palace features: sixteen acres of formal gardens and wooded areas, reflecting pools, swimming pools, greenhouses, tennis and badminton courts, man-made waterfalls, and two concrete-bottom lakes.

When Greystone was completed in June 1928, Edward Laurence Doheny, Sr., gave the mansion and its grounds to his son and only child, Ned. In its size, cost, and the builder's personal ambitions, Greystone surely represented the acme of the dream palace. But the younger Doheny—who moved into Greystone with his wife and five children late in 1928—did not enjoy his father's magnificent gift for long. Late one Saturday night, February 17, 1929, a muffled gunshot rang out in the house, quickly followed by another. Ned Doheny and his secretary, Hugh Plunkett, lay dead in Ned's bedroom suite.

By Monday morning, the episode was front-page news. According to a Doheny family spokesman, Ned Doheny had visited Plunkett at his Hollywood apartment early Saturday evening, and the two men had quarreled—about what, the newspapers didn't specify. Then Ned Doheny returned home to Greystone. Several hours later, Hugh

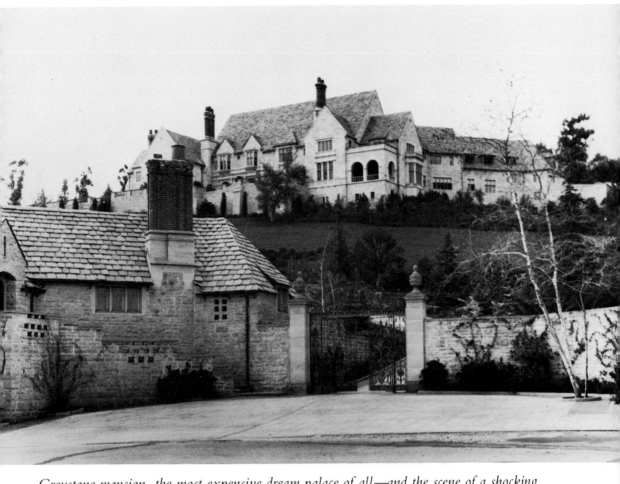

Greystone mansion, the most expensive dream palace of all—and the scene of a shocking tragedy.

Plunkett drove to Greystone, sneaked onto the grounds, silently let himself into the house with his key, found Ned Doheny in his bedroom, shot him to death, then killed himself.

But *why?* The Doheny family physician, Dr. E. C. Fishbaugh, reported that Plunkett had been "highly excited and nervous" in recent months, and was sick with influenza and strung-out on sleeping pills the night of the shooting. Ned Doheny, declared Dr. Fishbaugh, had been so worried about his secretary's condition that he was "attempting to induce Plunkett to retire," even to have him "placed in a sanitorium for rest."

But these newspaper stories did not explain what the two men had quarreled about earlier in the fatal evening or why Plunkett would have killed himself after shooting Doheny. But there were plenty of rumors about what really happened that night at Greystone. According to one story, Plunkett asked Doheny for a raise that Saturday evening, certainly not a hardship for someone who had just moved into a four-million-dollar house; but Plunkett was refused the increase, and that's what led to the quarrel and the later shootings.

That may well be the truth. But another version of Ned Doheny's death is still more farfetched, certainly more tantalizing, and it is the story some Los Angelenos who remember the incident still repeat: Ned Doheny and Hugh Plunkett were lovers, and the family had just found out. Rather than suffer public exposure or, at best, be forced to stop seeing one another, Ned Doheny and Hugh Plunkett decided to kill themselves. And that Saturday night at Greystone, Doheny shot and killed Plunkett, then put the gun to his head and pulled the trigger. But Doheny, Sr., when he saw the two men's bodies before the police arrived at Greystone, switched the gun to Plunkett's hand so that his son would appear to be a murder victim, not a suicide, and would receive a consecrated burial in the Roman Catholic church.

CHAPTER TWELVE

In 1931, Eric Lobban Cord, manufacturer of the luxurious Duesenberg and Cord automobiles, built a million-dollar mansion on his ten-acre North Hillcrest Road estate, above Sunset Boulevard in Beverly Hills. The thirty-room red brick mansion, designed by architect Paul R. Willams, was framed across its wide front by a neocolonial portico, and its thirty rooms were mahogany-paneled with white marble floors. Outside stood a spacious eighteen-car garage. But these luxuries were by now almost commonplace in Beverly Hills during the 1920s and 1930s. What really set Cord's estate apart from others were his chicken coops, constructed in the same style as the main house, with brick floors, wood paneling, and satin drapes. Raising chickens was one of Cord's passions, and his favorite birds reportedly ate and drank from gold dishes.

These chickens were living better than many Los Angelenos during the Depression, including the unemployed carpenters, masons, and plasterers that Cord had hired to build his house at a fraction of their usual wages. But these men accepted Cord's exploitative terms because they couldn't find work anywhere else. The volatile Los Angeles real-estate market had collapsed at the end of 1929. Consequently, construction of new houses and apartments declined from 15,234 units in 1929 to 11,257 in 1930 to 6,600 in 1931. Thousands of other men and women lost their jobs as oil production declined, factories shut down, and shops and small businesses closed their doors. Farmers couldn't sell their harvests, and some citrus exchanges actually dumped their

"No Help Wanted," MGM Studio.

Extras waiting for calls, circa 1920.

oranges in dry riverbeds and covered them with oil and tar to discourage the hungry from eating the unmarketable crops.

By the summer of 1934, more than a million and a quarter Californians were on relief, and 70 percent of these lived in the southern part of the state. Over 129,000 families received welfare in Los Angeles County alone that dismal summer. During the 1930s, more people in Southern California filed for bankruptcy, totaling more money, than in any other part of the nation.

As the financial crisis deepened, some of Los Angeles' biggest companies collapsed. Then came the shocking revelations that many of the city's most respected business leaders had been robbing their own firms for years. After the Richfield Oil Company declared bankruptcy in 1931, court-appointed trustees discovered that just the year before, executives had maintained a four-thousand-dollar-a-month hotel suite in downtown Los Angeles and had spent fifty thousand dollars a month on entertainment, even though the company had lost fifty-four million. For one party, Richfield executives chartered a yacht, and guests ate and danced their way to Catalina Island, twenty-seven miles offshore. While the ship was anchored off Catalina, an airplane flew overhead and dropped thousands of gardenias on guests below. And as if this weren't bad enough, the court learned that Richfield executives had charged their alimony payments, jewelry purchases, even speedboat repairs to the company up to the month of insolvency.

Richfield Oil was just the beginning of the scandals. Shortly thereafter, the Guaranty Building and Loan Association went into receivership. Its president had embezzled eight million dollars. Then the American Mortgage Company failed with losses of eighteen million. Next the Harold Ferguson Company went under, and its president served time at San Quentin Prison.

Unable to face financial ruin, hundreds of Los Angelenos shot themselves, took poison, or turned on the gas. Others chose more dramatic exits and jumped off Pasadena's Arroyo Secco Bridge. By the early 1930s, the death toll had reached seventy-nine, and the handsome high-arched structure became known as Suicide Bridge.

In the midst of all this social and political turmoil, many Southern Californians tried to ignore the Depression. Los Angeles Mayor John C.

Porter, attempting to put a brave face on the situation, declared that "it is not at all alarming," and an editorial in the Los Angeles *Times* insisted that "much of the Depression is psychological." But it was the motion picture industry that most carefully avoided mention of the Depression. Only a handful of Hollywood films in the 1930s ever treated the theme realistically, including director King Vidor's *Our Daily Bread* (1934), which he financed himself when the studios would not, and Charlie Chaplin's *Modern Times* (1936), a comedy that also explored subjects such as hunger, unemployment, and meaningless factory jobs.

At first, Hollywood had been Depression-proof, and studio profits and movie attendance totals were even higher in 1930 than in 1929, thanks to the introduction of the talkies with *The Jazz Singer* in 1927. Despite premium-price tickets, the public had flocked to talkies, any talkie, in the late 1920s. Every studio quickly changed to all-talking movies or slipped talking sequences into silent films that were already in production. Theaters switched over to talkies just as quickly. By the end of 1928, only 1,300 theaters out of the nation's 20,500 were wired for sound. Six months later, the number had risen to 9,000, including almost all the downtown houses and big neighborhood theaters.

The talkies, however, did not save Hollywood from the Depression for long. The novelty of the new technology soon wore off, particularly when millions of Americans were out of work, and studio profits and movie attendance figures declined in 1931, even though most studios and theaters still made money. But the next year, the studios and exhibition companies lost over eighty-five million dollars, and the figures were even worse in 1933. Four of Hollywood's eight largest studios—Paramount, RKO, Universal, and Fox—were in serious trouble. Almost one third of the nation's theaters closed in 1932 and 1933, despite promotions such as double features at a regular price or two-for-one tickets.

In a desperate attempt to lure the hard-pressed public into half-empty theaters, Hollywood studios made escapist films: crime-doesn't-pay gangster movies like *Little Caesar* (1930) and *The Public Enemy* (1931), stories about prostitutes and kept women like *Blonde Venus* (1932) and *Red Dust* (1932), lavish musicals like *42nd Street* (1933) and

Mary Pickford in Coquette *(1929), her first "talkie" and one of her last pictures.*

the Golddiggers series, and quick-paced, irreverent "screwball comedies" like *Bombshell* (1933).

Because movies like these took people's minds off their troubles, theater attendance figures rose in 1934. The studios showed modest profits that year, and most closed theaters reopened. The recovery of the motion picture industry had a kind of multiplier-effect for the rest of Los Angeles. The amount of new housing slowly increased; oil discoveries and the opening of automobile assembly and aircraft plants provided new jobs. Los Angelenos could also look to a proud future with the staging of the Tenth Olympics at Exposition Park in 1932, the completion of Griffith Planetarium in 1933, and the construction of the massive part-Moderne, part-Spanish Union Passenger Terminal, over the five years between 1934 and 1939. By the late 1930s, Los Angeles had escaped the worse effects of the Depression, a year or two ahead of most American cities.

Although Hollywood survived the transition to the talkies and the upheaval of the Depression, many silent stars did not. Nor did dream palaces or the notion that a star must live like a star come through those years unscathed. The Depression had taken away much of the money and optimism that had gone into the dream-palace building of the 1920s, and the new stars of the 1930s—Ronald Colman, Gary Cooper, Joan Crawford, Bette Davis, Cary Grant, Jean Harlow, Katharine Hepburn, William Powell, and James Stewart—did not feel compelled to build extravagant stage sets for their private lives, because they had more down-to-earth, more relaxed images than a haughty Swanson or an ever-so-romantic Valentino.

Besides, what 1930s star would want to invest all his money in a dream palace after seeing what had happened to Rudolph Valentino and his Falcon Lair? Valentino was virtually broke when he died of peritonitis in New York City on August 26, 1926. He had run through every penny of the million dollars he had earned the year before his death—and then some. To pay off the estate's debts, George Ullman, Valentino's manager and executor, decided to auction off Falcon Lair and all Valentino's possessions. Falcon Lair was worth $140,000 to $175,000, according to Ullman's estimate, and the cars, horses, furniture, antiques, and jewelry would bring, he expected, another $500,000. Not so. At a highly publicized six-day auction, Valentino's personal effects fetched less than a hundred thousand dollars, and no one bought Falcon Lair.

Even in death, however, Valentino's overzealous fans did not desert him. George Ullman had to hire guards for Falcon Lair, or else morbid souvenir-seekers would have taken the unoccupied house and grounds apart piece by piece. Even so, many guards saw that they could make a quick buck from the faithful standing at Falcon Lair's closed gates, and sold them silverware, candles, even articles of clothing guaranteed to have come from the now empty house. The favorite relics were feathers from Valentino's pillow. As if all this weren't humiliating enough, Juan Romero, an architect, bought Falcon Lair in 1934 for only eighteen thousand dollars, a pittance compared to the hundreds of thousands of dollars Valentino had lavished on the estate.

Rather than spend themselves deeply into debt and also risk the ire of Depression-weary moviegoers, most 1930s actors and actresses built large, but not too large, mansions, similar to the homes that stars and studio chiefs had occupied in the late teens before building their dream palaces in the 1920s. Architectural styles and interior decoration also became simpler, less flamboyant in the movie colony during the 1930s. The once voguish stucco-walled, red-tile-roofed Spanish-style haciendas began to lose popularity, and the eclectic mixing of several styles on one house or in one room was definitely unfashionable in cultivated Hollywood circles. Now stars and studio executives selected the more traditional neocolonial, Tudor, and Georgian architectural styles. In interior decoration, eighteenth-century English and French furniture, or reasonable facsimiles in most instances, were all the rage.

Joan Crawford was one of the first stars to sense the trend toward more conventional architecture and interior design. Shortly before her divorce from Douglas Fairbanks, Jr., in 1933, she asked William Haines to redecorate her Brentwood home. A matinee idol and a friend of Joan Crawford's from MGM, Haines became an interior decorator after his star waned in the early 1930s. Some said that he was a casualty of the talkies; others said Haines was getting too old to play boyish leads. Still others whispered about a reputed conversation between Haines and Louis B. Mayer. Too many people, Mayer told Haines, were talking about his boyfriend. The other man would have to go or the gossip would destroy his career. Haines refused to comply with Mayer's wishes. When Mayer insisted, Haines replied, "Mr. Mayer, what would you do if I told you to get rid of Mrs. Mayer?"

After agreeing to redecorate Joan Crawford's home, Haines promptly got rid of the kitschy 1920s furniture that she had bought in the first flush of her stardom several years earlier. Afterward, the drawing room—that's what Joan insisted on calling the living room—was painted white with Wedgwood-blue trim, and it was furnished in modern sofas and English antiques. A new wing was added for the dining-room, butler's pantry, and kitchen. The former dining room became the music room, where Joan occasionally played records of her singing opera to tensely smiling guests.

Joan Crawford even gave away her two thousand dolls to local hospitals. But she missed her surrogate children. Several years later, she adopted Christina, the first of the four children she raised behind the masonry wall encircling her home at 426 North Bristol Circle. Today her former Brentwood mansion is known as the "Mommie Dearest House."

Joan Crawford loved her big, fashionably decorated home and all the other perquisites of stardom in the 1930s. When some fans began to complain about Hollywood's lavish salaries in the midst of a Depression, she told the press that she ran her home on a budget and with only three servants. Not stopping there, Crawford was one of the few stars to defend publicly her generous life-style. In a statement in *Photoplay* titled "Spend!" she insisted that high salaries were essential for the movie industry and for America. The stars' fine homes, clothes, cars, and parties, she said, pleased the fans and stimulated the economy. "I, Joan Crawford, I believe in the dollar," she proclaimed. "Everything I earn, I spend!"

Other stars and studio executives did not let the Depression prevent them from enjoying their lucre either. Ronald Colman had lived in a secluded Spanish-style home on Mound Street in the Hollywood Hills since the mid-1920s, because he didn't want to borrow from his studio in order to buy something larger. But in the mid-1930s, Colman felt financially secure enough to buy silent star Corinne Griffith's ivy-

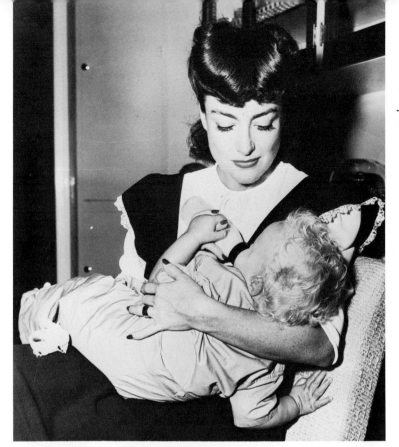

A determined-looking Joan Crawford takes on the role of mother.

Joan Crawford and her adopted daughter, Christina, later author of Mommie Dearest.

Romantic leading man
Ramon Novarro, who
starred in the 1925
Ben-Hur, *stands
outside his avowedly
Moderne-style home at
5609 Valley Oak
Drive in the Holly-
wood Hills.*

INSET: *Ramon
Novarro at home.*

covered Tudor-style mansion at 1033 Summit Drive, down the road from Pickfair. Standing at the end of a long driveway, the house had half-timbered walls, mullioned windows, and a sloping slate roof. What could be more appropriate for the leader of Hollywood's substantial British contingent? Colman accentuated the illusion of Olde England by ripping out the Southern California bougainvilleas and oleanders and planting formally trimmed yew hedges. Then he purchased Chippendale and Sheraton furniture and hung eighteenth- and nineteenth-century British paintings on the walls.

At first, Colman lived in this house by himself. His first marriage had ended unpleasantly, and he wasn't ready for another romance just yet. But events overtook him. In the late 1930s, he started seeing actress Benita Hume, who coincidentally lived in a little Spanish house behind his own. Colman installed a big oak door in the wall between the two properties so that they could discreetly visit back and forth. In 1938, Benita became the second Mrs. Colman, and she moved up the hill and into the big house.

The glove-dealer-turned-movie-mogul, Sam Goldwyn, also moved up the hill, metaphorically speaking, from a 1920s Spanish-style mansion on slowly decaying Hollywood Boulevard to a Colonial house at 1200 Laurel Way in Beverly Hills. According to Hollywood tradition, he asked a real-estate broker to find several secluded acres in Beverly Hills in 1932. The agent just happened to know of such a parcel in the still largely empty hills above Sunset Boulevard, and he and Goldwyn drove up the narrow dirt roads to a knoll overlooking Coldwater Canyon. The five-acre lot cost five thousand dollars. Goldwyn liked the property immediately, agreed to pay the asking price, and then decided to buy the adjacent lot as well. After signing the deal that afternoon, Goldwyn headed back home to tell his wife Frances what he had just done. He walked in the front door and shouted, "Get in the car. I have a surprise for you!"

"What kind of surprise?" Frances Goldwyn asked.

"I bought a lot," he replied. "Come, drive me there. I'll show it to you."

The Goldwyns drove off in her roadster, but finding the property again wasn't so easy: One twisting dirt road above Sunset Boulevard

The Sam and Frances Goldwyn residence, Beverly Hills.

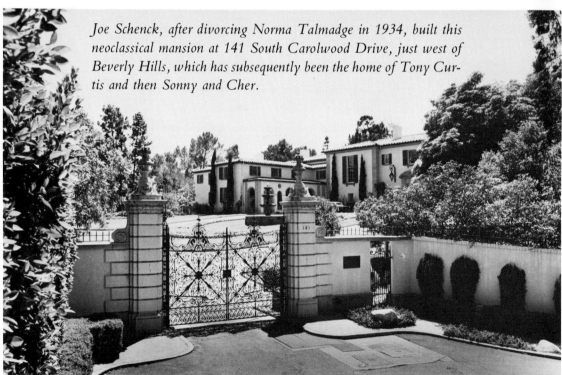

Joe Schenck, after divorcing Norma Talmadge in 1934, built this neoclassical mansion at 141 South Carolwood Drive, just west of Beverly Hills, which has subsequently been the home of Tony Curtis and then Sonny and Cher.

looked like any other to the couple, and the Goldwyns spent several hours searching for their new homesite before they gave up and called the realtor for help.

Building the new house proved just as difficult. Sam and Frances Goldwyn argued over architect Douglas Honnold's plans, particularly about the location of the screening room. He wanted to show his pictures in the living room, but she planned to hang their Renoirs, Picasso, and Matisse on the walls and didn't want any movie projector peepholes in the room. After one argument too many, Sam Goldwyn told Frances that he didn't want to be bothered with the house any longer. He'd give her the money, and she could do as she pleased.

How times had changed. Even busy producers like Thomas Ince and Mack Sennett had found the time to plan their dream palaces. But Frances Goldwyn was delighted to be put in charge, and she completed the two-story, six thousand-square-foot, neoclassical-style house for a thrifty twenty-eight thousand dollars. The tennis court cost another five thousand, because it had to be cantilevered over a hillside.

Sam Goldwyn had reportedly forgotten about the new house during the year of construction until one evening Frances picked him up at the studio in their limousine. After they had gone some distance, he realized that the car wasn't following the usual route home.

"Where're you going? Where's he going?" Goldwyn shouted.

"Take it easy, Sam. It's all right," Frances replied.

"I don't want to go for any joyrides tonight," he groaned "I'm tired. I want to go home."

Frances Goldwyn took her husband's hand, looked into his eyes, and said, "That's exactly where we are going, Sam. Home." The new house was finished.

Earlier that day, the movers had carried all their furniture and clothing from the Hollywood Boulevard mansion to Laurel Lane. When the Goldwyns arrived that evening, everything was in place. The maid opened the front door and curtsied. Goldwyn shook her hand rather formally and walked in. The living room was furnished in antiques, and the Renoirs, Picasso, and Matisse hung on the walls. The formal dining room was large enough to seat twenty-four, and that night the table was laid with their best china, crystal, and silver.

Promotion still for Pacific Palisades, 1927, adjacent to the Will Rogers ranch.

Promotion still for Brentwood's stylish Riviera tract, 1929.

Sam didn't say a word as he inspected all the downstairs rooms, including his wood-paneled den that doubled as a screening room. So far, so good, thought Frances. Then he headed up the winding staircase to the second floor and started prowling through the his and hers master bedrooms, the bedroom for son Sam, Jr., and the several guest rooms. Frances Goldwyn stood downstairs, waiting for the verdict. Suddenly she heard Sam shout, "Frances!" from the upstairs landing.

"Something wrong, Sam?" she asked.

"Yes," he answered. "There's no soap in my soap dish!"

By the late 1930s and 1940s, some movie stars and studio executives no longer wanted to build their large traditional-looking homes in Beverly Hills. They wanted to escape the movie colony rat race and the megaphone-equipped open tour buses and left Beverly Hills altogether. Many moved to Bel Air, located in the hills above Sunset Boulevard about a mile west of Beverly Hills, and found privacy behind the hedges and walls of the several-acre estates scattered along that community's winding roads.

Bel Air had changed considerably since oil millionaire Alfonzo Bell opened the neighborhood to development in 1922 and laid down his tacit no-movie-people edict. Selling land to these *nouveaux riches*, Bell feared, would ruin his plan to make Bel Air "the crowning achievement of suburban development." With architect Mark Daniel's help, he carved roads out of the hillsides and installed underground water, sewage, and electric lines. Then Bell planted thousands of shrubs and trees, quietly buying castoffs from the Beverly Hills Nursery whenever he could.

This was Bell's only economy. He divided the first two hundred-acre tract, just west of Beverly Glen and above Sunset Boulevard, into several-acre parcels, nothing smaller, and he encouraged buyers to purchase even larger five- and ten-acre lots. He laid out polo fields, tennis courts, and an eighteen-hole golf course, which became the Bel Air Country Club. In order to attract the horsey set, Bell built the Bel Air Stables on Stone Canyon Road and prepared sixty-five miles of bridle paths through the hills.

As one last splendid gesture, Bell erected a large, handsome gate at the Bel Air Road–Sunset Boulevard entrance to the community, just as rich men installed gates at the head of driveways to their estates. Uniformed guards checked cars in and out of the neighborhood here, and a private police force patrolled the streets and escorted visitors from the gates up the sometimes confusing roads to their destination. The Bel Air gate and the private patrol service were arrogant and elitist, and the rich residents loved it. Only the grandest dream palaces like Harold Lloyd's Greenacres and the Doheny family's Greystone would ever have such features.

Alfonzo Bell's no-movie-people rule worked just fine in the prosperous 1920s but proved disastrous during the Depression. So few businessmen wanted to buy land and build mansions that Bel Air almost went bankrupt. The private guards at the gate disappeared in an economy move. Bell couldn't afford to be so selective anymore, and his real-estate agents discreetly welcomed inquiries from film stars and studio executives. They were some of the only people in Los Angeles who could afford—and would pay—Bel Air prices.

Mary Duncan, a Broadway actress turned film performer, reportedly was the first movie person to get in. Then Colleen Moore, who had portrayed flappers in the 1920s, bought an estate on St. Pierre Road. In 1935, Warner Baxter, who played the popular Cisco Kid roles and got the starring part of Julian Marsh in *42nd Street* (1933), built a Gothic-style stone mansion on a five-acre estate at 688 Nimes Road.

These stars were the advance guard. By 1940 movie people were swarming into Bel Air, including seventeen-year-old Judy Garland, fresh from appearing opposite Mickey Rooney in a 1938 Andy Hardy Family film and from portraying Dorothy in *The Wizard of Oz* (1939). She built a ten-room Tudor-style house for herself and her mother, Ethel, at 1231 Stone Canyon Road, just up the street from the Bel Air Stables, which became the nucleus for the Bel Air Hotel.

The Stone Canyon Road house had everything a teenage girl could want: a tennis court, a badminton court, pinball machines, even a suite for Judy on the top floor, with its own separate entrance. Her bedroom also had a secret hideaway concealed behind a built-in bookcase that moved aside with the push of a button. For all its special features, though, Judy Garland never liked this house. Even though she had paid

Clark Gable and Carole Lombard at their San Fernando Valley ranch, where Clark occasionally milked a cow and Carole collected eggs in the henhouse for the benefit of reporters.

Clark Gable "working" at his San Fernando Valley ranch.

for its construction, she referred to the house as her mother's, because, she claimed, that's whom she really built it for.

During the 1930s and 1940s, top movie people also settled west of Bel Air, in Brentwood and Pacific Palisades, but these communities, lovely though they were, were a long drive every day to studios in Hollywood or the San Fernando Valley, which lay on the other side of the Santa Monica Mountains from Los Angeles and its rapidly developing coastal plain. So some movie people, quite logically, moved to the San Fernando Valley for the sake of convenience.

In 1939, Bette Davis bought a charming two-story red brick Tudor-style house behind a wall in the town of Glendale. During her previous ten years in Los Angeles, she had lived in twenty-five different places, ranging from modest apartments in Hollywood to Greta Garbo's Brentwood estate on San Vicente Boulevard. Now Bette Davis wanted to settle down, and she liked her new home—she modestly called it an "English farmhouse"—because it was only a five-minute drive from the Warner Brothers Studio and so allowed her an extra hour of sleep in the morning.

By the late 1930s, towns like Glendale, Burbank, and North Hollywood in the eastern end of the San Fernando Valley, which was geographically closest to Los Angeles, had become part of an expanding suburb. This part of the valley's population doubled from 54,217 residents in 1930 to 112,001 in 1940. But Sherman Oaks, Encino, and Tarzana in the western portion of the valley, farther away from Los Angeles, remained orange groves, barley fields, and poultry ranches until the post–World War II boom. Here was just the place for those stars and studio executives who wanted to avoid chic Beverly Hills and Bel Air and to enjoy unspoiled country living.

After Clark Gable and Carole Lombard were married on March 29, 1939, they moved to a thirty-acre ranch in Encino. Two of Hollywood's most popular stars, they could have settled in Beverly Hills and easily turned their home into that generation's Pickfair. But Gable and Lombard, unlike Douglas Fairbanks and Mary Pickford, did not want to live in the spotlight all the time.

Standing in the middle of a citrus grove, their nine-room white brick and frame neocolonial home was the opposite of the lordly Pickfair in location, architectural style, and interior decoration. The living room had canary yellow wall-to-wall carpeting, and the furniture was Early American and oversized for Clark's comfort. One room was set aside for his growing collection of firearms. About the only decorative concession to Carole Lombard's femininity was her bathroom, with its mirrored walls and ceiling. This bathroom was such a surprise, following room after room of the masculine Early American look, that Clark Gable saved it for last when he showed friends through the house. Evidently, however, the Gables did not want their company to stay too long, because the house didn't include any guest rooms.

Clark Gable and Carole Lombard enjoyed their casual home and the acres of alfalfa and citrus groves, the horses, the cow barn, even the pigsty with no pigs. But they were Hollywood stars, too, and knew how to make use of their ranch as a stage show for country living. During some interviews, Clark went to the barn with the reporter and milked a cow. Carole often took important guests from the studio into the hen house to gather eggs. And for a while she even thought about getting more chickens and selling "The King's Eggs."

CHAPTER THIRTEEN

Now that some top-rank actors and actresses lived on ranches in the San Fernando Valley, even raised cows and chickens, the veteran, sometimes fading stars of the 1920s felt increasingly estranged from the movie colony. The change was too dramatic for Gloria Swanson, who had virtually invented the glamorous star life-style before her career declined in the early 1930s. She held a farewell-to-Hollywood party in her North Crescent Drive mansion in 1936, and thereafter closed the house and moved to New York. But most former stars did not want to leave their friends or the scenes of their earlier triumphs, and they retreated into their mansions and their memories.

By the mid-1930s, John Gilbert's Tower Grove Road estate had become a "somber place," according to David Niven, who occasionally played tennis with the ex-MGM romantic lead. The mood inside Gilbert's Spanish-style mansion was no cheerier. "The decor," according to Niven, "was heavy, and the gloom of the place was intensified by curtains permanently drawn against the light."

John Gilbert's career was one of the most tragic casualties of the transition from silents to talkies. With his jet-black hair, flashing dark eyes, and gleaming white teeth, he was known as "screenland's perfect lover" just ten years earlier, starring in classics like *The Merry Widow* (1925) with Mae Murray, *La Bohème* (1926) with Lillian Gish, and *Flesh and the Devil* (1927) with Greta Garbo. By 1927 and 1928, Gilbert was earning ten thousand a week from MGM, and he bought his stylish

Tall, dark, and handsome—yet tragically doomed—John Gilbert in the garden of his Beverly Hills home.

Tower Grove Road estate just up the hill from John Barrymore's Belle Vista.

Except for the money and the attention, Gilbert hated being a movie star, or so he said. What he really wanted to do was to direct pictures, but MGM wouldn't give him the chance, because he was more valuable to the studio in front of the cameras. Gilbert had endured a series of failed marriages, and a much-publicized and heartbreaking romance with Greta Garbo. Often depressed and moody even at the height of his fame, Gilbert found solace in the bottle, and one morning at three a.m. he showed up at the Beverly Hills police station and asked to be thrown into jail for drunkenness. He was.

Soon John Gilbert faced more serious problems than just his love life and his love of alcohol. During his European honeymoon with actress Ina Claire, wife number three, the stock market crashed, and he lost most of his money. But he had a lucrative contract with MGM to fall back on, and his latest film—and first talkie—*His Glorious Night* was just about to be released.

The film opened in New York the same day that Gilbert's ship docked, and he sneaked into the theater to see what the audience thought of the film. It wasn't good. On the movie soundtrack, his voice sounded high-pitched and tinny, not at all what the audience had expected from Valentino's successor, and when Gilbert whispered, "I love you! I love you! I love you!" to his leading lady, Catharine Dale Owen, the audience snickered and broke into howls of laughter. Gilbert crept out of the theater, and some critics labeled *His Glorious Night* "not a talkie but a shriekie."

John Gilbert's voice was quite normal in his few subsequent films, including *Queen Christina* (1934), where he starred opposite Greta Garbo. She had insisted that Gilbert be awarded the part of Don Antonio in hopes that he could make his comeback, but it didn't work. But what *had* happened with the sound in *His Glorious Night* several years earlier? Some faulted the primitive recording equipment. Others believe that MGM executives purposely tampered with the soundtrack to destroy the high-paid star they no longer wanted.

One thing is certain: John Gilbert never recovered from the blow to his pride when his career collapsed. Always a heavy drinker, he sealed himself up in his Tower Grove Road mansion for week-long binges. One afternoon in 1932 he called the Beverly Hills police and reported that a burglar was trying to break into the house. A squad car raced up the hill only to find that the culprit was a woodpecker enthusiastically at work.

Before Gilbert died of a heart attack at his Tower Grove Road home in 1936 at the age of forty-one, his alcoholic-induced delusions grew worse, and he started to believe that people were plotting against him. One night he saw a strange car parked on the road near his house, and he fired a round of shots at the suspicious vehicle. The occupants of the car, it turned out, were a young man and woman who thought they had found a safe place to neck on the quiet, deserted road. Gilbert spent several thousand dollars to repair the car and to soothe their shattered nerves.

Life was not much happier down the hill at John Barrymore's Belle Vista. Although he appeared in *Grand Hotel* (1932) with Greta Garbo, *A Bill of Divorcement* (1932), with Katharine Hepburn, *Twentieth Century* (1934) with Carole Lombard, his career was declining and his drinking was increasing. And he had started to emotionally abuse his wife, Dolores Costello, and to even occasionally beat her. As Barrymore once remarked, Dolores was "too beautiful for words . . . but not for arguments." At the same time, he was incredibly possessive of Dolores, and he installed iron bars over all the windows of the Marriage House, lest any other man try to sneak in and molest her. Their seven-year marriage ended in divorce on October 9, 1935.

By then, Belle Vista had only a shadow of its former elegance and whimsy. As the gardening staff dwindled, the grounds became overgrown, and the half-dozen reflecting pools and the several fish ponds were empty. From the outside, the Marriage House looked the same as in the 1920s, but inside it was virtually empty after Dolores removed her things and Barrymore's business manager, Harry Hotchener, put the rest of the furniture in storage. As Elaine Barrie, the fourth Mrs. Barrymore, later remembered: "Fixtures had been stripped from the walls, loose wires were all over the place, furniture dragged across the floor already bare of rugs, walls denuded of pictures and hangings. . . . A Meissen chandelier . . . still hung in the empty dining room,

RIGHT: *John Barrymore at Belle Vista, circa 1940.*

BELOW: *John Barrymore, broke and in failing health, at his slowly decaying Belle Vista estate, circa 1940.*

because . . . it had evidently been impossible to remove without destroying it."

By the late 1930s, Barrymore could have used some of the money he had spent improving Belle Vista. Since 1920 he had earned over three million dollars from his acting and movie career, but he was broke and in debt by 1937, and falling deeper into debt every month. Because of his drinking, Barrymore's health and even his memory were beginning to fail him, and his income had precipitously dropped off from the several hundred thousand dollars per year he had earned in the late 1920s and early 1930s. But Barrymore didn't scale down his living expenses accordingly, not with his alimony, child support, and the upkeep, by then, of two houses and his yacht, *The Infanta*. Then the Internal Revenue Service began to harass him for back taxes and ordered him to auction off *The Infanta*. Barrymore also starting selling his prized antiques and art treasures for a fraction of what he had paid for them.

In 1937, John Barrymore declared bankruptcy and Belle Vista was put up for auction. By then he referred to the house on which he had lavished so much attention and so much of his fortune as "that Chinese tenement" and "a kind of nightmare." But eccentric dream palaces were by then hopelessly impractical, and nobody bought Belle Vista, the estate that had cost him an estimated $448,000 over the years, not counting the hundreds of thousands spent on furnishings.

As Barrymore's drinking increased, his behavior became more and more erratic. One visit to Errol Flynn was described by that actor as "the most frightening three weeks I had since I was in the New Guinea jungle." Late one night he awoke to hear Barrymore screaming: "Let me out, you bastard, let me out! Flynn, you traitor, let me out of here!"

Running down the hall and into the guest room, Flynn discovered that Barrymore had gotten out of bed to go to the bathroom but was so drunk that he had walked into the closet instead. By the time Flynn reached the room, Barrymore was pounding on the closet walls, shouting: "Bats! Your house is full of bats!" While wandering around the closet looking for the toilet, he had backed into some coat hangers and felt a ticklish "batlike" sensation on the neck. None of this would have happened if Barrymore had followed his usual practice of urinating out the bedroom window.

Sometimes Barrymore's alcohol-induced confusion was quite amusing—as when, shortly after the bombing of Pearl Harbor, he offered his hilltop Belle Vista estate to the Army as a place to install antiaircraft guns to protect Beverly Hills from enemy attack. But Barrymore's decline was truly heartbreaking. By 1942 the career of this once great Shakespearean actor and movie star was all but over, and he had been reduced to being the butt of jokes on Rudy Vallee's radio program. Barrymore "took years dying, stalling his exit," according to Errol Flynn, and he suffered his final collapse on May 19, 1942, just before going on the radio. He died on May 29 at the age of sixty. His physician, Dr. Hugo M. Kersten, blamed his death on myocarditis, an inflammation of the heart muscle, but listed chronic nephritis, cirrhosis of the liver, and a gastric ulcer as contributing factors.

Unlike other silent stars, Mary Pickford did not allow her home to become run-down or to look out of date. In early 1932, just in time for all the entertaining that accompanied Los Angeles' hosting of the Tenth Olympics, society decorator Elsie de Wolfe completed the transformation of Pickfair to the eighteenth-century French mode that Doug and Mary had begun in the mid-1920s. The original 1919 country-gentleman motif was now gone.

Mary Pickford kept up a happy public front in the early 1930s, but these years were difficult for her. Having reigned as America's Sweetheart for twenty-five years, her career was in serious trouble. After she played a fifteen-year-old girl in *Sparrows* (1926), she started to play more mature roles in her films, and even cut off her eighteen nearly waist-length curls on June 21, 1928. Sporting a stylish short bob, Mary Pickford now looked like the beautiful thirty-five-year-old woman she really was, but Doug didn't approve of the change in her appearance. Nor did her fans: They stayed away from her grown-up sound pictures like *Coquette* (1929), *The Taming of the Shrew* (1929), which was her only film with Doug, *Kiki* (1931), and *Secrets* (1933). Even though Mary turned forty in 1933, her fans felt that she had deserted them by giving up Little Mary. They didn't want to see her any other way. If

Mary's fans allowed her to age, they would have to admit to themselves that they, too, were getting older.

After these four sound pictures, Mary Pickford retired from the screen in 1933. "I knew it was time," she later recalled. "I left the screen because I didn't want what happened to Chaplin to happen to me. When he discarded the little tramp, the little tramp turned around and killed him. The little girl made me. I wasn't waiting for the little girl to kill me. I'd already been pigeonholed."

During these difficult professional years, Mary Pickford's personal life was just as vexed. Her beloved mother, Charlotte, died on March 21, 1928. Her thrice-married, scandal-plagued brother, Jack, died on January 3, 1933, at the age of thirty-six, as did her four-times-married sister, Lottie, on December 9, 1936, at forty-two. Mary even lost Doug to other women. After over a decade by her side, he had begun to chase younger women and to travel for months at a time. He made films like *Around the World in 80 Minutes* (1931) and *Mr. Robinson Crusoe* (1932) just to travel for location shooting. Douglas Fairbanks may have been unhappy with Mary, but he was also definitely anxious about middle age. After all, he did turn fifty in 1933.

With Doug away more and more, Mary Pickford stayed closer than ever to Pickfair. Although she had several close friends, she craved the deeper affection and understanding that her mother and Doug had once provided. Not surprisingly, she fell in love with Charles "Buddy" Rogers, a handsome actor eleven years her junior, with brown eyes and curly black hair, who had been her leading man in *My Best Girl* (1927).

Mary Pickford also started drinking heavily in the early 1930s. This wasn't her first experience with liquor. Even when Doug refused to stock alcoholic beverages at Pickfair in the early 1920s, Mary had found ways to bring it in. She would have a tumbler or two with her mother, who loved to drink, as did brother Jack and sister Lottie. When Mary smuggled liquor into Pickfair, she didn't limit her private stash to the cheap brands that Doug insisted on serving their exalted guests after he relaxed his no-liquor rule in 1923 and 1924. According to actress May McAvoy: "After dinner, the men would go off by themselves—I thought it was rude and crude—and Mary would take us up to her room. She'd go into the bathroom and take a big slug of something, then rinse her mouth out with mouthwash."

Jack Pickford supplied Mary with all the hard liquor she wanted. One day he and director Eddie Sutherland were drinking, and they ran out. It was Prohibition, so they couldn't simply run out to the local liquor store and buy some more. But "Jack said not to worry, and we drove over to Pickfair," Sutherland recalled years later. "Mary wasn't home, and Jack went right on in the front door, didn't even knock, and we went straight up to her room and into her bathroom. 'Gin or whiskey?' he asked. 'The hydrogen peroxide bottle's gin, the Listerine bottle's scotch.' We sat down in the bathroom, Jack on the tub, me on the commode, and finished off both bottles. I was worried about Mary. I know what it's like to go looking for a drink and not find it. But Jack said it was okay, there was plenty more where that came from."

Douglas Fairbanks didn't try to stop Mary from drinking in the early 1930s, because he was away from home so often to make his movies and to see Sylvia Hawkes Ashley in London. Daughter of a livery-stable employee, an ex-chorus girl, and the estranged wife of Lord Ashley, Sylvia—Lady Ashley—was blond, beautiful, and twenty-one years younger than Doug. Shortly after Mary learned about the affair, she filed for divorce in December 1933.

By then Mary Pickford was seeing Buddy Rogers regularly, but she still went out with other men, including Leslie Howard, who appeared opposite her in *Secrets* (1933). According to her niece, Gwynne Pickford Ornstein, Mary had another special admirer, too. One Thursday night in 1934, the telephone rang at Pickfair, and it was Clark Gable, who had just won an Oscar for *It Happened One Night.*

"It's Thursday night, right?" he asked Mary. "The servants are out."

"Yes," she replied.

"I'll be right over," he said.

"No you won't," Mary answered. "I won't open the door if you do come."

Gable was a persistent suitor, and he called the next few Thursday nights in a row before giving up. Mary Pickford never forgot this.

Mary Pickford and her brother, Jack, practicing his lines for Garrison's Finish *(1923) on the diving board over the Pickfair swimming pool. Jack Pickford was better at drinking than at acting, and he smuggled booze into Pickfair for Mary in the 1920s, against Douglas Fairbanks' wishes.*

Many years later, she'd say, "Here it is Thursday night and still no Gable. You mean I actually turned Clark Gable down?"

Douglas Fairbanks and Mary Pickford attempted several reconciliations before their divorce became final in January 1936. She received Pickfair in the settlement, and he kept the Santa Monica beach house. On March 7, 1936, Doug married Sylvia Ashley in Paris, and they stayed at the beach house whenever they visited Los Angeles. With the outbreak of the Second World War in Europe in 1939, Doug and Sylvia returned to California, and he died of a heart attack at the beach house on December 12, 1939, at the age of fifty-six. Sylvia Ashley later became the fourth Mrs. Clark Gable.

Buddy Rogers and Mary Pickford were married on June 26, 1937. "I have never been so happy. I never expect to be so happy again," said Mary at the wedding. By then Pickfair was beginning to look a little dated, despite the redecoration five years earlier, and it was filled with memories of Douglas Fairbanks, Sr. So Buddy and Mary started thinking about building another home, perhaps in Bel Air. Their new house, Buddy Rogers told the New York *American*, would not be as "pretentious as Pickfair. Mercy no; only four master bedrooms, and of course tennis courts, swimming pool, and things like that."

Buddy Rogers and Mary Pickford decided to stay at Pickfair, but the estate never regained the glamour and excitement of the Doug days. And Mary Pickford knew that she had become a famous has-been when stars and studio chiefs began to turn down her dinner invitations in the 1930s and 1940s. Katharine Hepburn was one, although she remembered her manners and always sent Mary a note saying, "I never go out to dine." One Sunday morning, Katharine Hepburn's doorbell rang, and she found Mary Pickford on the front steps. After exchanging pleasantries, Mary asked, "Won't you come up?" Katharine Hepburn could hardly say no to this plaintive invitation, and that evening she went to Pickfair for dinner and a movie, the same routine that Mary had followed for the last twenty years! David Niven was another visitor to Pickfair in these years, and he remembers the once famous home as "a sad, overfurnished, and melancholy place of memories and closed doors."

Although the new stars of the 1930s lived in solid, sensibly sized

Mary Pickford's comfortable world was crumbling by 1930. Her mother, Charlotte, had died in 1928. Doug was running around with other women. And her career was on the skids.

Douglas Fairbanks, Sr., still the athlete at age fifty-six, with his new wife, Sylvia Ashley, in 1939, less than a year before his death.

mansions, the dream-palace ideal was not dead—at least not yet. Just as it had been an oil millionaire, Edward Laurence Doheny, Sr., who built the ultimate 1920s dream palace, the four-million-dollar Greystone, now, ten years later, another rich Los Angeleno outside the movie colony built that decade's most extravagant palace.

Hilda Olsen Boldt Weber, mistress of the sumptuous home at 10644 Bellagio Road in Bel Air built in 1937–1938, was a Cinderella-like figure. A large, plain-looking woman, Hilda did not have Cinderella's beauty, but her warmth and kindness won her a Prince Charming nonetheless. Hilda Olsen had been a hospital nurse in New York City in 1920 when she met Charles Boldt, a multimillionaire Cincinnati glass manufacturer, who was a cardiac patient. Boldt was thirty years older than Hilda Olsen, and his wife had just died. He fell in love with Hilda, married her shortly after he was discharged from the hospital, and they returned to Cincinnati to live. Like many East Coast and Midwestern businessmen, Boldt also owned a home in Los Angeles, and as his health deteriorated, he and Hilda spent more and more of their time at his Benedict Canyon estate. Just before the Depression, Boldt made a business trip to New York, against his doctor's orders, and he suffered a fatal heart attack at the Plaza Hotel. Hilda Olsen Boldt inherited his fortune.

A year later, she married her chauffeur, Otto Weber, and then decided to crash Southern California society. She bought a one-and-a-half-million-dollar estate up the coast in exclusive Santa Barbara, but the local society ladies would have nothing to do with her. She was common-born. She had married her chauffeur with unseemly haste. And she didn't know how to handle her servants. Hilda opened her own front door on many occasions, even permitted the servants to address her by her first name in front of guests.

After a year in Santa Barbara, Hilda Weber knew she wasn't getting anywhere, sold the estate, and returned to Beverly Hills, where money and power mattered more than background. But she grew unhappy with the estate at 1500 Benedict Canyon Drive. The house was too small—only twenty rooms—and its heavy, 1920s Tudor style looked old-fashioned by the lighter, more classically inspired standards of the 1930s.

So on March 22, 1934, Hilda Weber bought one of the finest sites in Bel Air: a ten-acre hillock at 10644 Bellagio Road which rose one hundred feet above the flat land of the Bel Air Country Club and was almost totally surrounded by the golf course. In 1936 she hired architect James Dolena to design a house, and a team of gardeners began landscaping the property. Hilda Weber laid a cornerstone on May 15, 1937. How many houses are grand enough to merit a cornerstone?

At a cost of two and a half million dollars for construction and furniture, Hilda Weber now owned one of Los Angeles' largest, most comfortable, and most attractive homes. Designed in a 1930s Moderne-influenced Georgian style, it stood at the end of a curving driveway with a neoclassical portico over the main entrance. The house had forty rooms—actually sixty if you counted the servants' wing and basement rooms. The first floor included a large, high-ceilinged living room, a drawing room, a dining room that sat fourteen guests, a library, and long sweeping galleries. Every room was paneled in rare woods.

On the second floor were Hilda's bedroom—its walls were upholstered in yellow silk—and husband Otto's bedroom, which were connected by a sitting room, and a "lady's guest bedroom" and a "man's guest bedroom," also connected by a sitting room, plus a breakfast room, a small kitchen, a massage room, and an ironing room. Because of the house's H-shape and its location on top of a small hill, each room on the first and second floors had a view of the gardens, the city, and the Pacific Ocean.

Unlike the dream palaces of the 1920s, which were filled with over-priced department-store reproductions, Hilda Weber's house was furnished elegantly and to order.

Just inside the front door, she placed fourteenth-century bronze Indian figures of the god Siva and the goddess Devi on a table at the foot of the oval staircase. All the first-floor furniture was custom-made in English sycamore, black walnut, acacia, and madrone burl. Hilda filled the floor-to-ceiling library shelves with beautifully bound sets of the classics, and she collected dozens of antique clocks and centuries-old Chinese porcelain and vases. She paid twenty-five thousand dollars for a lace tablecloth. Her eighteen-karat-gold-trimmed tea set had been made for the Russian Imperial family in 1840, and it had been used in the Winter Palace in St. Petersburg. She bought a sterling-silver service for eighty.

No one knew just how much Hilda Weber had inherited from Charles Boldt. The most accurate guess was five to six million, but some estimates ran as high as thirteen million. Whatever the real amount was, it wasn't enough, not the way she spent money. To maintain her investment, she hired a house staff of twenty-one, plus twenty-one full-time gardeners. And now that she lived like a princess, Hilda Weber moved to entertain like one, holding several big dinner-dances a month and two or three small dinners each week. Her dinner tables were usually decorated with one hundred orchids, all raised in her orchid house. For some meals, the butler wheeled in a turkey that was cut up and put back together again. When all the white meat was gone, he would wheel that turkey out and bring in another one. One time Hilda wanted popular singer John Charles Thomas to entertain at one of her upcoming parties. So she called Thomas at his Los Angeles hotel and hired him for five thousand dollars. "What the hell's five thousand?" Hilda Weber remarked to a friend after she hung up the telephone.

This kind of spending could not go on forever, particularly when she ran up heavy gambling debts and made bad investments. One con man took her for half a million on several dry oil wells. After the Second World War, Hilda began to run out of money, and she quietly put her estate up for sale in 1948. The asking price was a million and a half—about half of what she had spent for the land, the house, and the furnishings a decade earlier. But no one was interested. By early 1949 her asking price was a very negotiable seven hundred fifty thousand. Louis B. Mayer looked at the property. So did MGM's chief set designer, Cedric Gibbons, and his wife, Dolores del Rio. Still no takers. The price kept dropping, because Hilda had to sell.

In November 1950, Conrad Hilton bought the estate—and all of its furniture, art, and silver—for $225,000. Hilton was living in Los Angeles, and he put his clothes in a station wagon and drove over to the estate. Everything else he needed was already in the house—just like a hotel.

Hilda Weber's Cinderella-like story had an unhappy ending. Like so many silent stars whose high spirits and reckless extravagance she shared, Hilda had lost her dream palace and now returned to her earlier, simpler life. She moved back to Santa Barbara, this time into a bungalow in the flats, within sight of her earlier hillside mansion. Here she was continually reminded of her fall from glory, and she started gambling more than ever before. A year after she sold her Bel Air estate to Conrad Hilton, she had run through her last few hundred thousand dollars and was driving around with husband Otto in an old Dodge.

One morning, Hilda Weber went to Hilton and told him that she was flat broke. He gave her another ten thousand. By the afternoon, she was at the race track, betting at the hundred-dollar window, "trying to make some money," as she told one friend. After gambling away this last ten thousand, Hilda Weber drove back to the Santa Barbara bungalow with Otto and that evening slit her throat in the bathroom. Otto Weber remarried, moved to Chicago, and became a bartender.

Millionaire engineer and contractor Lynn Atkinson built the only other mansion to rival Hilda Weber's in the 1930s. In spite of the Depression, he had grown rich building dams, bridges, and tunnels throughout the West, and he decided that his comfortable home at 324 South Muirfield Road in Hancock Park wasn't good enough for him anymore.

In 1935, Atkinson bought a twelve-acre piece of land at 750 Bel Air Road, about half a mile above Sunset Boulevard, and hired architect Sumner Spaulding to prepare plans for a forty-room mansion. Atkinson didn't tell his wife what he was doing. He wanted the house to be a surprise. Three years and nearly two million dollars later, he had completed a French-style mansion that looked as though it had been carried from a fashionable Parisian boulevard to a Bel Air hillside. As befitted a contractor's home, the walls were reinforced concrete, faced with Indiana limestone, and the roof was copper. The cast-iron drainpipes were concealed in the walls so that they did not mar the beauty of the facade. Unlike most Bel Air estates, Atkinson's home was totally visible from the street: first the impressive gates to the property on Bel Air Road, then a long rectangular formal garden with the driveway on either side, and finally the elegant two-story limestone house itself.

Millionaire contractor Lynn Atkinson built this Bel Air mansion for his wife, Berenice, in the late 1930s, but it was Atkinson, and not Berenice, who got the surprise.

Cinderella-like Hilda Boldt Weber's ten-acre Bel Air estate under construction. Unlike Cinderella's, her story did not have a happy ending.

The front door opened into a 20-by-30-foot reception hall with a solid beige marble floor, frescoed walls, and a ceiling that rose three full stories to a skylight and a Baccarat crystal chandelier with one hundred twenty lights. Nearby, the 39-by-70-foot living room had walnut parquet floors, damask-covered walls, a marble fireplace, and an organ console. In this room, the ceilings were eighteen feet high, and a row of French doors opened onto a terrace along the back of the house overlooking the city below.

The dining room, which accommodated twenty-four comfortably, had walnut parquet floors, walnut-paneled walls, and two large Baccarat crystal chandeliers. In the middle of the ceiling, a fresco depicted a Madonna standing on a crescent moon. When guests walked into the dining room, the Madonna was upside down and looked awkward, until they realized that she faced whoever sat at the head of the table.

Atkinson's house was lavish down to the smallest detail. Every room had gold doorknobs, including the first-floor study, library, breakfast room, men's and women's cloakrooms, and garden room, which had a fountain in the middle of its dark green marble floor. Atkinson's mansion quickly became known around Los Angeles as "the house of the golden doorknobs." But gold was visible everywhere—in built-in mirror frames, ceilings, organ grilles, even bathroom fixtures. And because he'd invested in oil wells, he even installed a gold derrick in his bathroom to pump water into his bathtub!

Atkinson's home was built into a steep hillside, and therefore it was two stories tall in front and four stories in back. The floor below the main one included a 20-by-40-foot ballroom with a maple floor, marble and mirrored walls, and a gold-leaf ceiling; a card room; a billiard room; plus one furniture vault, one linen vault, one crystal vault, one china vault, and two silver vaults. Even Hilda Olsen Boldt Weber had only one silver vault.

After Atkinson had surreptitiously finished his house, he thought about exactly the right way to show their new dream palace to his wife, Berenice. He couldn't just drive them over in the car! So he decided to throw a housewarming party and not tell Berenice anything until she saw the house that evening, brilliantly lit, filled with dance music, and thronged with guests. As the Atkinsons drove over to Bel Air for the party, Berenice asked her husband who the hosts were. "It's a surprise," he replied, "but you know them."

When they arrived at the house, the courtyard was filled with dozens of gleaming Packards and Cadillacs leaving fashionably dressed men and women at the front door. Atkinson and his wife got out of their car and walked into the three-story-high reception hall where a band was playing. Still blissfully unaware of her surprise, Berenice Atkinson turned to her proud husband and whispered: "Who would ever live in a house like this? It's so pretentious."

Atkinson was crestfallen but managed to say: "Well, then, let's go. We don't have to stay at this party." And they left their own house-warming celebration.

When Berenice Atkinson later learned the truth, she made a more thorough inspection of the estate. But that didn't change her original opinion, and the Atkinsons continued to live on South Muirfield Road, while he unhappily paid real-estate taxes and guards' salaries for the unoccupied "house of the golden doorknobs." In July 1945, Atkinson sold the estate to hotel millionaire Arnold Kirkeby for two hundred thousand dollars.

Today's Lynn Atkinson's white elephant is the best-known house in Bel Air. On Saturdays and Sundays, dozens of cars stop in front of the gates, and tourists jump out and snap photographs. These people are not admirers of fine French architecture, but they do remember that the estate was used as the home of television's *Beverly Hillbillies* in the 1960s.

CHAPTER FOURTEEN

I had landed myself in the driveway of some big mansion that looked run-down and deserted. . . . It was big and still, one of those white elephants crazy movie people built in the crazy twenties." William Holden speaks these lines near the beginning of the classic 1950 film *Sunset Boulevard*. Portraying a down-and-out Hollywood screenwriter named Joe Gillis, Holden has unexpectedly turned his car into the driveway of an overgrown Beverly Hills estate, and into the eerie fantasy world of Norma Desmond, an almost forgotten, half-mad, aging silent-movie queen, played by Gloria Swanson.

Living in the once splendid but now decaying Spanish-style mansion that she built during her heyday in the 1920s, Norma Desmond still imagines herself a great star. Shortly after they meet, Holden looks at Swanson and says: "Wait a minute, haven't I seen you . . . ? I know your face. You're Norma Desmond. You used to be big in pictures. You used to be big." To which Swanson haughtily replies: "I *am* big. It's the pictures that got small."

Supported in these delusions by her faithful butler, Max, played by silent director Erich von Stroheim, Norma Desmond believes the public has "never forgiven me for deserting it," and she has written a script, based on the life of Salome, for a triumphant "return" to the screen. When Norma Desmond learns that Holden is a screenwriter, she asks him to stay at the house and edit her script, which consists of several hundred pages in her scrawling longhand. He agrees to take the job and within weeks he becomes Norma's kept man. She buys him fashionable clothing, takes him for rides in her Isotta Fraschini (shades of Valentino!), even throws a lavish New Year's Eve party just for the two of them. As several musicians play to an otherwise empty house, they dance the tango. "You know, this floor used to be wood," she tells him, "but I had it changed. Valentino said there was nothing like tiles for the tango."

Throughout *Sunset Boulevard*, Norma Desmond's mansion is a symbol of her own decline from stardom and her increasing distance from reality. Architectural styles had changed severely since the 1920s, but the house—like a museum dinosaur—bore silent witness to a new generation of the splendors of life in the dream palaces of the 1920s. The living room had heavy velvet-upholstered pseudo-Spanish furniture, a painting that slid up into the ceiling to reveal a movie screen, a pipe organ that moaned in the wind, heavy velvet curtains drawn tight against the sun, and dozens of elaborately framed photographs of the young Norma. A black marble staircase with a typically 1920s wrought-iron railing and worn velvet rope along the wall led to Norma's second-floor bedroom, which had a baroque fireplace, white brocade walls and curtains, and a bed in the form of a golden swan.

The mansion, like Norma Desmond herself, had the look of decaying elegance. The upholstery of the living-room furniture was beginning to fade and wear out. The white brocade walls and curtains in her bedroom had become dirty with the passing years, and the gold leaf of the swan bed was beginning to peel off.

Norma Desmond's palazzo, quite naturally, had a tennis court, now sadly overgrown, and a large swimming pool, where "Mabel Normand and John Gilbert must have swum . . . ten thousand midnights ago, and Vilma Banky and Rod La Rocque," mused Holden. This is the same swimming pool that Holden falls into when, at the film's climax, a distraught Norma Desmond shoots him in the back as he tries to leave her to return to his earlier work and friends.

After the fatal shooting, the police arrive at Norma's mansion, followed by newspaper reporters, newsreel cameramen, and ghoulish curiosity seekers. Norma's delusive madness is complete now, and it mercifully shields her from what is really happening around her. As the police stand by, she sits at her vanity table, thinking that she's back at the studio again making a film with her old-time director, Cecil B. De Mille. Looking into the mirror at her makeup and speaking to no one in particular, Desmond says: "The cameras have arrived? Tell Mr. De Mille I'll be on the set at once."

In her final performance, Norma Desmond descends the staircase to the first floor before the crowd of onlookers, some enjoying the macabre spectacle of the fallen star, others horrified by her total descent into a fantasy world. As newsreel lights blaze and cameras turn, Norma reaches the first floor and blurts out: "I can't go on with the scene, I'm too happy. . . . I just want to tell you how happy I am, to be back in the studio, making a picture again. You see, this is my life. There's nothing else, just us, and the cameras, and those wonderful people out there in the dark." The film ends with a close-up of Norma's crazed face fading into a blur.

A POPULAR FILM both in its original 1950 release and in the revival theaters today, *Sunset Boulevard* offers a moving and sometimes frightening look at Hollywood and at what had happened to some of the silent stars by the 1950s. But who was Norma Desmond modeled after? Was it Gloria Swanson herself? Probably not—although it was courageous for her to take the part, since her own brilliant career had ended in the 1930s. Actually, the Norma Desmond character in *Sunset Boulevard* was a composite of any number of silent stars, men as well as women, who still had their money and their dream palaces but had little to do but feast on their memories.

Marion Davies resembled Norma Desmond in many respects, except that she did not recall her twenty-year and forty-seven-feature Hollywood career with similar satisfaction. After Marion retired from the screen in 1937, she began to believe all the malicious talk about her lack of talent. Her four last films had been embarrassing. Not only were the scripts mediocre, but in each case she had been terribly miscast as an alluring young woman of about twenty. No amount of makeup or soft lighting could hide the fact that Marion had turned forty in 1937. Her eyes and thickening waist betrayed her years. Even so, she might have carried off these roles with her youthful vigor, but that quality, too, was gone.

Marion Davies still had her ever-adoring William Randolph Hearst after her retirement, but he was thirty-four years older than she and was now an old man, preoccupied with the struggle to save his publishing empire, now under siege because of the Depression, years of bad business management, and Hearst's own legendary extravagance. Now their roles were reversed.

When the banks wouldn't extend Hearst any more credit, Marion gave him a check for a million dollars. She didn't ask for an IOU. A few days later, Hearst needed another million, as more loans came due. Once again, Marion came to the rescue with another million-dollar check. Although she was still a very rich woman, she told Anita Loos: "Why do I need diamond brooches when I have plenty of safety pins?"

Although Hearst's empire was eventually saved, he could no longer satisfy his every whim at San Simeon or entertain any number of guests at Marion's beach house. The Second World War would have cramped his style anyway. In 1942, W.R. and Marion decided to leave San Simeon, fearing that the mountaintop castle would make an easy target for Japanese warships or offshore submarines. But they got a taste of warfare at the beach house nonetheless. One night in 1942, American antiaircraft guns in Santa Monica opened fire on an unidentified plane just off the coast. Hearst went up to the rooftop balcony of the beach house to watch, while Marion hid under a heavy table downstairs.

In 1946 they moved into a pink stucco red tile roof 1920s Spanish-style mansion on a seven-acre estate at 1017 North Beverly Drive, a block and a half behind the Beverly Hills Hotel. The three-story, U-shaped house had been built in 1927 at a cost of over a million dollars, but its hapless owner then went broke and lost the estate. But Marion Davies overlooked the house's sad history and outdated Spanish style. At a price of $120,000, the estate was a good buy, and she knew that Hearst wanted to live in something grander, something more reminiscent of San Simeon than the house she had owned, ever since first coming to Los Angeles twenty-five years before, at 1700 Lexington Road. To make him feel at home, Davies even placed some statuary from San Simeon around the formal gardens and pools of "the Beverly house," and sixteen armed guards provided around-the-clock security.

Marion Davies—with sad, sad eyes—at "the Beverly house."

Harold Lloyd and his year-round Christmas tree.

During their first year in the Beverly house, Hearst and Marion Davies entertained their friends frequently, although on a smaller scale than they had at the beach house, which she sold in 1946 to investors, who turned the rambling compound into a hotel. But by 1948, Marion had to cut back on the dinners and parties at the Beverly house and limit their social engagements to visits from close friends, particularly old Hollywood cronies like Mary Pickford, Contance Talmadge, Eleanor Boardman, Frances Marion, and Diana Fitzmaurice, widow of director George Fitzmaurice. By then W.R.'s health had measurably deteriorated, and he was virtually confined to his second-floor bedroom. Marion, in turn, was drinking more than ever and had two nurses in constant attendance.

When Hearst died on August 14, 1951, at the age of eighty-nine, Marion Davies was asleep in her own bedroom and did not waken until after Hearst's sons and the undertaker had already taken the body away. Except for the oldest son, George, the Hearst family now ignored Marion—even the other sons, whom she had entertained all those years at San Simeon and at the beach house. The complimentary copies of Hearst's Los Angeles *Herald* and Los Angeles *Examiner* stopped coming to the Beverly house the morning after his death, and when she wasn't invited to the funeral in San Francisco, Marion Davies decided not to attend on her own. As she told one reporter, "Why should I? Why should I go through that kind of dramatics when I had him alive all these years?"

Marion Davies wasn't very good at playing the role of grieving "widow." On October 31, 1951, just ten weeks after W.R.'s death, she made headlines across the nation when she married Horace Brown, who had only recently been her sister Rose's jilted suitor. An ex-merchant mariner and occasional movie extra, Captain Brown, with his solid build, narrow-set blue eyes, and long nose, looked remarkably like a younger version of the departed Hearst. But these physical qualities aside, many of Marion's friends immediately disliked Horace Brown, even called him a fortune hunter behind his back. At one party, Mary Pickford ran up to Brown and started beating him on the chest with her tiny fists, screaming, "You're all wrong for Marion! Wrong! Wrong!"

Captain Brown, however, lightened the often somber mood at the Beverly house. If he didn't like some of Marion's visiting friends he would turn a garden hose on them as they got out of their cars in the driveway. Earthy, fun-loving, but socially insecure in Beverly Hills, Captain Brown couldn't tolerate what he called "Hollywood phonies." Some of his best friends were Beverly Hills cops, who regularly dropped by the Beverly house to drink coffee and take him for rides in their squad cars.

Captain Brown also bought a monkey, which he named Junior and carried around the estate like the child they would never have. Junior was mischievous, even for a monkey. With the exception of Marion's bedroom, he had the run of the house, and he liked to jump out at startled guests, smear food on walls and windows, and climb up the drapes. On more than one occasion, Junior got into the dining-room chandelier during dinner and urinated on the table below.

Marion Davies was almost too drunk to notice. After W.R.'s death, she did not have much to live for except Captain Brown and making charitable donations from her estimated twenty-million-dollar fortune. She gave over two million to the Marion Davies Children's Clinic in Los Angeles, and if old friends asked for money—even those from her distant Ziegfeld days—she gladly took out her checkbook.

Throughout the 1950s, Marion's faithful Hollywood friends, and a handful of hostesses, including Zsa Zsa Gabor, Frances Goldwyn, Kay Spreckels, and Cobina Wright, invited her and Captain Brown to their dinners and parties. But most of Hollywood ignored her now, even people who had been regular guests in her homes or acquaintances whom she had helped out with a kind word to the right producer or studio executive. Perhaps some people chose to forget Marion Davies in the 1950s, because they did not want to see her as an aging, alcoholic parody of her former self—or to be reminded of what they themselves had been and had become with the passing years. Marion died on September 22, 1961, at the age of sixty-four.

Harold Lloyd became another semirecluse in the years before his death on March 8, 1971, at the age of seventy-seven. His career had ended in the early 1930s, when the verbal joke superseded the visual gag after the arrival of the talkies. But Lloyd's popularity might have faded anyway, because—turning forty years old in 1933—he could no longer convincingly portray the fumbling but well-intentioned adolescent character he had carved out for himself fifteen years earlier.

With his multimillion-dollar fortune and free time, Harold Lloyd collected vintage cars, which he rented out to studios, spent hours studying tiny plants and animals under microscopes, became interested in color theory and started painting, and even took up photography. Over the years, he made approximately six hundred thousand stereographs that cost him—in film and development costs—nearly two million dollars! And he started taking photographs of naked young women in his gardens during the 1960s.

Harold Lloyd did not disappear from sight entirely. He received a lot of publicity—and ridicule—for his active participation in the Shriners. Shortly before he was elected president of the national organization in 1950, Mildred Lloyd held a lunch at Greenacres for seven hundred Shriners' wives who were visiting Los Angeles for their national convention. That mob scene, and son Harold, Jr.'s, twenty-first birthday party in 1952, were some of the last large entertainments at Greenacres.

It may have been just as well, since the estate was slowly running downhill. Even though Lloyd had increased his movie millions with careful investments, he still couldn't afford the staff of twenty that his estate required. Anyway, he and Mildred didn't mind Greenacres' shabbiness. By the 1950s, the custom-made silk drapes in the baronial living room were falling apart, but the Lloyds did nothing to replace them. Nor did they fix the fraying upholstery on the furniture throughout the mansion.

One year Lloyd was "too busy" to take down the family Christmas tree, and this provided the excuse to start one of the strangest Greenacres customs: the year-round Christmas tree. Every year, Lloyd fireproofed and structurally reinforced a fifteen-foot-tall tree, and then, with a servant's help, took two weeks to hang over a thousand ornaments on the branches. The finished tree was quite a sight, because he had over ten thousand ornaments to choose from.

Harold Lloyd was never one to take up a hobby in a modest way. When he became interested in music during the 1960s, he installed a

Mary arranging breakfast table on Pickfair terrace.

Although Mary Pickford was worth millions of dollars, she insisted on selling off most of Pickfair's fourteen-acre grounds over the years to get even more money, 1940.

stereo system in the fifty-foot-long living room and eventually purchased over ten thousand record albums. "Mrs. Lloyd used to be after
me to clean up this stuff," he told a reporter in 1965 as they stood in
the living room, "but she gave up five years ago. Now it's my room."
Sometimes Lloyd played his thirty-six-speaker system so loud that
flakes of gold leaf fell onto the fraying Oriental carpet from the living-
room ceiling, just like the gold leaf peeling from Norma Desmond's
swan bed.

Mary Pickford came to resemble the Norma Desmond character,
too. Throughout the 1940s and 1950s, she talked of returning to films,
but nothing ever came of this. She was drinking heavily but continued
to hold charity functions and occasional parties at Pickfair, including a
poignant get-together on Easter Sunday, 1956, for two hundred silent
stars, including William Boyd, Francis X. Bushman, Marion Davies,
Hedda Hopper—she'd acted in several films before getting into the gos-
sip-column business—Harold Lloyd, Frances Marion, Anna Q. Nils-
son, Ramon Novarro, and Zasu Pitts. Some invited guests, though—
including Joan Blondell, Ronald Colman, and Norma Shearer—were
no-shows, because they didn't want to be classified as old-timers.

As the years passed, Mary Pickford entertained less frequently,
saw fewer of her friends, and almost never left Pickfair. By the 1970s,
she spent most of her time in bed—not surprising perhaps, for a
woman who turned eighty in 1973. But people started to gossip about
what was happening to her. Some said that she was so out of things
that she lay in bed drinking gin out of a baby bottle. Others refuted
this. Her health wasn't good, they said, but she retained her mental
powers and often spent part of the afternoon in a wheelchair at her desk
supervising her fifty-million-dollar fortune. The year before her death
she reportedly caught an error that her accountant had made in her
income-tax return.

Whatever Mary Pickford was like, Pickfair was unquestionably
going to seed in the few years before she died on May 29, 1979, at the
age of eighty-six. When sightseers caught a glimpse of the estate through
the Summit Drive gates, the smooth lawns and the large white-and-
green-trim house still looked as well maintained and glamorous as ever.
But visitors to Pickfair knew that this was only an illusion. Away from

the main house and out of sight of Summit Drive, the grounds were overgrown, even littered with fallen tree branches and an occasional beer can that someone had thrown over the estate's white wall. Even that masonry wall was buckling and heaving over in places. More often than not, the swimming pool was dirty and filled with dead leaves.

Inside the house, the rooms on the main floor were still lovely, if unlived-in; like period rooms in a museum, they were scarcely changed since Mary's 1932 redecoration. But on the ground floor, where guests entered the house from the driveway, some rooms had water-stained walls, and film memorabilia, paintings, sports equipment, and musical instruments were scattered on the floor. By the time of Mary Pickford's death, even the outside of the house was starting to go. The walls needed painting, and a window shutter had fallen off one of its hinges and dangled on the side of the house at an awkward angle.

Although Pickfair had become genteelly shabby, it still had not lost its old Hollywood mystique or the feeling that something wonderful had once happened there. Although Douglas Fairbanks, Sr., had not lived at Pickfair since the early 1930s, his presence was everywhere, particularly in the ground-floor Wild West saloon with his Frederic Remington paintings on the walls and the carved mahogany bar Mary had given him one year for his birthday. Outside on the lawn, some guests half expected to see Doug bound over one of the hedges and do a handstand on one of the lawn chairs. And no visitor to Pickfair could ever forget that Mary Pickford, once America's golden-curled sweetheart and the most popular movie star in the world, was a recluse in her second-floor bedroom, which overlooked the front lawn and the swimming pool. On her "better days" she often peeked out of the window whenever she heard strange voices outside. When visitors reached this part of the lawn, they invariably looked up to her bedroom window, hoping for a glimpse of one of Hollywood's most enduring legends.

MARY PICKFORD'S Pickfair and Harold Lloyd's Greenacres weren't the only dream palaces to deteriorate in the 1960s and 1970s. By then, dozens of prewar mansions were decaying in the Hollywood Hills, Beverly Hills, and Bel Air, all relics of Hollywood's silent era, outmoded architectural tastes, and vanished life-styles. As the tragically

Cecil B. De Mille's office circa 1925, much as it appears today. Every morning staff members turn the calendar pages and place fresh flowers on the desk, as if they were waiting for C.B.'s return.

spendthrift Hilda Olsen Boldt Weber and millionaire contractor Lynn Atkinson each discovered, almost no one wanted these lavish estates after the Second World War—at least nobody was willing to pay anywhere near what the mansions had originally cost to build.

A few contemporary stars still added outrageous features to their otherwise conventional homes in the 1950s and 1960s. Liberace built a piano-shaped swimming pool at his wonderfully overdecorated Hollywood Hills estate. Kim Novak installed an all-gray living room, an all-blue bedroom, and an all-purple study at her home on Tortuosa Drive in Bel Air. The study, though, was primed for an accent of a different shade: A specially built niche stood waiting for the gold Academy Award statuette she never won.

Sex goddess Jayne Mansfield took the one-color decorative scheme one step further when in the 1950s she transformed the eight-bedroom Spanish-style mansion that Rudy Vallee originally built at 10100 Sunset Boulevard into her Pink Palace. When Mansfield said pink, she meant it: The wall around the estate, the stucco facade, the rooms, the wall-to-wall carpeting on the floors and ceilings of the entrance hall and living room, the heart-shaped swimming pool, the heart-shaped bathtub, and even the heart-shaped toilet seats were all pink. Only occasionally did another color creep into the house, such as in the living room, with its plush purple-upholstered sofa, white and gold piano, crystal chandeliers, religious statuary, and pictures of Jayne. Although Jayne may have looked and acted the part of the dumb blonde, in remodeling the Pink Palace she knew how to get the most for her money. Her Hungarian muscleman husband, Mickey Hargitay, had been a builder, and he completed or supervised most of the work. Then Jayne's press agent, Jim Byron, asked fifteen hundred furniture and building supply houses for free samples. Think of the honor, he told them, of having your—fill in the blank—as a part of the Pink Palace. The pitch worked. Jayne received over a hundred fifty thousand dollars' worth of free merchandise.

When Jayne Mansfield started work on the Pink Palace in 1958, she modestly announced that it would be "more magnificent than Pickfair." Mary Pickford must have been pleased that someone, even Jayne Mansfield, still held her home in such high esteem. What Jayne eventually created at the Pink Palace, however, was not another Pickfair, but a parody of the 1920s dream palaces. Extravagant. A residential stage set. A star's private fantasies translated into stucco and plaster. Yes, the Pink Palace embodied all the qualities that had characterized a dream palace. But unlike Pickfair in the 1920s, the Pink Palace was embarrassingly out of touch with its time: This kind of self-indulgent architectural excess looked positively foolish after the Second World War.

As the Los Angeles *Times* observed in 1952, the old estates were an "anachronism. Today most movie stars live like other people. They weed their own gardens, cook their own hamburgers, take part in the local Community Chest drives, and frequent the neighborhood movie theaters. . . . Not a single one owns an automobile upholstered in leopard skins."

While some of this talk about down-home life-styles was exaggerated, and quite a few stars were happy indeed living in their large homes in Beverly Hills and Bel Air, the winding streets in the previously undeveloped upper reaches of these areas were built up to emulate middle-class suburban ranch houses, albeit on a more lavish scale. In Bel Air the difference between these postwar houses high in the hills above the Sunset Boulevard estate areas was so extreme that realtors—and residents of the far more expensive prewar estates—began to make the distinction between Old Bel Air and New Bel Air. Regardless of where they lived, however, every resident of the neighborhood enjoyed the privilege of driving through one of the two impressive gates on Sunset Boulevard on their way home.

One of the still-grand estates they might drive past belonged to Jack Ryan, inventor of Mattell's Barbie and Chatty Cathy dolls. Ryan purchased the Tudor-style Nimes Road estate—once owned by matinee idol Warner Baxter—in the mid-1970s, and for it he built a drawbridge to the front door, installed one hundred fifty telephones around the house and grounds, and even served formal dinner parties beneath a crystal chandelier in his tree house. These were luxuries that were a little extreme even for this neighborhood, and so were the one hundred fifty parties that Ryan held during his first year on Nimes Road.

Ryan's parties, however, were tame compared to what was happening in other nearby homes in the 1970s. At one of Beverly Hills'

Greenacres, 1980. The main house still stands at the end of the former estate driveway, but the twelve different formal gardens have been torn up, the canoe pond has been filled in, and the estate's remaining sixteen acres have been bulldozed into building lots.

most exalted 1920s mansions, the owner installed a sleazy Times Square–style massage parlor in one wing of the attic and filled the several cubicles with attractive women for weekend parties. And what would the upstanding residents of Bel Air have thought about the fully equipped—and frequently used—S&M dungeon in one of their neighborhood's finest homes?

As Los Angeles life-styles and tastes began to change in the postwar decades, pre-1940 houses became candidates for modernization, particularly those reflecting the Spanish style. All over Los Angeles, thousands of Spanish-style houses bore new, usually awkward-looking facades—from the humble bungalows that lined the streets in the Hollywood flats up to and including Charlie Chaplin's Beverly Hills mansion. One of that estate's later occupants suffered an attack of the pink epidemic: The facade was painted pink; many rooms were decorated in pink; even the Cadillacs in the 1950s carport that had been tacked onto the house were pink.

At least Charlie Chaplin's home is still standing today. Director Thomas Ince's "peephole house" at 1051 Benedict Canyon Drive was demolished in the late 1940s when no one wanted to buy it. Automobile magnate E. L. Cord's Colonial-style mansion at 811 North Hillcrest Drive—the one with the luxury chicken coops—was ripped down in 1962, and ranch-style houses were built on the property. Marion Davies' Santa Monica beach house was torn down in June 1956, amid much protest, because the Ocean House hotel had failed and nobody knew what to do with the eighty-room white elephant. One of the servants' wings, however, is still standing today as part of the Sand and Sea Club on Pacific Coast Highway.

Even the Doheny family's four-million-dollar Greystone faced the wrecker's ball in the 1960s. By then, the mansion had been empty for years, and mischievous teenagers and inadequate maintenance had taken their toll. Most of the marble sinks and gold-plated fixtures were gone from the bathrooms and dressing rooms. Even ornamental doorknobs and hinges were missing. During the rainy winter season, water poured into Greystone through open doors and broken windows, damaging plaster, rotting the remaining woodwork, and turning the carpeting into a vermin- and mildew-ridden swamp. Paint was literally peeling off the walls in most rooms.

Greystone was saved from the ravages of time when the American Film Institute leased the estate from the City of Beverly Hills in 1969 and repaired the mansion for its offices and classrooms. Throughout the 1970s, students, AFI employees, and curious visitors filled Greystone with activity. Bulletin boards and large blowups of stars and directors lined the main hall. The film library, editing department, and video equipment room filled the former servants' wing. Upstairs on the second floor, a writer used Ned Doheny's massage room as an office, and the built-in massage table was still in place. Just down the hall, the accounting office occupied Mrs. Doheny's marble-walled bathroom. A coffee urn, usually surrounded by dirty plastic cups, sat on the green marble sink with its gold-plated fixtures.

While Greystone achieved a second life, time had stopped at Cecil B. De Mille's mansion in Hollywood's elegant Laughlin Park neighborhood. De Mille died on January 21, 1959, at the age of seventy-seven. After his wife of fifty-six years, Constance, followed him the next year, the heirs decided not to fire the office emloyees and servants who had worked for the family so faithfully over the years. Part of the family moved onto the De Mille estate to give the house staff and gardeners something to do. De Mille's home, and his offices and guest quarters in the one-time Chaplin residence next door, remained essentially as he and Constance had left them.

The De Mille family servants have since died off or retired, and no one has lived on the estate recently except for a caretaker. But the De Mille family still maintains the house as it was. Every morning Florence Cole, who started working for C.B. in 1928, arrives at the house to work on family business. A smartly dressed woman of about eighty, Miss Cole turns the page on his desk calendar to the current date, puts fresh flowers on the desk, and makes sure the pencils are sharp. On De Mille's desk sits a dagger that turns into a cigarette lighter, a copy of the Ten Commandments—just one of the many references to this film scattered around the house—and the movie camera with which he shot the original 1913 *The Squaw Man*. De Mille insisted on using this camera for the first take on all his subsequent silent films for good luck.

Inside the desk drawers are several hundred snapshots of De Mille with his family and friends, dozens of matchbooks, and a freshly filled tobacco pouch. A small address book, its leather cover rotted off the binding, contains pencil entries like "Gary Cooper Arizona 31321," "Ernst Lubitsch 268 Bel Air Road," and "Jesse Lasky," his original movie partner from *The Squaw Man* days, with no address or telephone number.

An incongruously modern feature on C.B.'s otherwise old-fashioned desk is a pushbutton telephone that replaced the black rotary-dial model from the 1940s and 1950s. Evidently, when Florence Cole and the staff in the nearby offices got pushbutton telephones a few years ago, C.B. got one as well.

Unlike most film moguls, De Mille did not try to deny his business profession. No painting slides into the ceiling to reveal a movie screen in this office; his movie screen still covers one wall of the room, just as it always has. It's also very obvious who was the boss in this large, rather dark room with its peaked and beamed ceiling. At his desk, De Mille sat in a comfortable wing chair, the leaded-glass Gothic bay window back-lit behind him, and could look out at the movie screen to his right, or he might face a selection of his medals and testimonials on the wall directly opposite his desk. Unless De Mille made other arrangements, his visitors had to sit in an uncomfortable backless campaign chair and stare into the plain back of the desk clock, with C.B.'s head and shoulders rising above that.

The grounds and the facade of De Mille's mansion now look a little shabby for a house of its size and location, but besides his meticulously kept, unchanged office, he would feel right at home if he came through the front door today. The entire house is ready for him. His second-floor bedroom is still furnished with his simple double bed, the small, well-worn wooden desk where he did most of his work at home, two small Victorian rocking chairs, and a circa-1950 television set with a small round screen. It still works, like everything else in the house. Down in the first-floor butler's pantry, all the china and crystal are stacked neatly in cabinets. In the spotless kitchen, an apron hangs from a hook near the sink. The gas is on for the stove, and the refrigerators are plugged in and working, though empty of food. De Mille has been

Falcon Lair, 1980, now more serene than it ever was during Valentino's days.

gone for over twenty years, but his presence in this house is so strong that visitors often find themselves referring to him in the present tense, just as some of the staff and family do.

ONLY A HANDFUL of dream palaces will be fortunate enough to be rescued from reckless, ill-conceived alterations or outright destruction by turning them into public institutions, like Greystone, or into museums, much like the De Mille mansion. As their present owner-occupants know, it takes money, time, and imagination to buy and maintain these estates and to return the run-down ones to their former glory.

After several decades of neglect, there appears to be this kind of renaissance. All the "white elephant" arguments against these 1920s estates are still alarmingly true. The houses are old, at least by Southern California standards. Real-estate taxes are high. The houses and grounds do require lots of "help." But these familiar problems do not really matter when and if we can begin to appreciate these homes—for their irreplaceable workmanship, fine materials, and sense of grandeur—as the cultural artifacts they indeed are. These fabulous mansions of the 1920s now conjure up pleasing images of gracious and vivid living and reflect the resonances of a now distant romantic past.

Even though the future looks bright for these fabled homes, this does not mean that the survivors will regain their earlier architectural and social prominence. Los Angeles and its residents are very different from what they were like in the 1920s. And the movie stars, the very idea that "a star must live like a star," and the excitement and prosperity of 1920s Hollywood which gave birth to these houses and made them the center of the world's attention are gone forever. Today the remaining dream palaces are not much more than empty stage sets with their original players and expensive props long departed.

POSTSCRIPT

Despite their relative newness, the homes of the stars—like Europe's oldest royal families—have complicated genealogies, with one star following another at the same address.

Tobacco heiress Doris Duke has owned—and rarely lived in—Rudolph Valentino's Falcon Lair since 1953.

The Theda Bara/Fatty Arbuckle/Raoul Walsh–Miriam Cooper/Joe Schenck–Norma Talmadge house at 649 West Adams Boulevard is a convent.

After Natalie Talmadge Keaton sold the twenty-room Italian villa behind the Beverly Hills Hotel, the estate became the home successively of the dance team Fanchon and Marco, Barbara Hutton—whose fiancé Cary Grant was a frequent guest—a millionaire glass manufacturer, and James and Pamela Mason. The stretch of Hartford Way leading to the estate has been renamed Pamela Drive.

Residents of the John Gilbert estate on Tower Grove Road have included producer David O. Selznick and his actress-wife Jennifer Jones; Sammy Davis, Jr.; and, most recently, rock singer Elton John.

Singer-dancer Donald O'Connor now lives in the Joan Crawford *Mommie Dearest* house in Brentwood.

Louis B. Mayer's Santa Monica beach house was once owned by Peter Lawford and his then wife Patricia, where two of their favorite houseguests were her brothers, John and Robert Kennedy.

John Barrymore's aviary has been converted into a small house which has been the home of Katharine Hepburn, Marlon Brando, and Candice Bergen.

The Clark Gable–Carole Lombard ranch in Encino is today an expensive tract-housing development.

Singer Engelbert Humperdinck lives in Jayne Mansfield's Pink Palace at 10100 Sunset Boulevard.

Two years after Harold Lloyd's death in 1971, his Greenacres estate was opened to the public as the Harold Lloyd Museum, according to the terms of his will. But the nearby residents objected to hordes of tourists coming into their exclusive Benedict Canyon neighborhood, and the Harold Lloyd Museum closed in 1974, amid much controversy. Greenacres was subsequently sold to an investment group composed primarily of Iran's Nasrolla Afshani family, and the sixteen-acre estate was subdivided into small—and very costly—building lots. Bernard and Dona Solomon bought and restored Lloyd's forty-room mansion in 1980.

Several months after Conrad Hilton's death in 1979, his ten-acre Bel Air showplace was put up for sale for fifteen million dollars. Although interested buyers reportedly included the Shah of Iran, the estate did not sell at once, and the real-estate brokers raised the asking price to seventeen million—to keep pace with inflation, they said. In August 1980, land and office-building developer David Murdock bought the property for twelve million dollars, the highest price ever paid for a single-family residence in Los Angeles.

The garish Sheik's House at the northwest corner of Sunset Boulevard and Alpine Drive was destroyed in a spectacular fire on New Year's Day, 1980. Two weeks later, the Beverly Hills fire chief announced that the blaze had been deliberately set.

Pickfair's remaining 2.7 acres were put on the market for ten million dollars following Mary Pickford's death in 1979. Real-estate developer and sports entrepreneur Jerry Buss bought the estate for almost five and a half million a year later. With a million-dollar down payment and a twenty-year mortgage for the balance of the purchase price, Buss's monthly mortgage payments are $37,261.77. Will he rename the estate Bussfair?

NOTES

While   les, and scattered newspaper   on in *Dream Palaces*, certain o   pful to me. In order not
to bu   refrained from detailed
footn   ditional sources for the
follov   tations, see the Bibliography

CHAPTER ONE.   Descriptions of Falcon Lair and Valentino's wardrobe: *The Estate of Rudolph Valentino to Be Sold at Public Auction, Commencing December 10, 1926;* and Irving Shulman, *Valentino.*

CHAPTER TWO.   Los Angeles topography, climate, and history: Carey McWilliams, *Southern California: An Island on the Land;* and Bruce Torrence, *Hollywood: The First 100 Years.*

CHAPTER THREE.   Hollywood Hotel anecdotes: Anita Loos, *A Girl Like I.*

CHAPTER FOUR.   Synopsis of Theda Bara's *A Fool There Was: Motion Picture News,* January 23, 1915; and *The New Yorker,* October 18, 1952. Fatty Arbuckle's practical-joke dinner party for Adolph Zukor: Tom Dardis, *Keaton.* Norma Talmadge's jewelry: Miriam Cooper, *Dark Lady of the Silents.* Buster Keaton's various homes: Rudi Blesh, *Keaton.* Mack Sennett's mountaintop mansion: Gene Fowler, *Father Goose.*

CHAPTER SIX.   Pickfair: Gary Carey, *Doug and Mary. A Biography of Douglas Fairbanks and Mary Pickford;* Ralph Hancock and Letitia Fairbanks, *Douglas Fairbanks: The Fourth Musketeer;* Booten Herndon, *Mary Pickford and Douglas Fairbanks;* Mary Pickford, *Sunshine and Shadow;* Richard Schickel, *His Picture in the Papers;* Robert Windeler, *Sweetheart. The Story of Mary Pickford;* and *Photoplay,* May 1929.

CHAPTER SEVEN.   Gloria Swanson: Kenneth Anger, *Hollywood Babylon;* Gloria Swanson, *Swanson on Swanson;* and Robert Windeler, *Sweetheart. The Story of Mary Pickford.* Charlie Chaplin and Douglas Fairbanks' practical jokes: Charles Chaplin, Jr., *My Father, Charlie Chaplin.* Douglas Fairbanks and Tom Geraghty's joke on Chaplin: Ralph Hancock and Letitia Fairbanks, *Douglas Fairbanks: The Fourth Musketeer.* Charlie Chaplin's home: Charles Chaplin, *My Autobiography;* Charles Chaplin, Jr., *My Father, Charlie Chaplin;* Lita Grey Chaplin, *My Life With Chaplin;* John McCabe, *Charlie Chaplin;* and *Photoplay,* June 1929. Chaplin's bedroom furniture: Hedda Hopper, *The Whole Truth and Nothing But.* Chaplin's unfinished shower: King Vidor, *A Tree Is a Tree.* Chaplin's second marriage and divorce: Kenneth Anger, *Hollywood Babylon;* and John McCabe, *Charlie Chaplin.*

CHAPTER NINE.   Greta Garbo at the Beverly Hills Hotel: John Bainbridge, *Garbo.* John Barrymore buys King Vidor's Beverly Hills estate, plus Barrymore and the Good Samaritan: Gene Fowler, *Good Night, Sweet Prince.* Greenacres: Richard Schickel, *Harold Lloyd.*

CHAPTER TEN.   Buster Keaton's "surprise" house for Natalie: Rudi Blesh, *Keaton.* Keaton and life at the Hartford Way estate: Rudi Blesh, *Keaton;* and Tom Dardis, *Keaton.* Clara Bow's dinner party, plus the lovesick men outside her front door: Joe Morella and Edward Z. Epstein, *The "It" Girl.* Clara Bow's house: *Photoplay,* October 1929.

CHAPTER ELEVEN.   Marion Davies yells at William Randolph Hearst: Charles Chaplin, *My Autobiography.* Marion's beach house: Fred Guiles, *Marion Davies.*

CHAPTER TWELVE.   Falcon Lair after Valentino's death: Irving Shulman, *Valentino.* Frances Goldwyn's surprise house for husband, Sam: Garson Kanin, *Hollywood.*

CHAPTER THIRTEEN.   Mary Pickford's drinking: Booten Herndon, *Mary Pickford and Douglas Fairbanks*. Clark Gable's calls: Robert Windeler, *Sweetheart. The Story of Mary Pickford*. Mary Pickford invites Katharine Hepburn to dinner: Charles Higham, *Kate*.

CHAPTER FOURTEEN.   Marion Davies at the Beverly house: Fred Guiles, *Marion Davies*. Harold Lloyd's later years: Richard Schickel, *Harold Lloyd*. Jayne Mansfield and the Pink Palace: May Mann, *Jayne Mansfield*.

BIBLIOGRAPHY

Anderson, Clinton. *Beverly Hills Is My Beat*. Englewood Cliffs, New Jersey, 1960.

Anger, Kenneth. *Hollywood Babylon*. San Francisco, 1975.

Arliss, George. *My Ten Years in the Studios*. Boston, 1940.

Astaire, Fred. *Steps in Time*. New York, 1959.

Astor, Mary. *My Story*. Garden City, New York, 1959.

Bacon, James. *Hollywood Is a Four-Letter Town*. Chicago, 1976.

Bainbridge, John. *Garbo*. Garden City, New York, 1955.

Banham, Reyner. *Los Angeles: The Architecture of Four Ecologies*. New York, 1976.

Barrymore, Diana. *Too Much, Too Soon*. New York, 1957.

Barrymore, Elaine. *All My Sins Remembered*. New York, 1964.

Bawden, Liz-Anne, ed. *Oxford Companion To Film*. New York, 1976.

Baxter, John. *Hollywood in the Thirties*. New York, 1970.

Beaton, Cecil. *Photobiography*. Garden City, New York, 1951.

————. *The Wandering Years*. London, 1961.

Blesh, Rudi. *Keaton*. New York, 1971.

Brown, Karl. *Adventures With D. W. Griffith*. New York, 1973.

Brownlow, Kevin. *The Parade's Gone By*. New York, 1968.

————, and Kobal, John. *Hollywood: The Pioneers*. New York, 1979.

Cagney, James. *Cagney by Cagney*. Garden City, New York, 1976.

Carey, Gary. *Doug and Mary. A Biography of Douglas Fairbanks and Mary Pickford*. New York, 1977.

Cary, Diana Serra. *The Hollywood Posse*. Boston, 1975.

Chaplin, Charles. *My Autobiography*. New York, 1964.

Chaplin, Charles, Jr. *My Father, Charlie Chaplin*. New York, 1960.

Chaplin, Lita Grey. *My Life With Chaplin*. New York, 1966.

Colman, Juliet Benita. *Ronald Colman*. New York, 1975.

Cooper, Miriam. *Dark Lady of the Silents*. Indianapolis, 1973.

Crawford, Joan. *A Portrait of Joan*. Garden City, New York, 1962.

Crowther, Bosley. *Hollywood Rajah: The Life and Times of Louis B. Mayer*. New York, 1960.

Croy, Homer. *Our Will Rogers*. New York, 1953.

Dardis, Tom. *Keaton*. New York, 1979.

Davidson, William. *The Real and the Unreal*. New York, 1957.

Davies, Marion. *The Times We Had*. New York, 1975.

De Mille, Cecil B. *Autobiography*. Englewood Cliffs, New Jersey, 1959.

Dempsey, Jack. *Dempsey*. New York, 1977.

Erte. *Things I Remember*. New York, 1975.

The Estate of Rudolph Valentino to Be Sold at Public Auction, Commencing December 10, 1926.

Everson, William K. *American Silent Film*. New York, 1978.

Farrar, Geraldine. *Such Sweet Compulsion*. New York, 1938.

Flynn, Errol. *My Wicked, Wicked Ways*. New York, 1959.

Fowler, Gene. *Father Goose: The Story of Mack Sennett*. New York, 1934.

———. *Good Night, Sweet Prince: The Life & Times of John Barrymore*. New York, 1944.

Gebhard, David, and Winter, Robert. *A Guide to Architecture in Los Angeles & Southern California*. Santa Barbara, 1977.

———, and von Breton, Harriet. *Los Angeles in the 1930s*. Santa Barbara, 1975.

Gish, Lillian. *The Movies, Mr. Griffith, and Me*. Englewood Cliffs, New Jersey, 1969.

Goodman, Ezra. *The Fifty-Year Decline and Fall of Hollywood*. New York, 1961.

Graham, Sheilah. *The Garden of Allah*. New York, 1970.

Guiles, Fred Lawrence. *Marion Davies*. New York, 1972.

Halliwell, Leslie. *The Filmgoer's Companion*. New York, 1977.

Hancock, Ralph, and Fairbanks, Letitia. *Douglas Fairbanks: The Fourth Musketeer*. New York, 1953.

Haskell, Molly. *From Reverence to Rape*. New York, 1974.

Hellman, Lillian. *An Unfinished Woman*. Boston, 1969.

Herndon, Booten. *Mary Pickford and Douglas Fairbanks*. New York, 1977.

Higham, Charles. *Cecil B. De Mille*. New York, 1973.

———. *Kate*. New York, 1975.

Hopper, Hedda. *From Under My Hat*. Garden City, New York, 1952.

————, and Brough, James. *The Whole Truth and Nothing But*. Garden City, New York, 1953.

Kanin, Garson. *Hollywood*. New York, 1974.

————. *Tracy and Hepburn*. New York, 1970.

Keats, John. *Howard Hughes*. New York, 1972.

Kerr, Walter. *The Silent Clowns*. New York, 1975.

Keylin, Arleen, ed. *Hollywood Album*. New York, 1977.

Knight, Arthur. *The Liveliest Art*. New York, 1978.

Kobler, John. *Damned in Paradise: The Life of John Barrymore*. New York, 1977.

Koury, Phil. *Yes, Mr. De Mille*. New York, 1959.

Lasky, Jesse L. *I Blow My Own Horn*. Garden City, New York, 1957.

Lasky, Jesse L., Jr. *Whatever Happened to Hollywood?* New York, 1975.

LeRoy, Mervyn. *Mervyn LeRoy: Take One*. New York, 1974.

Loos, Anita. *A Girl Like I*. New York, 1966.

————. *Kiss Hollywood Goodbye*. New York, 1974.

Macgowan, Kenneth. *Behind The Scenes*. New York, 1965.

Mann, May. *Jayne Mansfield*. New York, 1973.

McCabe, John. *Charlie Chaplin*. Garden City, New York, 1978.

McCoy, Esther. *Five California Architects*. New York, 1960.

McWilliams, Carey. *Southern California: An Island on the Land*. Santa Barbara, 1979.

Milland, Ray. *Wide-Eyed in Babylon*. New York, 1974.

Mix, Olive Stokes. *The Fabulous Tom Mix*. Englewood Cliffs, New Jersey, 1957.

Moews, Daniel. *Keaton*. Berkeley, 1977.

Moore, Colleen. *Silent Star*. Garden City, New York, 1968.

Morella, Joe, and Epstein, Edward Z. *The "It" Girl*. New York, 1976.

Motion Picture Magazine. Various issues.

Negri, Pola. *Memoirs of a Star*. Garden City, New York, 1970.

Niven, David. *The Moon's a Balloon*. New York, 1972.

O'Brien, P. J. *Will Rogers*. Chicago, 1935.

Paine, Albert Bigelow. *Life and Lillian Gish*. New York, 1932.

Palmer, Edwin O. *History of Hollywood*. 2 vols. Los Angeles, 1937.

Parsons, Louella. *Tell It to Louella*. New York, 1961.

Photoplay Magazine. Various issues.

Pickford, Mary. *Sunshine and Shadow*. Garden City, New York, 1955.

Powdermaker, Hortense. *Hollywood: The Dream Factory*. Boston, 1950.

Regan, Michael. *Stars, Moguls, Magnates*. Los Angeles, 1966.

Robinson, Edward G. *All My Yesterdays*. New York, 1973.

Rogers, Betty. *Will Rogers: His Wife's Story.* Indianapolis, 1941.

Rosen, Marjorie. *Popcorn Venus.* New York, 1973.

Rosenberg, Bernard, and Silverstein, Harry. *The Real Tinsel.* New York, 1970.

Rosten, Leo C. *Hollywood.* New York, 1941.

St. Johns, Adela Rogers. *The Honeycomb.* Garden City, New York, 1969.

Saxton, Martha. *Jayne Mansfield and the American Fifties.* Boston, 1975.

Schickel, Richard. *Harold Lloyd.* Boston, 1974.

———. *His Picture in the Papers.* New York, 1973.

———. *The Stars.* New York, 1962.

Sennett, Mack. *King of Comedy.* Garden City, New York, 1954.

Shulman, Irving. *Harlow.* New York, 1964.

———. *Valentino.* New York, 1967.

Sklar, Robert. *Movie-Made America.* New York, 1975.

Stine, Whitney. *Mother Goddam.* New York, 1974.

Swanberg, W. A. *Citizen Hearst.* New York, 1961.

Swanson, Gloria. *Swanson on Swanson.* New York, 1980.

Thomas, Bob. *Selznick.* Garden City, New York, 1970.

Torrence, Bruce T. *Hollywood: The First 100 Years.* Los Angeles, 1979.

Ullman, S. George. *Valentino As I Knew Him.* New York, 1926.

Vidor, King. *A Tree Is a Tree.* New York, 1953.

Wagner, Walter. *Beverly Hills: Inside the Golden Ghetto.* New York, 1976.

Walsh, Raoul. *Each Man in His Time.* New York, 1974.

Windeler, Robert. *Sweetheart: The Story of Mary Pickford.* New York, 1974.

Wright, Frank Lloyd. *An Autobiography.* New York, 1977.

Writers' Program of the Work Projects Administration. *Los Angeles: A Guide to the City and Its Environs.* New York, 1941.

Yablonsky, Lewis. *George Raft.* New York, 1974.

Zolotow, Maurice. *Billy Wilder in Hollywood.* New York, 1977.

PICTURE CREDITS

INDEX